I0130035

CONTENTS.

EXPLANATIONS.

The families in this Memorial are arranged in the order of seniority, in the first five generations, the head of the family, having a consecutive number, being in German text, thus—V. 60. **Elijah Burke,** shows that Elijah Burke is of the fifth generation, and that 60 is his consecutive number, and that by turning back to the number 60, his name will be found in his father's family. The other head of the family is in old English, and is printed in the middle of a line.

This mark †, following a consecutive, and immediately before a person's name, denotes that the person will be subsequently noticed as a head of a family, his or her name being printed in German text, in the middle of the line, preceded by the consecutive number.

When a woman's name occurs thus, Thankful (Wait) Burke, it will be understood, that the name in parenthesis was her original or maiden name, and the name following was acquired by marriage.

When a woman's name occurs thus, Mary (——) Alvord, the horizontal line included in a parenthesis denotes that her original or maiden name is not known to the compiler.

Previous to the year 1752, there were two methods of reckoning time. According to one of these methods, the year began on the 25th of March, February being the twelfth month; this was called the *civil* or *legal* year. According to the other method, the year began on the 1st of January, December being the twelfth month; this was the *historical* year. Upon our ancient records these methods are often combined thus, January 8th, 1727-8. According as we now reckon time it would be 1728, but according to the first mode it would be 1727.

ERRATA.

On the 58th page, 19th line from the top, Kentucky should be Tennessee.

On page 139, 7th line from the top, Tinkham should be Tinker.

On 143d page, the consecutive number 145 should be 147.

On 144th page, 3d line from the top, the word died should be omitted.

On 161st page, Nos. 661, 662, Paschal should be Pascal.

PREFACE.

MANY years since, my father, Benjamin Burke, Esq., began to collect and record some genealogical account of his ancestors and relatives. What he had thus collected was quite brief and imperfect, his opportunity for examining such records as would have assisted him being very limited.

Before his decease he placed in my hands what he had gathered, and was very desirous that I should complete what I well knew, from my earliest recollection, had been a favorite object with him.

Very fortunately I obtained the services of John A. Boutelle, Esq., of Woburn, Mass., by whose genealogical skill, assiduity, and untiring perseverance the following account of the Burke and Alvord families has been collected, and to whom all the credit is due for collecting the material for this book. No one, but those who have made the trial, can have a just conception of the labor and investigation required to prepare with tolerable accuracy a genealogical work of even so limited an extent as the present one.

The historical account of the De Burghs (or Burkes) has been prepared from authentic records, collected by Mr. Boutelle. Some readers may think it fanciful or far sought, while to others it may be interesting to learn the origin of a name that was unfrequent in New England forty or fifty years since, but is now quite common.

The genealogy of the Alvord family here given is not a complete one.

In looking up the genealogy of my mother I only purposed to make a brief record of her ancestors. It was owing to having followed another branch of the Alvord family that quite an amount of information was collected, that it was thought best to print for future reference by those who might be interested in it.

In the Appendix are genealogical accounts of minor importance, with sundry wills, deeds, &c., that it may be interesting to some persons to read. These were collected by Mr. Boutelle in the course of his researches in Probate Court and Church Records.

Upon the title-page to the Burke Genealogy will be seen the coat of arms of the De Burghs, with the motto—UNG ROY, UNG FOY, UNG LOY—that is, one king, one faith, one law—and on that of the Alvord Genealogy, the coat of arms of the Alvord family, as described in Sir Bernard Burke's "General Armory."

My thanks are due to all who have in any way assisted to furnish such information as has contributed to make up this book.

No doubt the persistence with which it has been sought has annoyed some who can see little or no use in collecting records of past generations. "Let the dead rest," perhaps they may think or say. But in almost every instance information has been cheerfully given, with a desire to possess the "book" as soon as it could be published.

There are some omissions (and no doubt many inaccuracies) in this book, and many of them might have been filled up (or corrected) by taking more time; but as more than a year and a half has now been occupied in collecting such facts as are here presented, I thought best to bring the work to an end.

WILLIAM A. BURKE,

LOWELL, MASS.

MAY, 1864.

The Burke and Alvord Memorial

A Genealogical Account of the Descendants of

Richard Burke

of Sudbury, Massachusetts

and the

Descendants of

Alexander Alvord

of Windsor, Connecticut

John Alonzo Boutelle

HERITAGE BOOKS
2020

HERITAGE BOOKS
AN IMPRINT OF HERITAGE BOOKS, INC.

Books, CDs, and more—Worldwide

For our listing of thousands of titles see our website
at
www.HeritageBooks.com

A Facsimile Reprint
Published 2020 by
HERITAGE BOOKS, INC.
Publishing Division
5810 Ruatan Street
Berwyn Heights, Md. 20740

Originally published 1864

— Publisher's Notice —
In reprints such as this, it is often not possible to remove blemishes from the original. We feel the contents of this book warrant its reissue despite these blemishes and hope you will agree and read it with pleasure.

International Standard Book Numbers
Paperbound: 978-0-7884-1557-9
Clothbound: 978-0-7884-6096-8

INTRODUCTORY HISTORY OF THE NAME OF BURKE.

THE name of Burke, Bourke, or Bourck, as it is variously spelt, was originally written De Burgh, and under that form is an ancient name, and of much note in the old world. It may be traced back to the eighth century, and has for its head Charles, Duke d'Ingheim, fifth son of the Emperor Charlemagne. In the fourth generation from him, we find Baldwin de Bourg, his great-grandson, a renowned crusader, whose son Baldwin founded the house of Blois in France, and was a progenitor of the noble families of Burgh and Vesey in Ireland.

Early in the fourteenth century, lived and died John, Earl of Comyn, and Baron of Tonsburgh in Normandy, a descendant of the above, "who, being general of the king's forces, and governor of his chief towns, obtained the surname of de Burgh," a name particularly pertinent, not only on account of its meaning, which signifies "pertaining to a city," but also because the name had belonged to one of the earliest progenitors of the family. Being, therefore, a prominent Norman family, it is not unnatural to suppose that they found their way to England when the connection between the two countries became so intimate, that the first Norman kings of England passed a great part of their time in what was to them their old home. Accordingly we find them mentioned in early English history from time to time, verifying their descent from the staunch old crusader by deeds of bravery, piety, and fidelity to their king. The celebrated Hubert de Burgh, afterwards King's Justiciary, was a marked instance of loyalty and integrity. His father and uncle had been in places of trust under Henry II., and in the latter part of the troublous reign of King John, when his Barons had confederated against him, and leagued with the King of

France to put *his* son on the throne, Hubert was Governor of Dover Castle, which, with that of Windsor, held out against the French. Prince Louis tried to corrupt him, but always found in that brave man a loyalty proof against all temptation. Force had been equally unavailing, and the attempt had been more than once relinquished, when, the death of King John happening, Louis hoped the Governor would become more tractable. Accordingly, he again ordered him to surrender, representing to him that since he was released from his oath by the death of his King, he might without scruple swear fealty to a Prince, whom his countrymen had owned for sovereign, and who would be glad to show him marks of his esteem. Hubert replied that the esteem of a brave Prince could not be gained by baseness, and that his allegiance was due to the successor of the late King, whose cause he would maintain to the last drop of his blood. Louis then tried intimidation, and threatened to put to death his brother, Thomas de Burgh, who was a prisoner in his hands. Threats were also ineffectual in moving the faithful Governor, and Louis raised the siege, and shortly agreed upon a truce. This check upon the success of the French no doubt contributed greatly to the peace which followed, and to the establishment of the young King, Henry III., upon the throne.

Hubert was made Chief Justiciary of England, and rose speedily to such power and influence with the King as to excite the jealousy of the Barons. He was made Earl of Kent, and received in marriage the eldest sister of the King of Scotland; an honor which procured him the alliance of two monarchs, the King of Scotland having espoused the sister of Henry of England. Hubert, through the influence of the nobles, lost the King's favor, and was imprisoned in the Tower, but not long after was released, and was subsequently reconciled to the King, although he seems never again to have mingled in public affairs.

A son of his, John de Burgh, is mentioned with distinction in subsequent wars with the French.

In the reign of Henry II., a branch of the De Burghs went over into Ireland. Prior, in his "Life of Edmund Burke," says,

"The Burkes, or Bourkes, though now thickly strewn over the whole of Ireland, particularly the southern part of it, were not an aboriginal, or as their English invaders termed them, a *mere Irish* family; but descended from the Norman Burghs, or De Burghs, (of which Burke is merely a corruption,) who went thither as adventurers under Strongbow, in the reign of Henry II.; not as temporary marauders, whose visitations might soon be over, but to conquer an inheritance, to seize upon such possessions as their strength would permit, and permanently to hold what they had thus seized." The name figures in Irish history from this time down, until it is merged in other equally famous, and perhaps more familiar to modern ears. Even then it is retained as the family name. It is frequently involved in the wars and struggles which pervaded that riotous kingdom, and in most cases is found on the side of law and order, when law and order was the dangerous and unpopular side.

It was William Fitzaldelm, uncle of Hubert the Justiciary, who, accompanying Strongbow into Ireland, remained there with the little English colony, was appointed Governor of Wexford by the King, and afterwards entrusted with the management of affairs in that kingdom. In 1177, he was appointed Governor of Ireland, and about that time founded the monastery of St. Thomas, near Dublin. He obtained a great part of the province of Connaught, and died in England in 1204. His son, Richard de Burgh, Lord of Connaught and Trim, had the conquests of his father confirmed to him by King John in 1215, on condition of his doing homage therefor and paying the yearly rent of 300 marks. He was made Lord Lieutenant of Ireland in 1227, and died on a voyage to France in 1243.

His two sons, Walter and William, became incorporated into the two noble families of Ulster and Clanricarde. Walter, the elder of the two, by his marriage with Maud, daughter of the Earl of Ulster, became Earl of Ulster in her right, upon the death of her father. He died in 1271, and was succeeded by his son, Richard de Burgh. William, brother of Walter, and younger son of Richard, served with his father in France, and was in many battles with his brother, and died in 1270.

His son, William, was appointed Custos of Ireland, and performed many signal services with the Irish. He died in 1324. His son, Ulick de Burgh, was Lord of Clanricarde, and of great power. Then follow several Ulicks in direct succession, one of whom, living in the reign of Henry VIII., and being Governor of Connaught, the possession of his ancestors for so many centuries, was made by that king, Earl of Clanricarde and Baron of Dunkellin. He died in 1544. His son, Richard de Burgh, second Earl of Clanricarde, occupied the position so frequently conferred upon members of this family, that of Lord Lieutenant of Ireland. His son and heir, Ulick, third Earl of Clanricarde, dying in 1601, left five sons. Richard, the eldest, distinguished himself eminently in the service of the Crown, during the rebellion of O'Neil, Earl of Tyrone, and received many favors from his king, Charles I. He had the command of the county and town of Galway, where most of his estates lay. In 1624, he was advanced to the dignity of peer of England, by the title of Baron of Somerhill, (a manor of his in Kent,) and Viscount Tunbridge, to which were added, four years later, Viscount of Galway, and Earl of St. Albans. He died at Somerhill in 1635. His only son, Ulick, born in London, was a general of the king's army in Ireland, and zealous in opposing the Irish rebels. In reward of his loyalty, he was created Marquis of Clanricarde in 1644. He was made Lord Lieutenant of Ireland in 1650, but was finally driven from the country, his estates sequestered, and he retired to his manor in Kent, where he died in 1657. The line of succession then swerved into the family of his uncle, William, third of the five sons of Ulick, third Earl of Clanricarde, from whom, in direct line, the title has come to the present Earl, Ulick John, fourteenth Earl, born in 1802.

The Earls of Mayo are descended from a collateral branch of the De Burghs, having, with the Earls of Clanricarde, a common ancestor in the William, who was Custos of Ireland in 1308, and died in 1324.

This brief sketch of this ancient family will perhaps be interesting to those who, having the same name or one identical, are presumed to be connected by some one of those innumerable and constantly increasing lines, which, accumulating from generation to generation, are yet all traceable, were the materials at hand, to a common source. Many a genealogical tree, like the far-famed tree of India, *seems* to have many roots, because its branches have planted themselves in other spots, and been the source of life to other branches, but none the less did the life come originally from one root, none the less is it one tree. Throughout the genealogical records, the name Burgh is frequently spelt Bourke; and we find in the Life of the great statesman already alluded to, that the identity was acknowledged by the Earl of Clanricarde of the last century, who frequently addressed Mr. Burke as "cousin."

The early records of this country, owing to various causes, are not always to be found. Sometimes, no doubt, they were very imperfectly kept, sometimes they were destroyed in the wars with the Indians, and sometimes the very precautions taken to save them were the cause of their loss. The church records, which are very valuable sources of information, were often kept on detached pieces of paper, and were lost in passing from hand to hand. In one instance, (Greenland, N. H.,) the record of baptisms is found upon a roll of paper, two or three yards in length, consisting of narrow pieces, pasted together. The oldest burial-place of Sudbury, now in the town of Wayland, whose inscriptions have yielded valuable facts, has been deprived of a portion of its testimony by having some of its stones appropriated to private uses.

One supposition may have some weight in deciding the causes of the difficulty of tracing the connection of names this side the water with names on the other. Most of those who came to this country, had some strong reason for leaving their own. It is not unlikely that some, beginning as it were a new life here, may have made some slight alteration in their name, or have taken one already in their family though not strictly theirs. There seems no other way of accounting for the fact, that some names, traceable to an early period in this country, are not to be found at all in the other, either in records or even in present use.

But this cannot be said of the name of Burke, although the precise time of its transit to this country cannot be ascertained. The first possessor of the name to be found on this side, is Richard Burke, of Sudbury, of whom nothing is known previous to the date of his marriage in Sudbury, in 1670. Connecting his appearance here with the fact that, less than twenty years before, Ulick de Burgh, Earl of Clanricarde, was driven from his country, his estates sequestered, and his home thoroughly broken up, we are led to wonder, whether in the consequent dispersion of his retainers, one of his relatives did not find his way to this country, and seek to establish a new home in a new world. Or, supposing the passage to have been made earlier than 1650, might not a stray Protestant have been found in the Roman Catholic family of Clanricarde, to whom Ireland would prove an uncongenial if not an uncomfortable home? But the field of conjecture is limitless, and, once let loose in it, the fancy finds it very enticing. It were best then to draw back, and confine inquiry simply to the facts which have been collected, and which are presented to the reader in the following pages.

THE BURKE MEMORIAL.

I. 1. Richard Burke,

Of Sudbury, Mass.

Born, supposed about the year 1640; died at Sudbury, Mass., 1693-4. [For his inventory and settlement of his estate, see Appendix A.] He was probably of Anglo-Norman origin.

He owned land in Sudbury, Mass., and also in Stow, Mass.

"An Indenture made between Henry Loker of Sudbury, Glover, and Hannah his wife, and Richard Burke of Sudbury, Oct. 24, 1670, witnesses that for a valuable sum or consideration Henry Loker and Hannah his wife have sold" &c., "unto Ri. Burke one hundred and thirty acres of land in Pompassitticut, and in the two miles last granted to the town of Sudbury." [Reg. Mid. Co., Vol. 7, page 243.

Town Records of Stow, Mass.—Given, granted ye 1st March 1685–6 vnto Richard Burke Sen. & to his heirs and assigns forever Thirty acres of upland & swamp land for an house lott. Ten acres thereof is allowed him instead of meadow ground within, in this town wth all Rights and Priviledges belonging to a Twenty acre lott provided y^{t} hee doe com, & build, dwell, & settle vpon ye said hous lott, and make Improvement of ye same, & y^{t} hee also doe from time to time pay (or caus to be pd) into all rates & to all Town charges y^{t} shall at all times hereafter as is by due proportion with others according to y^{t} Hon^{ed} comm^{ttees} orders."

His son Richard Burke sold the above land in Stow, June 4, 1708.

Another grant upon Stow Town Records, "July 26, 1687 It is voted, & hereby given, & granted, to Richard Burke, y^{t} small tract of land y^{t} was viewed, and is to bee laid out to him by

Boaze Brown, Senr. and Jno. Butterick, who are appointed by ye Town for such work, & are hereby ordered to bring in ye Bounds ther of with his whole Lott under their bonds for ye Town approbation y^t so it may be recorded together."

For Richard Burke's inventory and settlement of estate, see Appendix A.

He was married at Sudbury, Mass., June 24, 1670, to

Mary Parmenter,

Born Sudbury, Mass., (June 10, 1644 ?) died ——.

(She was the daughter of John and Amy (——) Parmenter, and granddaughter of Dea. John Parmenter, born 1588, who was one of the first settlers of Sudbury in 1639?) She administered on her husband's estate, and afterwards married a Mr. Allen.

Children—

2. †Richard, born Sudbury, Mass., April 16, 1671; died ——; resided in Stow, Sudbury, and in Brookfield. He married Abigail Sawtell.
3. †John, born (Sudbury?) I have not the date of his birth or death. He is named in the settlement of his father's estate. He married Rebecca ——.
4. Joseph, born Sudbury, Mass., April 1, 1676; died ——. He received a division of land in his father's estate, "Lands lying on ye north side of ye farm joyning to ye new grant of Left. John Ruddock on ye North Easterly sid: and runs Easterly: hom to the hy way that divides ye new Grant lots; and Southerly buts on his brother Thomas his division and westerly on his brother John's division."

   "Of ye moveable estate"

   "by 2 chaines: grinstone beetle rings wedges horse traces 2£. 10^s. 06^d."

   In 1695–6, aged about 20, he chose a guardian.
6. Mary, born Sudbury, Sept. 25, 1680. Named in the settlement of her father's estate. In 1695–6, aged about 15, chose a guardian. She married George Parmenter, Jr.

7. †Jonas, born Sudbury, Mass., Jan. 4, 1683–4; died at Stow, Mass. Resided in Sudbury, and in Stow. He married, Dec. 23, 1709, Hannah Johnson, who outlived him.

8. †Thomas, born Sudbury, Mass., Nov. 1, 1686; died Stow, Mass., April 29, 1753; married Mercy Parmenter, May 11, 1718.

II. 2. Richard Burke,

Born Sudbury, Mass., April 16, 1671; died ——. Son of Richard and Mary (Parmenter) Burke. He resided at Stow, Sudbury, and at Brookfield, Mass. The earliest births now upon Stow Town Records commence May 22, 1713. The births of some of his children are upon Sudbury Town Records. The following is an extract from a deed of the heirs of his wife's father's estate, in which we find the name written Burt and Burk, but signed Burk.

"Richard Whitney and Elizabeth Whitney his wife, and Samuel Hall and Hannah Hall his wife, and Samuel Cutler and Sarah Cutler his wife, and Richard Burt and Abigail Burt his wife, now of Stow, husbandmen, For and in consideration of the sum of Thirteen pounds, ten shillings to us all ready and truly paid in hand by Cap. Jonas Prescott of ye town of Groton blacksmith, convey Two acres of Land with a stable and a dwelling house in ye Town Hill (?) Groton, (also a piece of land lying in the Indian Hill six acres be it more or less which Jonathan Sawtell Sen. bought of Justin Holden of Groton) in the township of Groton," &c., &c., &c. [Mid. Co. Reg. Deeds, Vol. 13, 197. Dec. 8, 1698.

Upon Stow Town Records, June 10, 1700, we find the name, Richard Burke, the 7th on a list of 32 names with regard to the support of Rev. Mr. Eveleth.

Richard Burke of Stow, and Abigail, his wife, convey several parcels of land in Stow, to Israel Held of Stow; said land being near Marlboro' line, Feb. 18, 1705–6. [Vol. 14, 593, Mid. Reg. Deeds.

June 4, 1708. Richard Burck of Sudbury, carpenter, with Abigail Burck, sell all that thirty acres of land, swamp and meadow, granted by the town of Stow, for a house lott, be it more or less, &c., to Moses Whitney.

Richard Burk of Brookfield, Co. of Hampshire, carpenter, John Burk of Groton, husbandman, George Parmenter, Jun., of Sudbury, cooper, with Mary, his wife, convey to Thomas Burk of Sudbury, a quit claim of all the interest that we have to any of the estate of which our honored mother, Mary Allen of Sudbury, widow, deceased, died possessed of. Sept. 19, 1727. [Vol. 32, 461, Mid. Reg. Deeds.

From the Town Records of Brookfield.—Jan. 20, 1720–1. Then laid out to Richard Burk one piece of upland on the five mile River, being on y[e] east and west sides, fifty foure Rods in length and on the north and south sides eighty rods in length; bounded northerly on Thomas Gibse's land easterly on the town line, southerly on common land westerly partly on Hopstil Hind's land and partly on common land having on the north west and south west corners a hemlock tree; at y[e] north east corner a white oak tree and at ye south east corner a pitch pine tree, each tree marked H being twenty seven acres in quantity and twenty three in quality. By us committee. John Willcolt, Hopestill Hinds, Thomas Gibbs. Recorded by order of y[e] selectmen.

Richard Burke married

Abigail Sawtell,

Born Groton, March 5, 1671–2; died Sudbury (April 1, 1716?) She was the daughter of Jonathan and Mary (——) Sawtell, who was an original proprietor of Groton, and granddaughter of Richard Sawtell, who was a proprietor of Watertown in 1636–7, and one of the first settlers of Groton, where he was town clerk the first three years after its organization.

Children—

9. Abigail, born (Stow, Mass.?) ——; died ——; (married John Parmenter, June 1, 1709?)
10. †Richard, born (Stow, Mass.?) ——; died ——; resided in Brookfield, &c. He married Mary ——.

11. †Jonathan, born (Stow, Mass.?) Jan. 1701; died Windsor, Vt., May 18, 1775; married, May 10, 1731, Thankful Wait.
12. Sarah, born Sudbury, May, 1708; bapt. May 3, 1708. [Church Records, Sudbury.
13. Keziah, born Sudbury, Feb. 24, 1710–11; died Sudbury, Nov. 1, 1717.
14. Uzziah, born Sudbury, Feb. 24, 1710–11; bapt. March 4, 1711. [Sudbury Church Records.

II. 3. John Burke,

Born Sudbury, Mass. ——; died ——. Son of Richard and Mary (Parmenter) Burke. He and his mother, Mary, administered on his father's estate. He was appointed, April 6, 1696, a guardian of his brother, Jonas Burke, and was also guardian of his brother Thomas.

He resided in Sudbury and in Groton. In Sudbury he resided on part of the estate which formerly belonged to his father, Richard Burke, situated in Sudbury, near Stow line, and bounded in part by land of his brothers, John, Jonas, and Thomas's division. He sold, March 23, 1721–2, his estate in Sudbury to Edward Fuller of Salem. In April following, he purchased an estate in Groton, of Samuel Farnsworth, for four hundred pounds, and subsequently moved to Groton, Mass.

He married

Rebecca ——.

Children—

15. Rebecca, born Sudbury, April 7, 1690.
16. Elizabeth, born Sudbury, March 22, 1701.
17. Margaret, born Sudbury, May 17, 1702.
18. John, born Sudbury, April 16, 1704.
19. Phineas, born Sudbury, Nov. 3, 1706.
20. Dinah, born Sudbury, April 15, 1709.
21. Azubah, born Sudbury, May 13, 1711; bapt. July 12 1713. [Church Records.

II. 7. Jonas Burke,

Born Sudbury, Mass., Jan. 4, 1683–4; died Stow, Mass. Son of Richard and Mary (Parmenter) Burke. He received the following division of land in his father's estate: land "butting on ye east with the land of his brother John burk on ye south with ye lands of Mr. Abraham Holman, westerly with the lands of Stow, northerly with ye lands of Lieut. Ruddock." "Of ye moveable estate," "by one cow, 2 : 10 : 00."

He resided in Sudbury and in Stow. As early as the year 1722, he sold land in Sudbury to his brother, John Burk. His inventory is on file, dated March 3, 1729–30. A letter, which is on file, dated Nov. 15, 1739, says, that the oldest son had sold his share and moved out of the province. Another statement is, that he has sold his interest, and is beyond the sea. A division and settlement of the estate was made April 10, 1741. Amos Brown, who purchased the estate of Jonas Burke, gave security for that which belonged to Mary, the eldest daughter.

Mr. Burke was married at Sudbury, Dec. 23, 1709, to

Hannah Johnson.

She outlived her husband and administered on the estate.

Children—

22. Mary, named as eldest daughter in the division of the estate.
23. Hannah, one of the heirs, married a Wright.
24. Sybil, born Stow, (Nov. 3, 1714?) not named in the settlement of the estate.
25. Joseph, named as eldest son in the settlement, &c.
26. Abigail, named as third daughter.
27. Elizabeth, named as fourth daughter.
28. Hephsibah, named as fifth daughter.
29. Jonas, born Stow, Mass., Nov. 25, 1728; named as youngest son in the division of his father's estate, April 10, 1741.

II. 8. Thomas Burke,

Born Sudbury, Nov. 1, 1686; died Stow, Mass., April 29, 1753. Son of Richard and Mary (Parmenter) Burke. He received the following division of land in his father's estate: "Land bounded on ye south with ye lands of Mr. Abraham holman; easterly with ye middle hy way of ye new grant lots and northerly with the lands of Joseph Burk, and westerly with the lands of John Burke." Moveables—"by pillows, bed & bedding. 2:12:00. Sept. 9, 1695, at the age of nine years, his brother John was appointed his guardian.

He resided in Sudbury and in Stow, Mass.

He was married at Sudbury, May 1st or 11th, 1718, to

Mercy Parmenter,

Born Sudbury, Dec. 8, 1687; died Stow, Mass., June 25, 1761.

She was the daughter of Benjamin and Thomasine (Rice) Parmenter, who was the son of John and Amy (——) Parmenter, who was the son of Dea. John Parmenter of Sudbury, the immigrant, who was born about the year 1588. She outlived her husband, and her inventory is dated Aug. 11, 1761.

Children—

30. Mercy, born Sudbury, (?) March 23, 1718–9.
31. Thomas, born Sudbury, (?) June 13, 1727.

III. 10. Richard Burke,

Born Stow, Mass. (?) (The date of his birth we have not.) Son of Richard and Abigail (Sawtell) Burke; who was son of Richard and Mary (Parmenter) Burke; resided in Brookfield (Quabbin now Greenwich) and in Ware.

From Town Records of Brookfield, Feb. 12, 1721–2.—"Laid out to Richard Burk Jun., one piece of land bounded northerly on Arthur Tooker's land, being two hundred rods in length, and forty rods in width, having" &c.

June 6, 1727. Samuel Bush, of the town of Brookfield, husbandman, to Richard Burke, Jun., carpenter, land in Brookfield. [Wor. Co., Vol. 4, 168.

March 28, 1729. Richard Burk, Jun., of Brookfield, carpenter, sells several parcels of land in Brookfield to Sargeant Thomas Gibbs, and in bounding the same, names the land of John Hind, and of Samuel Bush. Wife Mary relinquishes her right of dower. [Wor. Co. Reg. of Deeds, Vol. 4, 170.

Feb. 15, 1722. Richard Burk, Jun., of Brookfield, conveys land in Brookfield to Capt. Thomas Baker of Brookfield. [Vol. D, page 80, Hampshire Co. Reg. of Deeds.

Sept. 8, 1726. Richard Burk, Jun., carpenter, to Jonathan Burk, carpenter, all of Brookfield, conveys land in exchange. [Vol. D, 638 Ham. Co. Reg. of Deeds.

March 4, 1733. Richard Burk, Jun., of Ware-River, so called, in the bounds of Kingsfield, so called, in the county of Hampshire, conveys his title to a certain piece of land lying and being in Kingsfield, to Samuel Barnard, of Hadley. [Vol. G, p. 302, Ham. Co. Reg. of Deeds.

Aug. 6, 1740. Richard Burk, living at Quabbin, within ye county of Hampshire, and in actual possession of ye within granted land, conveys his right and title, &c., to Sam. Wait. [Vol. M, 93.

Nov. 15, 1741. Samuel Wait, of Quabbin, conveys fifty acres of land to Richard Burke. [Vol. M, 598, Ham. Co. Reg. of Deeds.

Dec. 2, 1743. Richard Burke, of Quabbin, conveys fifty acres of land in Quabbin to James Redaway of Rehoboth. [Vol. N, p. 442.

Richard Burke of Brookfield married

Mary ——.

Issue—

32. Seth. Seth Burk, a minor, more than fourteen years old, one of the heirs of Richard Burk, late of Ware River, so called, in the county of Hampshire, deceased, made choice of Dea. Supply Kingsley of Northampton, to be his guardian, April 14, 1756. See Hampshire Probate, Vol. 8, 174, at Northampton, Mass. Seth Burk was of Chesterfield in 1770, of Northampton in 1774, of Westampton in 1782, and in 1785. He married in Northampton, Jan. 25, 1762,

Rebecca Stearns

Child—

33. Sibel Burk, baptized Sept. 19, 1762. [Northampton Church Records.

III. 11. Jonathan Burke,

Born Stow, Mass.,(?) Jan. 1701; died Windsor, Vt., May 18, 1775, aged 73. Son of Richard and Abigail (Sawtell) Burke, and grandson of Richard and Mary Parmenter Burke; resided in Brookfield, Brimfield, South Brimfield, Mass., and in Westminster, and Windsor, Vermont.

March 12, 1725. Richard Burk, of Brookfield, carpenter, conveys land in Brookfield, to Jonathan Burk, of Brookfield, carpenter. [Vol. 21, 495, Worcester Co. Reg. of Deeds.

March 11, 1725. Thomas Gibbs, of Brookfield, in the county of Hampshire, conveys to Jonathan Burk, of Brookfield, one tract of land in Brookfield, lying on Five Mile River, east on the town line, south on Richard Burk's land, west, part on Hopestill Hind's land, north on Witham Ayres' land, &c. [Vol. 21, 495.

Sept. 8, 1726. Jonathan Burk, of Brookfield, carpenter, conveys land unto Richard Burk, of Brookfield. [Hampshire Co., Vol. D, 636.

Feb. 15, 1731-2. He sold land in Medway to Widow Sarah, relict of Josiah Rocket, of Medway; and on the same day he sold land in Brookfield to Richard fforce, [A. H. Ward, Esq., says it should be Vose] of Medway.

From Brookfield Town Records.—Jan. 11. 1742. "Laid out to Jonathan Burk, five acres of land in Brookfield, northerly of his house, being one hundred and twenty rods in length, east and west, the whole length of his lot to a point at each corner; and fifteen rods in the middle running northerly to a white oak tree marked B., bounded southerly on said Burk's own land, northerly on common land. *Note.*—There is an allowance for a highway across said land north and south. By us Thomas Gibbs, Wm. Old. Recorded by order of ye selectmen."

Aug. 28, 1742. Jonathan Burk, of Brookfield, in the county of Worcester, carpenter, conveys to Thomas Powers, of Quabbin, one certain lot of land in the north westerly part of Quabbin, it being lot No. 35, containing one hundred acres. [Hampshire Co., Vol. S, 472.

May 24, 1739. Benjamin Martain, of Grooden, county of Mid., grants unto Jonathan Burk, of Brookfield, in the county of Worcester, wheelwright, all the whole share of Walter Joyce in a certain township granted to the Narragansett soldiers number 4, and said township lieth in two parts; one part at a place called Quabbin, and the other part of said grant lieth west of Hatfield. [Vol. S, 470.

April 14, 1748. Jonathan Burke, of Brookfield, purchases his real estate in Brimfield. Samuel Moulton, of Brimfield, with Mary, his wife, for thirteen hundred and fifty pounds, paid by Jonathan Burk, conveys one hundred and forty-two acres of land, lying south from Charles meadow, and is in the south easterly part of Bromfield, and bounded as follows: westerly by Joseph Haynes' land; northerly part by sd. Haynes' land, and part by Ebenezer Bishop's land, and part by common land; easterly by James Thompson's land, and southerly by John Donelson's fifth division lot, and common land; said Burk is to have the above premises with the buildings thereon. [Vol. S, 317.

July 10, 1759. Jonathan Burk, of Brimfield, with Thankful, his wife, conveys unto his beloved son, Jonathan Burk, Jun., of said Brimfield, husbandman, eighty acres of land, lying in the south easterly part of said town. [Ham. Co. Reg., Vol. 7, 516.

From Wales Town Records.—Formerly South Brimfield. South Brimfield was incorporated Sept. 18, 1762. Incorporated as the town of Wales in 1828.

The following is an abstract probably of the first warrant for a town meeting in South Brimfield. "Sept. 28th 1762 Hampshire S.S. To Jonathan Burke, one of the principal Inhabitants of the District of South Brimfield, in the county of Hampshire," "Greeting &c. By the authority granted me the subscriber, one of his majesties Justices of the peace for the county aforesaid, by an order by the great and General Court, passed the 18th day of Sept. inst. You are required in his majesty's name, forthwith, to warn and give notice to the inhabitants of said district of S. B. qualified to vote, &c., &c., Josiah Dwight."

Mr. Burke was often appointed a committee on town and church affairs, in Brimfield and in South Brimfield.

Dec. 15, 1769. We find Mr. Burke in what is now called

Westminster, Vermont, selling his real estate in South Brimfield. "Jonathan Burke, of Westminster, in the county of Cumberland and province of New York, for the sume of four hundred and ten pounds, sells to Ruth Swinnerton of South Brimfield, &c., a parcel of land situated in South Brimfield, containing one hundred and sixty acres, and in bounding the same names James Thompson, James Marcy, John Nelson, and John Hinds. [Vol. XI., 284.

His grave-stone is in the ancient burial ground at Windsor, Vt.

"In Memory of Mr Jonathan Burke who died
May ye 18th 1775 in ye 74th year of his age."

"Death is the Debt to Natver Due which
I Have paid and so must you."

Thankful Wait,

Born Northampton, Jan. 27, 1706; (?) died Windsor, Vt., Jan. 29, 1783. Supposed daughter of William and Ann (Webb) Wait. She was married to Jonathan Burke, in Northampton, Mass., May 10, 1731. Her grave-stone, likewise, is in the ancient burial-ground at Windsor, Vt.

"Here lies buried Mrs. Thankful the Wife of
Mr Jonathan Burk who died January 29th
1783 in the 75 year of her age."

Children—

34. Keziah, born Brookfield, Mass., March 3, 1732, died at Windsor, Vt. She married Ozel Morse. She was much afflicted with sickness, and for many long years was confined to her bed.

35. †Jonathan, born Brookfield, Mass., Feb, 26, 1733–4; died at Hartland, Vt.; married, 1, Sarah ——; 2, Sarah Gould, Brookfield, May 29, 1763.

36. †Simeon, born Brookfield, Mass., May 3, 1736; died Westminster, Vt., April 15, 1781; resided in South Brimfield and in Westminster, Vt. He married Martha Strong.

37. †Jesse, born Brookfield, Mass., April 8, 1738; died Westminster, Vt., Jan. 20, 1811; married at Brookfield, Mass., May, 1761, Widow Leah Rice, and resided at Westminster, Vt.

38. †Isaiah, born Brookfield, Mass., June 13, 1740; died Hartland, Vt. (?) Probate, July, 1802. Married Anna (?) Mason, and resided in Windsor, Woodstock, and in Hartland, Vt.

39. Richard, born ——; "Deceast. April 13, 1741." The record of this death occurs between the record of the births of Isaiah and Solomon, sons of Jonathan and Thankful Burke, but whether it is the death of a son of Jonathan Burke, or the death of his father, Richard Burke, I know not. We are informed that Jonathan had a son Richard, who died young, in Brookfield, Mass.

40. †Solomon, born Brookfield, Mass., Dec. 2, 1742; died Windsor, Vt., Feb. 8, 1819; married Keziah Benjamin, and resided in Windsor, Vt.

41. †Silas, born Brookfield, Mass., Nov. 22, 1744; married Mary Eastman, and resided in Westminster, Vt.

42. Elijah, born Brookfield, Mass.

43. Anna, born Brimfield, Sept. 2, 1748; married —— Belknap; resided in Mass.

IV. 35. Jonathan Burke,

Born Brookfield, Mass., Feb. 26, 1733–4; died at Hartland, Vt. Son of Jonathan and Thankful (Wait) Burke; who was the son of Richard and Abigail (Sawtell) Burke, who was the son of Richard and Mary (Parmenter) Burke. He resided in Brimfield, Mass., and in Hartland, Vt. He received of his father, Jonathan Burke, July 10, 1759, eighty acres of land, situated in the southeast part of Brimfield. He sold the above premises, Sept. 13, 1768, to John Hinds of Brimfield; he then residing in South Brimfield. [Hampshire Co., Vol. 12, 78, Reg. Deeds.] He married, 1,

Sarah ——,

Born ——; died at Brimfield, Mass., Nov. 12, 1761.

He was married, 2d, by Jedediah Foster, Brookfield, March 29, 1763, to

Sarah (Gilbert) Gould,

Supposed to be the widow of Samuel Gould.

Children by first wife—

43. Sarah, born Brimfield, Mass., Jan. 18, 1755.
44. Jonathan, born Brimfield, Mass., June 7, 1756.
45. †Joseph, born Brimfield, Mass., April 27, 1758; died in Warner, N. H.; resided in Hartland, Vt., and in Warner, N. H. He married Judith Barrell.
46. Abigail, born Brimfield, Mass., Nov. 12, 1761.

Children by second wife—

47. Elizabeth, born Brimfield, Mass., March 29, 1763.
48. Olive, born Hartland, Vt., May 22, 1773. She was a healthy and very strong woman. Married, 1, Edmund Barrell, Aug. 9, 1789, at Hartland, Vt.; 2, Elnathan Walker.

IV. 36. Simeon Burke,

Born Brookfield, Mass., May 3, 1736; died Westminster, Vt., April 15, 1781. Son of Jonathan and Thankful (Wait) Burke, who was the son of Richard and Abigail (Sawtell) Burke, who was the son of Richard and Mary (Parmenter) Burke. He resided in Brimfield, Mass., and in Westminster, Vt. His gravestone is in the ancient burial ground in Westminster.

"Here lies buried Mr Simeon Burke
who died April 15. 1781 in the 45 year of his age."

Martha Strong.

She, with her husband, Simeon Burke, belonged to the first church in Westminster, Vt., having been received under the first pastor.

Children—

49. Thankful, born Brimfield, Mass., Aug. 21, 1757.
50. †Lucy, born Brimfield, Mass., Aug. 13, 1758; died Bridgewater, Vt., Nov. 26, 1850; married, Feb. 26, 1778, Phineas Sanderson.
51. Martha, born Brimfield, Mass., July 15, 1760.
52. Amy, born Brimfield, Mass., July 27, 1762; died Sept. 18, 1792; married Phineas Onispus Shaw, Feb. 14, 1786.
53. Samuel, born ——, 1763; died Westminster, Vt., June 18, 1821. He resided in Westminster, Vt., and about

the year 1801 he moved to Stow, Vt., where he lived a few years, and then returned to Westminster, Vt., where he died and was buried.

Samuel Burk died June 18. A. D. 1821,
in the 58 year of his age.
"Virtue lives beyond the grave."

Huldah, consort of Samuel Burk died
Dec. 30. 1821. In the 54 year of her age.
"Believe & look will triumph in the grave."

54. †Ebedmelech, born Westminster, Feb. 1766; died South Woodstock, Vt., March 20, 1822; married, 1, Prudence Dunbar; 2, Polly Hammond, Oct. 17, 1802.
55. Betsey, born Westminster, ——; married —— Kingsley.
56. †Simeon, born Westminster, Vt.(?) —— 1769; died Stow, Vt., March 29, 1850; resided in Westminster and in Stow, Vt.; married Lucy ——.
57. Hannah, born Westminster, Vt.(?) married —— Josselyn, and resided in Morristown, Vt.
58. Polly, born Westminster, Vt.(?) married, 1, —— Jones; 2, —— Fenton.
59. Elisha, born Westminster, Vt., 1773; died Westminster, Vt., July 24, 1777.

Here lies buried Elisha son of Mr Simeon and
Mrs Martha Burk who died July 24, 1777, aged 4 years.

60. †Elijah, born Westminster, Vt., March 13, 1775; died Gainesville, N. Y., Sept. 1861; married Hannah Root.

IV. 37. Capt. Jesse Burke,

Born Brookfield, Mass., April 8, 1738; died Westminster, Vt., Jan. 20, 1811. Son of Jonathan and Thankful (Wait) Burke, grandson of Richard and Abigail (Sawtell) Burke, and great-grandson of Richard and Mary (Parmenter) Burke. He resided in Westminster, Vt., of which town he was one of the first settlers.

June 21, 1771. Jonathan Burk, of Westminster, Co. of Cumberland, and Province of New York, conveys several parcels of land situated in Westminster, unto his beloved son, Jesse Burk, of said town.

Capt. Burke was a farmer by occupation, and a large land owner, being proprietor of a large part of the land comprised in the lower settlement or village of the East Parish in that town. He was a man of intelligence for those times, and of marked decision of character.

In the political agitations which preceded the outbreak of the American Revolution, he was a decided liberal, or whig, and of course allied himself to the Revolutionary party. The first military company in that vicinity of which there is any record, was raised in Westminster, of which company he was captain.

At that period of time, the King's Courts were held in Westminster, and for that reason that town was the centre and rallying point of the leaders of the party adhering to the king. And in that town the first blood was shed in the political collisions which took place in the county on the eve of the outbreak of the Revolution. William French, a citizen of Westminster, and a whig, was the first victim, and martyr of liberty. He was most barbarously murdered by a mob of tories, headed by the sheriff of the county. This event occurred in April, 1775. It was about this period that the military company was formed, of which Jesse Burke was captain. He had the confidence of the Committee of Public Safety, and Imbursements; and his name appears in the public archives as a recipient of orders from them. He was also the friend and confidant of the celebrated Ethan Allen, who made Captain Burke's house his head-quarters during the collision between the people of Vermont and the authorities of New York, prior to the independence and admittance of the State of Vermont into the Union as a State.

He was a man of morality and integrity, lived respected, and died lamented by his townsmen, and was buried in the ancient burial-place at Westminster.

"Erected in memory of Capt. Jesse Burk who died
January 20, 1811 in the 73 year of his age."

Leah (Jennings) Rice.

Her maiden name was Jennings (and she was the widow of Charles (?) Rice. She was married at Brookfield, May, 1761, to Jesse Burke.

> "Erected in memory of Mrs. Leah Jennings' wife of Capt. Jesse Burk who died Aug. 5. 1811 in the 75 year of her age."

Children—

61. Anna, born ——. Her father gave her a farm as well as to his sons. She married first, Calvin Chaffee, by whom she had children, and moved out west, where her husband died. She, with her children, returned to Westminster, where she married a Mr. Cobb.
62. †Joseph, born Westminster, Vt. (?) June 22, 1762; died Sept. 8, 1845. Married, Abigail Petty, and moved to Morristown, Vt., in 1800.
63. Jonathan, born ——; married, May 26, 1811, Widow Laurana Butterfield, who had children by a former husband. He had an only child, a daughter. He was a soldier in the American Revolution, and was, for his patriotic services, a recipient of a pension from the first enactment of the pension law in the United States to the day of his death. After the close of the Revolution, he engaged as a seaman, in the mercantile service. Having made a voyage to England, he was there impressed into the naval service of that country, where he remained eight years, and was not allowed to go ashore, where it was suspected that there was any opportunity for him to escape; but he did desert in England. He was from home some sixteen years. During the time he was in the British naval service, he was in the fleet commanded by Lord Nelson. He was present and fought at the battle of Copenhagen. At his decease, the newspapers of the day announced the event, with the expressive addition, "a revolutionary soldier and an honest man."
64. Eliab, born Westminster, Vt., 1766; died Westminster,

Jan. 28, 1804. He was never married, and was of feeble health.

"In memory of Eliab Burk, son of Mr. Jesse and Mrs. Leah Burk who died January 28, 1804 in the 38th year of his age."

65. †Jesse, born Westminster, Vt., Dec. 20, 1770; died Westminster, Vt., 1816; married Sarah Hatch, and left a large family.

66. †Eli, born Westminster, Vt., Oct. 21, 1771; died Pomfret, Vt., Sept. 29, 1855; resided at Andover, Vt., and a few years at Pomfret, Vt. He married Mary Adams.

67. †Elijah, born Westminster, Vt., March 3, 1774; died March 21, 1843; married Grace Jeffers, Sept., 1795.

IV. 38. Isaiah Burke,

Born Brookfield, Mass., June 13, 1740; died Hartland, Vt., 1802. Son of Jonathan and Thankful (Wait) Burke, who was the son of Richard and Abigail (Sawtell) Burke, who was the son of Richard and Mary (Parmenter) Burke. He resided in Windsor, Hartland, and in Woodstock, Vt. He was a large land owner. He bought, Nov. 12, 1772, of Nathan Stone, a large tract, or tracts of land, situated in Windsor, County of Cumberland and Province of New York, and in bounding the same, names Burk's Brook, the great river, and the dividing line lately made between his and Solomon Burk's land. [See Reg. of Deeds, Vol. 2, page 88.

Abel Farwell of Hartland, was appointed administrator of the estate of Isaiah Burke of Hartland, deceased, the widow Mary Burk declining being present. [Prob. Rec., Woodstock, Vt., Vol. 3, p. 45.

He married

Anna Mason.

Wife Mary is named in the settlement of the estate.

Children—

68. †David, born Jan. 26, 1772; died April 28, 1854, aged 82; married Olive Short.

69. Lydia, married John Lazell, who died in Massachusetts.

70. Miriam, born 1769; died Windsor, Vt., Sept. 4, 1838, aged 69. She was highly esteemed by those who knew her. She was a member of the first church at Windsor, and was a consistent christian. The following lines are upon her grave-stone:

"Dearest sister, thou hast left us,
Here thy loss we deeply feel,
But, 'tis God, that hath bereft us,
He will all our sorrows heal."

71. †Ezra, born ——; resided in Mount Holly and in Ludlow.
72. †Anna, born ——; married Abel Farwell.
73. Nathan, born ——; never married; died in Mass.

IV. 40. Solomon Burke,

Born Brookfield, Mass., Dec. 2, 1742; died Windsor, Vt., Feb. 8, 1819. Son of Jonathan and Thankful (Wait) Burke, grandson of Richard and Abigail (Sawtell) Burke, and great-grandson of Richard and Mary (Parmenter) Burke.

Tradition says, that a family, or families, of the name of Burke, came up the Connecticut River in a boat, or boats, to Westminster, Vt., where some of them made a permanent settlement, and others soon moved farther up the Connecticut valley.

Jesse, Simeon, and Silas, remained at Westminster, but Jonathan, Sen., Jonathan, Jr., Isaiah and Solomon Burke, moved farther up the Connecticut river.

Solomon Burke settled, May, 1771, in Windsor, Vt. The first permanent settlement of Windsor, Vt., was made by Capt. Steele Smith, in August, 1764. "Capt. Smith came up the Connecticut from Farmington, Conn., about 1763, with two others, in a canoe; and being remarkably agile, he sprang ashore to cut the first tree, leaving his companions some distance behind. In August, 1764, he came with his family. There was then no road north of Number Four (Charlestown, N. H.) The next season, Maj. Elisha Hawley, Capt. Israel Curtis, Dea. Hezekiah Thomson, and Mr. Thomas Cooper, with some others, came and began improvement. A man by the name of Solomon Emmons had however previously built a hut, and was living here when Capt. Smith arrived; but he had not purchased the land, nor made any improvements with a view to a permanent settlement. Mrs. Emmons, his wife, was the first, and for some time, the only, white woman in town."

Windsor, Vt., "was chartered by authority of the Province of New Hampshire to Samuel Ashley and 58 others, July 6, 1761, containing 23,500 acres. It was re-granted by Gov. Tryon of the Province of New York, March 28, 1772, to Col. Nathan Stone and 28 others. Thomas Cooper was the first Town Clerk.

The first male child born in town was Mr. Samuel Smith, son of Capt. Steel Smith. He was born July 2, 1765, and died in Windsor, Jan. 6, 1842, aged 77 years. The first female child born in Windsor was Mrs. Mary Wait, relict of the late Capt. Marshal Wait, and daughter of Col. Nathan Stone. She was born April 26th, 1767, and was living in 1855." [Church Manual, Windsor, Vt.

Rev. James Wellman was installed Sept. 29, 1768, and preached in Cornish, N. H., and in Windsor. By written agreement he was to preach in Windsor one-third part of the Lord's day, for five years, for which he was to receive, annually, twenty pounds good and lawful money of New York, &c. April 3d, 1774, the church of Cornish and Windsor, voted to comply with the request of those who desired a dismission with a view to join with others in forming a church in Windsor.

"Mr. Wellman used to ford the Connecticut on horseback in coming to Windsor to preach," and "sometimes he was obliged to enter the pulpit little short of dripping wet."

Mr. Solomon Burke was a member of the first Congregational church at Windsor, and was often appointed on committees of the church. In 1793, Mr. Solomon Burke, with Mr. Reuben Smith, were chosen a committee to call upon those who absented themselves from the church at Windsor. May 28, 1800, he with Seth Tinkham, was chosen to attend the Association at Alstead, N. H.

Nov. 12, 1772, Nathan Stone of Windsor, in the Province of

New York, conveys unto Solomon Burke of said Windsor, all that, and those lots of land, situated in said Windsor, county of Cumberland, being bounded as follows: Beginning at the corner on the bank of the Great River, which is the boundary between said Solomon and Isaiah Burke, &c. His land was bounded on the Great River, on the town line between Windsor and Hertford, also on the land of his brother, Isaiah Burke. He owned land in Hertford (now in the town of Hartland).

Dec. 30, 1803, Solomon Burke of Windsor, conveys land in Windsor and in Hartland to Jonathan Burke of Windsor.

April 25, 1804. An indenture was made between Jonathan Burke and Solomon Burke, that Jonathan Burke in consideration of two thousand dollars already received of Solomon Burke, doth lease unto said Solomon the whole of the land which he has this day deeded to him, the said Jonathan, situated in Windsor and in Hartland, with such part of the buildings as are necessary for the use of the said Solomon and Keziah, his wife, to make them comfortable during their natural lives. He is to deliver annually to them during their lives one-third part of all the productions of said farm in a state fit for market; likewise one-third part of the pasturing is to be theirs. The said Jonathan is to take care and tend one horse and two cows, summer and winter, for them, provided the said Solomon provides the said horse and cows for him to tend, &c., &c. Moses Burke, son of said Solomon, is to live and work on said farm until he arrives at the age of 21 years; said Jonathan is to furnish him with decent victuals, drink, and clothing, and to support him in sickness and in health. When said Moses shall come of age, said Jonathan is to pay him $200. Jonathan Burke is to support and maintain a negro woman by the name of Flora Brackey, who now lives with the said Solomon. (See Appendix B.)

March 30, 1812. Jonathan Burke deeded back the farm, &c., to Solomon Burke, and the same day Solomon Burke conveys the same premises to Nahum and Moses Burke, in consideration of like maintenance.

March 24, 1824. Moses and Nahum Burke deeded the above premises to Wm. Sabine of Hartland, for three thousand dollars.

Widow Keziah Burke released her claim for three hundred dollars, paid by William Sabine.

March 8, 1825. Moses Burke conveys the estate which he bought of Wm. H. Gallup, to his mother, Keziah Burke, for her maintenance, "and she is to have the south room," &c.

The following inscription is upon a stone in the old burial-ground in Windsor, Vt.:

> "Solomon Burke was born in Brookfield Mass
> Dec. 2. 1742. settled in this town May 1771
> died Feb. 8th 1819 in the 77 year of his age."

Keziah Benjamin,

Born Hardwick, Mass., May 6, 1749; baptized June 24, 1749; died Sept. 24, 1835. She was the daughter of Caleb and Abigail (Livermore?) Benjamin, who was the son of Abel and Abigail (——) Benjamin, who was the son of John and Lydia (Allen) Benjamin, who was the son of John Benjamin the immigrant. (See Appendix C.)

Children—

74. †Caleb, born Windsor, Vt., May 7, 1773; died Columbus, Wisconsin; married, 1, Aug. 28, 1797, Celia Stowell, who died Oct. 19, 1799, at Windsor, Vt. 2, Feb. 4, 1807, Charlotte Comins, who died Sept. 16, 1820, at Windsor, Vt. 3, Nov. 12, 1820, Lois Knight.
75. †Benjamin, born Windsor, Vt., Feb. 21, 1775; died Nashua, N. H., Sept. 28, 1855. (See Appendix D.) He married Roxana Alvord, Oct. 20, 1798.
76. †Rachel, born Windsor, Vt., March 5, 1778; married Zebulon Lee, and had a large family of children, some of whom lived in Barnard, Vt., Rutland, and in Quincy, Mass.
77. †Jonathan, born Windsor, Vt., July 7, 1780; died in New Orleans; married Gratia Cady.
78. †Solomon Wait, born Windsor, Vt., June 11, 1782; died Feb. 3, 1820, at Woodstock, Vt.; married Mary Craige, Westminster, Vt., Feb. 26, 1805.
79. †Alice, born Windsor, Vt., Jan. 21, 1785. She is now living at West Windsor; married Josiah Perkins, Dec 6, 1810.

80. †Moses, born Windsor, Vt., March 10, 1787; married Laura Lull.
81. †Nahum, born Windsor, Vt., July 13, 1789; married, 1, Evelina P. E. Taylor, Woodstock, Vt., April 19, 1818; 2, Mary S. Bailey, Nashua, N. H., March 5, 1848.
82. Abel, born Windsor, Vt., March 27, 1792; died Philadelphia, Jan. 27, 1817. He was a minister of the Gospel (of the Christian Baptist persuasion?). He was set apart to the work of the ministry, at Barnard, Vt., Sept. 15, 1814.

IV. 41. Silas Burke,

Born Brookfield, Mass., Nov. 22, 1744. Son of Jonathan and Thankful (Wait) Burke, who was the son of Richard and Abigail (Sawtell) Burke, who was the son of Richard and Mary (Parmenter) Burke; resided in Westminster, Vt.

June 21, 1771. He received several lots of land of his father, Jonathan Burke.

Nov. 25, 1815. An indenture was made between Silas Burke and Silas Burke, Jr., in which Silas Burke, Jr., was to support his parents during their natural lives. A proviso was also made with regard to the maintenance of his sisters, Lucy and Thankful Burke, as long as they lived single.

Silas Burke, and Mary Burke, his wife, were members of the first church at Westminster, Vt., at the settlement of the third pastor. He married

Mary Eastman,

Born Jan. 1743;(?) died Oct. 3, 1840, aged 97 years and five months.

Children—

83. Philip Eastman Burke, born Nov. 4, 1766; went to Lucerne, N. Y.; married, 1, Sarah Swan; 2, ——.

Children of Philip Eastman Burke—

84. 1. Fanny, married Abner Cunningham; resides at Saxton River, Vt.
85. 2. Harry, married ——; went out west.

86. 3. Ira, married ——; went out west.
87. 4. Laura, married ——; went to Canada.
88. 5. Orpha, married —— Kilbourn; resided in Townsend, Mass.
89. 6. Persis, married, 1, Asa Wheeler; 2, Franklin Perry; resides Saxton's River, Vt.
90. 7. Lucretia, married and went out west.
91. 8. Emily, married ——.
92. 9. George, married and left her.
93. 10. Mary Ann, married —— Clark; lives in Townsend, Mass.

94. Mary, born Westminster, Vt., March 9, 1769; married Eusebius Ball, and lived in Steuben, N. Y.
Children of Eusebius and Mary Burke Ball—
95. 1. Eusebius Ball, married Keturah Weed.
96. 2. Silas Ball, married Sarah Dod.
97. 3. Thaddeus Ball, married Cynthia Tuttle.
98. 4. Justus Ball, never married.
99. 5. Curtis Ball, married and lived in Ohio.
100. 6. Horace Ball, single.

101. Keziah, born Westminster, Vt., June 17, 1771; married Ariel Aldrich, and resided at St. Johnsbury, Vt.
Children of Ariel and Keziah (Burke) Aldrich—
102. 1. Almira Aldrich, married James Works, and lives in Waterford, Vt.
103. 2. Caroline Aldrich, married Emery Goss, and lives at St. Johnsbury, Vt.
104. 3. William Aldrich, married, 1, ——; 2, ——; resides at St. Johnsbury, Vt.
105. 4. Alanson Aldrich, married; resides at St. Johnsbury, Vt.
106. 5. Sophia Aldrich, married —— Starks.

107. Silas, born Westminster, Vt., Sept. 14, 1773; never married; resided in Westminster, Vt.
108. Justice, born Westminster, Vt., July 10, 1776; died young.

109. Sarah, born Westminster, Vt., July 8, 1778; married Timothy Clarke, and resided in Rockingham, Vt.

Children of Timothy and Sarah (Burke) Clarke.

110. 1. Timothy; 2. Silas; 3. Sarah; 4. Charles; 5. Mary;
115. 6. Lucinda.
116. 7. Joseph, married and resides at Westminster, Vt.
117. 8. Benjamin; 9. Julia Ann; 10. Albert.

120. Lucy, born Westminster, Vt., Sept. 11, 1780; single; living in Westminster, Vt., Dec. 19, 1862, with the family of her nephew, Joseph Clark, who has no children.

121. Thankful, born Westminster, Vt., June 17, 1783.

123. Anna, born Westminster, Vt., Sept. 28, 1785; married, March 23, 1815, Luther Brown of Westmoreland, N. H., and moved to the State of New York.

Children of Luther and Anna (Burke) Brown—

124. 1. Luther; 2. George; 3. Mary Ann; 4. Arabel, married Aaron Gilman.
129. 5. Harrison.

V. 45. Joseph Burke,

Born Brimfield, Mass., April 27, 1758; died Warner, N. H. Son of Jonathan and Sarah (——) Burke, who was the son of Jonathan and Thankful (Wait) Burke, who was the son of Richard and Abigail (Sawtell) Burke, who was the son of Richard and Mary (Parmenter) Burke. He resided in Hartland, Vt., and in Warner, N. H. He was in the Revolutionary war, and also in the war of 1812. When he returned home from the war of the Revolution, he left his wife, (Judith,) and went to Warner, N. H., where he lived and died.

He was married in Hartland, Vt., April 25, 1784, to

Judith Barrell.

Children—

130. Jonathan, born Hartland, Vt., Oct. 25, 1784, died Hartland, Oct. 23, 1861; resided in Hartland; married, Jan. 1808, Polly Grow.

Children of Jonathan and Polly (Grow) Burke—

131. 1. Albert B. Burke, born Nov. 13, 1808; married and resides at Hartland Four Corners, where he is a Justice of the Peace, Town Clerk, and Postmaster.

Child of Albert B. Burke—

132. 1. Marcia E. Burke, born Aug. 31, 1831.

133. 2. George G., born Feb. 25, 1810; died in 1855.

134. 3. Mary Jane, born July 17, 1812.

135. 4. Jacob Putnam Hadley, born Oct. 1814.

136. Sally [Smith?] Burke, born Hartland, Vt., Jan. 6, 1789; married, 1, Nathaniel Grow; 2, David Hopkinson.

V. 50. Lucy Burke,

Born Brimfield, Mass., Aug. 13, 1758; died Bridgewater, Vt., Nov. 26, 1850. She was the daughter of Simeon and Martha (Strong) Burke, who was the son of Jonathan and Thankful (Wait) Burke, who was the son of Richard and Abigail (Sawtell) Burke, who was the son of Richard and Mary (Parmenter) Burke. Although she lived to an advanced age, (92 years and 3 months,) she retained the faculties of her mind to the very last. "She had nine children, who lived to be more than sixty years of age, and who enjoyed good health, and a fair share of the good things of this life, with good reputation, and good character."

She was married, Feb. 26, 1778, to

Phineas Sanderson,

Born April, 1771; died Dec. 11, 1840, aged 89 years, 8 months. He moved with his family to Bridgewater, Vt., Sept. 18, 1792.

Children—

137. Phineas, born Jan. 3, 1779; died at Stockbridge, April, 1850, aged 71; married Lurana Macomber, Jan. 1, 1805, and had six children.

138. John, born Aug. 10, 1780; died in Ohio, 1850, aged 74 years; married Olive Macomber, 1807, and had two children.

139. Artemas, born May 2, 1782; died Feb. 4, 1844, aged 62; married Phebe Newton, and had two children.

140. Lucy, born May 22, 1784; died Sept. 5, 1855, aged 71; married Avon Lamb.

141. Anna, born Aug. 8, 1786; died in New Haven, April, 1856, aged 70; married William Grow, and had nine children; four living, March, 1863.

142. Susan, born Aug. 10, 1788; living in Bridgewater, Vt., March, 1863; married Thomas V. Vose, Jan. 10, 1817. She had five children. The first died in infancy; the second, Sally Miranda, died Oct. 15, 1852, aged 32; Phebe Wertley, Pliny Fisk, and Thomas Pickering.

148. Elisha, born June 17, 1790; died June 7, 1856, aged 66; married Sally Grosvenor, Jan. 1816; moved to Ohio; died on his way to visit his friends in Vermont.

149. Benjamin, born March 12, 1792; died Bridgewater, Vt., April 5, 1794, aged 2 years.

150. Lucinda, born Bridgewater, Vt., April 8, 1794; married Joseph Eaton, and resides in the State of Ohio.

151. Asenath, born Bridgewater, Vt., March 30, 1796; died Nov. 23, 1858; single.

152. Elijah, born Bridgewater, Vt., Aug. 22, 1798; married Sophronia Blair, and went to Ohio, and is now, if living, in Minnesota.

V. 54. Ebedmelech Burke,

Born Westminster, Vt., Feb. 1766; died Woodstock, Vt., March 20, 1822. Son of Simeon and Martha (Strong) Burke, who was the son of Jonathan and Thankful (Wait) Burke, who was the son of Richard and Abigail (Sawtell) Burke, who was the son of Richard and Mary (Parmenter) Burke; resided in Woodstock, Vt.

In the year 1792, he purchased land in the eastern part of Woodstock, and, in 1800, he purchased of Warren Cottle, (formerly of Woodstock, but then of Pensacola, Spanish Dominions), one-fourth of a grist-mill, standing near a meeting-house, in the south part of the town. He was generally known as Captain Burke. Capt. Ebed M. Burke died in South Woodstock, of consumption, March 20, 1822, aged 56.

His will, Jan. 12, 1822, names wife Mary, sons Elisha, Ora M., Albert G., and Ebed M., also daughter Calista Burke; also item, John, and Polly Marvin, my daughter, three notes of hand, dated in 1816.

He married, first,

Prudence Dunbar,

Born 1769; died at South Woodstock, Vt., May 14, 1802.

The following inscription is upon a grave-stone in South Woodstock:

"In memory of Prudence wife of Ebed M. Burk
died May 14. 1802 aged 33."

He was married, second, by Jabez Cottle, Justice of the Peace, Oct. 17, 1802, to

Polly Hammond,

Born May 3, 1767; died Jan. 11, 1851.

She administered on the estate of her husband, Capt. Burke, and subsequently married Noah Winslow.

Children by first wife—

153. Elisha, born Woodstock, Vt., May 19, 1790; married and went out west, near Cleveland, Ohio.

154. Polly, born Woodstock, Vt., Feb. 18, 1792; married John Marvin, and moved to Pennsylvania.

155. Mascalora, or Ora Mascal, born Woodstock, Vt., April 10, 1794; married, 1, Sally Willard; 2, Widow Howard, maiden name Clark; 3, Mary Ann Howard.

Children of Mascalora and Sally (Willard) Burke—

156. 1. Sarah, married James Hazleton; not living.(?)

157. 2. Ammi, single.

158. 3. Eliza, married Charles Smith; lives in Amherst, Mass.

159. 4. Albert G., born Rockingham, Vt.; married Caroline Blagg, who was born in Portland, Me. He practised law in Boston.

160. Seth, born in Woodstock, Vt., and died in infancy.

161. Eliza, born Woodstock, Vt., May 29, 1797; died at Walpole in 1820; married John Rice of Walpole, and had a son, Ebed Burke Rice, who lived to grow up, and died, it is supposed, in Cavendish, Vt.

163. Calista, born Woodstock, Vt., June 28, 1817; died in Pennsylvania, married Jasper Fletcher of Woodstock, Vt., and had one son, named Jasper Fletcher. She did not live with her husband, but went to Pennsylvania and married again, but died soon.

Children by second wife, Polly Hammond—

164. Albert Gallatin, born Woodstock, Vt., May 5, 1804; died Sept. 11, 1837. He was a lawyer by profession, and practised in Cherry Valley, N. Y.; married, Oct. 1827, Maria L. Babcock, and had children.

165. 1. Ellen, born Jan. 23, 1831.

166. 2. Albert G., born Jan. 8, 1833; married, March, 1862.

167. 3. Olivia, born in 1836; died in 1841.

168. Ebed Melech, born Woodstock, Vt., Feb. 11, 1806; Town Records say Jan. 12, 1806. His Post Office address is Gowanda, New York. He married, Sept. 22, 1823, Priscilla C. Briggs, (born Sept. 9, 1809), by whom he had the following children:

169. 1. Mary Hammond, born July 9, 1830; married, April 16, 1848, H. W. King, and had a son, born July 14, 1861, who died Sept. 10, 1861.

171. 2. Rosine, born Jan. 30, 1833; married, Oct. 16, 1851, Lyman Stevens, and had children, Charley Carleton, born Jan. 12, 1853; Charley died Aug. 16, 1853; Hiram, born Aug. 28, 1861; died Dec. 20, 1861.

175. 3. Elizabeth, born March 19, 1835; married, Jan. 25, 1857, W. H. Terwillign.

176. 4. Ebed M., born Dec. 26, 1827; married, June 26, 1861, Emeline Stewart.

177. 5. Albert G., born Dec. 3, 1842.

V. 56. Simeon Burke,

Born Westminster, Vt., 1769; died Stow, Vt., March 29, 1850, aged 81. Son of Simeon and Martha (Strong) Burke, who was the son of Jonathan and Thankful (Wait) Burke, who was the son of Richard and Abigail (Sawtell) Burke, who was the son of Richard and Mary (Parmenter) Burke; removed from Westminster, Vt., to Stow, Vt., March, 1801.

He married

Lucy ——,

Born ——, 1773; died in Stow, Vt., Jan. 4, 1843, aged 70.

Children—

178. Naomi, born Westminster, Vt.; died Westminster, Vt., Sept. 27, 1792.

179. Horatio, born Westminster, Vt.; died Westminster, Vt., Nov. 27, 1799, aged 10 months, 10 days.

180. Gracia, born Westminster, Vt., Sept. 8, 1800; married Horatio Sawtell, and lives, a widow, in Shefford, C. E., and has one daughter living in the same place, viz.: Lucia Louisa, born Aug. 2, 1835, who married Isaac A. Closson. They have one daughter, named Florence Gertrude Closson, born Nov. 1856.

183. Simeon S., born Stow, Vt., June 25, 1803; married, and has no children; resides in Stow.

184. Abishai, born Stow, Vt., June 15, 1805; resides in Stow, Vermont.

185. Curtis, born Aug. 25, 1807; died Stow, March 9, 1846.

186. Alanson, born Oct. 5, 1809; married and has no children; resides in Berlin, Vt.

187. Lucy, born March 2, 1812; died in Morristown, Vt., Nov. 29, 1859; married Daniel Cole of Morristown, and had children:
188. 1. Gustavus B., born Aug. 12, 1838.
189. 2. Charles Henry, born Feb. 14, 1844.
190. 3. Lucy Jane, born Nov. 25, 1846.

V. 60. Elijah Burke,

Born Westminster, Vt., March 13, 1775; died Gainesville, N. Y., Sept. 7, 1861. Son of Simeon and Martha (Strong) Burke, who was the son of Jonathan and Thankful (Wait) Burke, who was the son of Richard and Abigail (Sawtell) Burke, who was the son of Richard and Mary (Parmenter) Burke; resided in Woodstock, Vt., Barry, Vt., Mexico, N. Y., and in Gainesville, Wyoming Co., N. Y. He was married at Woodstock, Vt., to

Hannah Root,

Born Coventry, Conn., May 23, 1771; died Gainesville, N. Y., April 9, 1829.

Children—

191. Norman, born Woodstock, Vt., Sept. 25, 1796; married, July 19, 1821, Lucinda Sweet, (born Hebron, N. Y., Oct. 6, 1803, died Lakeport, Oct. 8, 1851), and had children, viz.:
192. 1. Harriet, born Leroy, N. Y., Jan. 2, 1823; married, Aug. 15, 1843, Austin Buzzell of Armada, Mich., and died at Romeo, Mich., Sept. 15, 1846.
193. 2. Caroline, born Perry, N. Y., Feb. 6, 1825; married John M. Wilson of Lapeer, March 20, 1861; they reside in Lapeer, Mich.
194. 3. Hiram, born Portage, N. Y., Jan. 25, 1827; married Elizabeth Flint, Lakeport, 1860, and died April 13, 1861.
195. 4. Graham, born Portage, N. Y., Feb. 7, 1829; his residence is Lakeport, Mich.

196. 5. Adelia, born Romeo, Mich., Dec. 28, 1831; married Charles Hitchcock, Oct. 10, 1849, and resides in Memphis, Mich.

197. 6. Norman, born Armada, Mich., Oct. 4, 1836; his residence is Lakeport, Mich.

198. 7. Eunice, born Armada, Mich., June 4, 1837; married William McDonah, Aug. 17, 1858; resides at Lakeport, Mich.

199. 8. Hannah, born Armada, Mich., June 15, 1840; resides at Lakeport, Mich.

200. 9. Charles, born Armada, Mich., July 14, 1843.

201. Betsey, born Barry, Vt., Feb. 17, 1801; married at Perry, Wyoming Co., N. Y., June 19, 1819, Daniel Wheeler, who was born at New Salem, Mass., Sept. 20, 1795, and resided in Perry, N. Y., and Gainesville, N. Y.

Children of Daniel and Betsey (Burke) Wheeler—

202. 1. Theodore, born Perry, N. Y., March 27, 1820; married in Warsaw, N. Y., Oct. 29, 1840, Lorana Conable, and resides in Greenlake, Wis.

203. 2. Lydia, born Perry, N. Y., Feb. 11, 1822; married in Gainesville, N. Y., March 1, 1849, James H. Howell, and resides in Sharon, Wis.

204. 3. Julia A., born Gainesville, March 12, 1824; married in Gainesville, March 1, 1845, George Dinsmore, and resides in Sharon, Wis.

215. 4. Amanda M., born Perry, N. Y., Dec. 24, 1826; married in Gainesville, N. Y., Oct. 18, 1849, Daniel C. Nichols, and resides at Chicago, Ill.

216. 5. Hannah, born Gainesville, N. Y., Aug. 11, 1828; married at Gainesville, N. Y., Oct, 30, 1851, John Howell, and resides at Gainesville.

217. 6. Daniel, born Gainesville, N. Y., Oct. 31, 1832; married at Gainesville, Nov. 18, 1854, Lucy A. Inglesby, and resides at Chicago, Ill.

218. 7. Hiram B., born Gainesville, N. Y., July 25, 1834; married, Gainesville, N. Y., June 19, 1856, Emeline Dunning.

219. 8. Edwin P., born Gainesville, N. Y., July 19, 1840; resides at Gainesville.

220. Hannah, born Barry, Vt., March 18, 1802; married, Nov. 12, 1826, Edwin Painter, and resides in Warsaw, N. Y., and had children, viz.:

221. 1. Thalia, born Perry, N. Y., Aug. 24, 1827; died Warsaw, N. Y., Aug. 11, 1850.

222. 2. Sarah, born Perry, N. Y., Oct. 7, 1832; married Warsaw, N. Y., Feb. 15, 1853, James N. Barrett, and resides in Warsaw, N. Y.

223. 3. Mary, born Warsaw, N. Y., Aug. 27, 1837.

224. 4. Jane, born Warsaw, N. Y., Sept. 3, 1839.

226. Elijah, born Mexico, N. Y., June 13, 1807; died Armada, Mich., Sept. 19, 1848; he married, Dec. 20, 1829, Betsey Burdick, (born Nov. 2, 1812).

Children—

227. 1. Phebe, born March 28, 1833; married, Sept. 25, 1850, Joseph Banister, and resides in Armada.

228. 2. George, born May 2, 1836; married, Dec. 22, 1858. His wife died April, 1860. He is in the First Michigan Cavalry on the Potomac.

229. 3. Elizabeth, born Jan. 26, 1840; married, March 7, 1858, J. B. Jackson, and resides in East Saginaw, Michigan.

230. 4. Dwight, born Dec. 19, 1842; single.

231. Hiram, born Mexico, N. Y., Feb. 17, 1810; married Harriet Woodruff, who was born Washington, Litchfield Co., Conn., July 15, 1815, and had children:

232. 1. Hortense, born Richmond, Mich., Sept., 22, 1845; died Nov. 15, 1848.

233. 2. Francelia, born Aug. 23, 1849.

234. 3. Eugenie, born March 6, 1854.

Mr. Hiram Burke's Post Office address is (Jan. 1864) Memphis, Michigan.

V. 62. Joseph Burke,

Born Westminster, Vt., June 22, 1762, died Morristown, Vt., Sept. 8, 1845. Son of Jesse and Leah Jennings (Rice) Burke, who was the son of Jonathan and Thankful (Wait) Burke, who was the son of Richard and Abigail (Sawtell) Burke, who was the son of Richard and Mary (Parmenter) Burke; moved from Westminster, Vt., about the year 1800, and settled in Morristown, Vt. He married

Abigail Petty,

Born May 25, 1769, died June 30, 1857.

Children—

235. Laurinia, born Westminster, Vt., May 13, 1789; died Hyde Park, March 16, 1853; married, Dec. 1814, Thaddeus Newland of Hyde Park, who was born March 10, 1796. Their children:

236. 1. Lucius, born Oct. 28, 1815; married, Aug. 29, 1841, Diama Adams, who was born Nov. 5, 1818, and had children, Lucius Augustus, born Nov. 9, 1842; Laura Augusta, born July 9, 1850.

239. 2. Thaddeus, born April 22, 1817; married, Jan. 1, 1861, Isabel L. Randall, born Nov. 9, 1840, and had George, born Jan. 31, 1863.

241. 3. George W., born Oct. 6, 1818; married, Nov. 9, 1842, Orpha C. Whipple, who was born Jan. 16, 1826, and had George Herbert, born July 28, 1849. The father died Aug. 3, 1853.

244. 4. Orrilla C., born Oct. 30, 1823, married William L. Beals, July, 1827, who was born Jan. 8, 1820, and had children, Viola A., born July 30, 1849; Frederick A., born May 8, 1852; Franklin, born March 3, 1860.

248. 5. Orra Wilmot, born 1825; died May, 1840.

249. 6. Levi Augustus, born March 14, 1829; married, Aug. 25, 1860, Jane Tice, who was born Aug. 30, 1838.

250. 7. Lorinda C., born July 14, 1833; married, Dec. 26, 1858, Augustus H. Kingsley, who was born Feb. 14, 1829.

251. Sampson, born July 24, 1790; married, Jan. 18, 1818, Louisa H. Haskins, who was born July 6, 1798. They reside in Morrisville, Vt., and have children, viz.:

252. 1. Hiram R., born Sept. 16, 1818; married, Oct. 15, 1845, Lucy A. Newland, who was born Sept. 3, 1826, and had children, Ville De Forrest, born Aug. 17, 1846, and died March 19, 1847; Clarence Vernon, born March 31, 1852, and died April 27, 1852; Emma Marion, born Aug. 2, 1860.

256. 2. Charles L., born Feb. 19, 1821; married, March 14, 1849, Vienna G. Montgomery, who was born Aug. 3, 1823, and had Ann Elizabeth, born Aug. 15, 1854; died Sept. 11, 1861.

258. 3. Asahel Munroe, born June 28, 1823.

259. 4. Sylvester W., born Sept. 18, 1825; died Oct. 28, 1850.

260. 5. Annis Louisa, born Nov. 24, 1827; married, Oct. 2, 1849, Joseph F. Hagar, born July 25, 1815, and had children, Ella Louisa, born July 22, 1850; Laura Vienna, born Feb. 9, 1852; died April 13, 1862; Joseph Sylvester, born March 3, 1854; Charles Carrol, born Dec. 31, 1856; Edna Rose, born May 7, 1860.

266. 6. Joseph Orlo, born Aug. 28, 1831.

267. 7. Aaron M., born Jan. 31, 1834; died Feb. 23, 1834.

268. 8. Sophia Abigail, born March 1, 1835.

269. 9. Seth Ozro, born Sept. 20, 1837.

270. 10. Carlos C., born July 15, 1840.

271. Abigail, born Westminster, Vt., Dec. 25, 1792; died Feb. 11, 1852; no family.

272. Joseph, born Nov. 9, 1794, Westminster, Vt.; no family.

273. Asahel, born Westminster, Vt., Sept. 13, 1796; married Dec. 4, 1823, Zeriah Walker, who was born Jan. 2, 1800; they reside in Hyde Park, and have children:

274. 1. Lavinia S., born Dec. 23, 1824; married, Oct. 12, 1846, Hezekiah Barnes, who was born Feb. 9, 1816.

275. 2. Milo A., born Oct. 22, 1826.

276. 3. Hannah L., born March 27, 1828; died July 16, 1850.

277. 4. Albert E., born Jan. 13, 1834.

278. Leah, born Westminster, Vt., Sept. 20, 1798; resides in Stow, Vt., and has no family.

279. Clara, born Sept. 1, 1800; resides in Morristown; no family.

280. Morris, born Morristown, May 25, 1802; resides in Morristown; no family.

281. Amasa, born Morristown, Vt., March 25, 1804; married, March 25, 1831, Ruth Hubbell, who was born June 15, 1807; they reside in Hyde Park, Vt., and have children:

282. 1. Salmon Augustus, born Sept. 23, 1834; died March 9, 1835.

283. 2. Ransom Van Ness, born Sept. 9, 1841.

284. 3. Clara Ellen, born Sept. 19, 1849.

285. Laura, born Aug. 25, 1807, and resides in Morristown; no family.

286. Ransom, born Feb. 9, 1809, and resides in Morristown; no family.

287. Calista, born March 17, 1812, and resides in Morristown; no family.

We are indebted for information with regard to Joseph Burke's descendants, to Miss Leah Burke, through Rev. James T. Ford; also, to Miss Sophia A. Burke, and Mr. R. V. N. Burke.

V. 65. Jesse Burke,

Born Westminster, Vt.,(?) Dec. 20, 1770; died Westminster, Vt., 1816. Son of Jesse and Leah Jennings (Rice) Burke, who was the son of Jonathan and Thankful (Wait) Burke, who was the son of Richard and Abigail (Sawtell) Burke, who was the son of Richard and Mary (Parmenter) Burke; resided in Westminster. He was a teacher of music, of which he was passionately fond. He married

Sally Hatch,

Born Dec. 12, 1778. She outlived her husband.

Children—

288. Infant, born Westminster, Vt.; died Westminster, Vt., 1796.

289. Infant daughter, born Westminster, Vt.; died Westminster, Vt., Dec. 28, 1797.

290. Ahira, born Westminster, Vt., April 21, 1799; he was baptized Sept. 2, 1832, on the profession of his faith. June 15, 1833, he was dismissed from the first church at Westminster, Vt., to the Presbyterian Church in Thompson, Ohio. June 17, 1836, Ahira Burke of Thompson, Ohio, signs a quit-claim of his interest in a certain parcel of land in Westminster, Vt., including the Widow Sarah's reversion of her dowry, unto Courtland Burke of Westminster, Vt. He married Lucinda Hamilton, and had Ahira Harris, baptized at Westminster, Vt., Oct. 6, 1832; Mary, born, &c.

293. Harris, born Westminster, Vt., Oct. 17, 1801; died Westminster, Vt., 1827.

294. Laura, born Westminster, Vt.,(?) Oct. 13, 1803; died Barnard, Vt., Nov. 19, 1850; married Cyrus Paige, born Jan. 19, 1799, and had children:

295. 1. Infant daughter, born Sept. 22, 1826, and died Sept. 23, 1826.

296. 2. Sarah Hatch, born Dec. 17, 1828; married Hiram Chester Young of Boston, July 23, 1851, and had Sanford Edmund, born Boston, Dec. 5, 1855.

298. 3. Laura Lorana, born Oct. 19, 1831; married July 3, 1854, Isaac H. Burroughs of Boston, and had Marshall Arthur Lewis, born in Boston, July 3, 1854.

300. 4. Amanda Cornelia, born Sept. 17, 1833; married Horatio Nelson Merrill of Hanover, N. H., and had children: 1, Elbridge Nelson, born Hanover, N. H., April, 1857; 2, Edwin Harlan, born Hanover, N. H., Sept. 1859; 3, Laura Ellen, born Hanover, N. H., Aug. 1862.

304. 5. Asa, born Feb. 16, 1836; married, Jan. 1, 1862, Mary L. Webster of Canaan, N. H., and had no children.

305. 6. Harlan P., born Oct. 22, 1838. Enlisted in the army for three years. Single.

306. Huldah, born Westminster, Vt., July 20, 1806; died Medford, Mass., June, 1846; she married Benjamin Sherman; resided in Medford, Mass., and had three children: Sarah, Benjamin, the name of the other not known.

310. Roxana Hatch, born Westminster, Vt., Sept. 9, 1808; she married in Westminster, Vt., Oct. 23, 1832, John Gordon Allbe, born in Peterborough, N. H., March 19, 1802; they reside in Chicopee, Mass., and have children:

311. 1. James Gordon, born Chesterfield, N. H., Aug. 15, 1833; married Nashua, N. H., July 1, 1854, Sarah Jones, and resides at Chicopee, Mass. He is a printer, publisher, and editor, by trade and profession. He published and edited a paper in Illinois nearly five years.

312. 2. Joseph Goodhue, born Chesterfield, N. H., April 14, 1835; married Chicopee, Mass., June 11, 1856, Jane A. Mixter.

313. 3. Juliet Gratia, born Westminster, Vt., July 13, 1837; died Chicopee, Mass., Aug. 6, 1841.

314. 4. Edward Payson, born Westminster, Vt., Dec. 3, 1839.

315. 5. Sarah Emily, born Chicopee, Mass., Aug. 22, 1843.

316. 6. Harlan Page, born Chicopee, Mass., Sept. 20, 1845.

317. 7. Silas David Mosman, born Chicopee, Mass., Sept. 26, 1848.

318. 8. Lucy Ann, born Chicopee, Mass., April 3, 1851.

319. Courtland, born Westminster, Vt., Jan. 9, 1810; married, Sept. 28, 1834, Mitty Ann P. Harris, who was born April 8, 1813; they resided in Westminster, Vt., and at Collins' Centre, N. Y., and had children:

320. 1. Sarah A., born Aug. 12, 1836; married, March 5, 1856, Francis A. Hoyt, and had a daughter, Georgianna.

322. 2. Willis A., born March 3, 1838; married, Feb. 14, 1859, Cornelia J. Pierce, and had children: 1, Ellis W., born Feb. 11, 1862; 2, Ada M., born May 2, 1863.

325. 3. Ellis W., born Jan. 23, 1840.

326. 4. Esther M., born Aug. 7, 1842; married, Jan. 1, 1862, Nathan M. Bailey.

327. 5. Ann Eliza, born Feb. 20, 1845; married, March 31, 1861, Royal C. Payne.

328. Luthera, born Westminster, Vt., June 28 or 20, 1811; has been twice married, and resides in New Hampshire.

329. Quartus, born Westminster, Vt., March 31, 1813; married an English lady, and resides in Canada.(?) They have six children.

336. Lorana, born Westminster, Vt., March 15, 1816; married, Oct. 9, 1837, Charles C. Hinds. They left Vermont, Nov. 1855, and now reside in Hardin, Clayton Co., Iowa. With a true patriotic spirit, she gave her boys—her all—to fight for her country, to put down the Rebellion. Children—

337. 1. Charles Barritt Hinds, born Jan. 31, 1839; enlisted in Company B, 21st Regiment Iowa Volunteers. "He, with the rest of his Company, marched all night, and fought all the next day, (May 1st, 1863,) at the commencement of the siege at Vicksburg, and three days after he was carried back to the Hospital, at Grand Gulf, where he died, May 14, 1863, of quick consumption. He

was called a brave soldier, and was always cheerful and ready, and never faltered when duty called."

338. 2. Edwin Burke Hinds, born Nov. 21, 1842; enlisted in Company M, Iowa Cavalry, in Aug. 1862, and his Company is now (Nov. 2, 1863) at Little Rock, Arkansas.

V. 66. Eli Burke,

Born Westminster, Vt., Oct. 21, 1771; died Pomfret, Vt., Sept. 29, 1855. Son of Jesse and Leah Jennings (Rice) Burke, who was the son of Jonathan and Thankful (Wait) Burke, who was the son of Richard and Abigail (Sawtell) Burke, who was the son of Richard and Mary (Parmenter) Burke.

"He resided in Westminster, Vt., until about the year 1800, when he removed to Chester, Vt., and commenced on a wild uncultivated tract of land, which he mostly cleared up; and about the year 1814, he moved to Andover, Vt., where he resided some sixteen years; during which time (about 1819 or 1820) he became lame in one knee, and had to go with crutches some 12 or 15 years. He removed from Andover, Vt., to Chester, Vt., where he lived about two years; from thence he moved to Bethel, Vt., and purchased a good meadow-farm on White River, where he lived some eight years. He returned to Chester, Vt., where he stayed about two years, and from thence he removed to Pomfret, Vt., where he purchased a good farm, of about one hundred and seventy acres, and there spent the remainder of his days." He married

Mary Adams,

Born Nov. 15, 1776; died at Pomfret, Vt., March 18, 1863.

Children—

339. Charles, born Westminster, Vt., March 21, 1796; died Pomfret, Vt., May 20, 1836; married Sally Gassett, born Jan. 11, 1796, and died Andover, Vt., July 7, 1843. They had children:

340. 1. Lawson C., born Sept. 14, 1830; married Fannie Carriel, who was born May 4, 1834, and had children: 1, Emma Jennett Burke, born Dec. 15, 1856; 2, Rose Alice Burke, born Feb. 9, 1859; 3, Charles Henry Burke, born Sept. 1, 1861. Mr. Lawson C. Burke resides at Goodhue, Min.

344. 2. Sarah M. Burke, born June 26, 1832; died Grafton, Vt., July 5, 1845.

345. 3. Darius O. Burke, born March 3, 1834.

346. 4. Alonzo L. Burke, born Dec. 30, 1835.

347. Clarissa, born Westminster, Vt., Feb. 21, 1798; married, Jesse Hall, who died Oct. 30, 1861. She is now a widow, and has a number of children. They are all married except one.

348. Sylvester, born Aug. 14, 1800; resides at North Springfield, Vt. He enjoyed good health until about the age of 18, when, being engaged at hard labor in a brickyard, he was taken with a liver complaint, which subsequently settled in his knee, and caused his leg to become emaciated, and of no use whatever. He continued to grow more feeble, until he engaged in a light employment, which brought him into the open air. He used crutches some 20 years. He now enjoys good health. From the fall of 1831 to the spring of 1856, he was successively engaged in mercantile business. He has held various offices of trust. He married Esther H. Shipman, who was born Jan. 12, 1803, and had children:

349. 1. Louisa, born Feb. 14, 1825; married Ballard B. Chidel, resides in Springfield, Vt., and has three children.

353. 2. Elizabeth S., born Jan. 23, 1831; married John W. Lockwood; they reside in Springfield, Vt., and have no children.

354. 3. Esther A., born Jan. 9, 1835; died Springfield, Vt., March 30, 1835.

355. 4. Amelia M., born May 18, 1841; married John C. Watson, and died Dec. 3, 1861, leaving a little son nearly two months old. The parents gave the child to Mr. and Mrs. Sylvester Burke. The child's name is Fred Elsworth Watson.

357. 5. Sidney Sylvester, born Sept. 7, 1844.

358. Hubbard, born Chester, Vt., Aug. 8, 1802; married Amelia Davis, who was born Oct. 17, 1826; they reside in Pomfret, Vt., on the old farm where his father and mother died. They had children:

359. 1. Mary A. Burke, born Aug. 31, 1859.

360. 2. Cleaves D. Burke, born June 6, 1861.

361. Ora, born Chester, Vt., April 1, 1805; married Alvira Riggs, born Sept. 10, 1804. They reside in East Barnard, Vt., and have children:

362. 1. Elvira A., born Oct. 28, 1828; married Alanson Barton.

363. 2. Mary Jane, born Sept. 15, 1830; married Aurin Culver.

364. 3. Eliza A., born May 17, 1832; married Ezra Kimton.

365. 4. Ora O., born March 6, 1835; died July 10, 1843.

366. 5. Ellen A., born March 10, 1837; married Seymour Culver.

367. 6. Mason P., born May 5, 1841.

368. 7. Oscar F., born Nov. 12, 1846.

369. Harriet Burke, born Chester, Vt., March 30, 1807; died at Andover, Vt., 1814.

370. Abigail, born Chester, Vt., Sept. 2, 1809.

371. Asa, born Chester, Vt., Oct. 13, 1811; married Rosanna Robinson, born Feb. 17, 1808. Child—

372. 1. Charles Asa, born Aug. 12, 1837; died May 16, 1848. Mr. Burke resides in Dorchester, Mass.

373. Eliakim, born Jan. 29, 1814; died at Pomfret, Vt., Sept. 1835.

374. Harriet, born Andover, Vt., July 14, 1815; married Sylvester W. Sterling, who was born Dec. 7, 1821; they live in Sharon, Vt., and have no children.

375. Dexter, born Andover, Vt., Dec. 17, 1817; married, 1, Aurilla Bugbee, who was born March 23, 1821, and died Sharon Vt., Sept. 25, 1859. He married, 2, Emily Houghton, born Nov. 23, 1836. They reside in Sharon, Vt. Children by first wife:

376. 1. Alma E. Burke, born Feb. 19, 1844; married Alonzo Dinsmore.

377. 2. Edmund D. Burke, born May 8, 1846.

378. 3. Martha A. Burke, born June 19, 1848.

379. 4. Mary A. Burke, born April 21, 1851; died at Sharon, Vt., Oct. 15, 1854.

380. 5. Edna C. Burke, born Dec. 29, 1853.

381. 6. Clarance E. Burke, born Sept. 25, 1859.

V. 67. Elijah Burke,

Born Westminster, Vt., March 3, 1774; died March 21, 1843. Son of Jesse and Leah Jennings (Rice) Burke, grandson of Jonathan and Thankful (Wait) Burke, great-grandson of Richard and Abigail (Sawtell) Burke, and great-great-grandson of Richard and Mary (Parmenter) Burke. He resided in Westminster, Vt., was a farmer by occupation, and lived a quiet and unobtrusive life. "He was a man of much more than ordinary reading and intelligence, for one in his condition in life. His character was without blemish. For these reasons, he always enjoyed the respect and confidence of his townsmen, by whom he was often tendered such public offices as were in their gift. These, he almost invariably declined, never accepting any, except the most humble and practically useful. In his early life, his farming operations were quite active. He was among the first to engage in the introduction and growth of the merino sheep, in the State of Vermont, and for many years was owner of large flocks of that valuable animal. His whole life was one of exemplary virtue and practical utility."

He married, Sept. 1795,

Grace Jeffers,

Born Sept. 14, 1777. She now lives with her son, Edmund, at Newport, N. H., and is a devoted, exemplary, christian lady. She was the daughter of Moses and Lucy Jeffers of New London, Conn. She was a member of the first church at Westminster, Vt., where her children were baptized.

Children—

382. Russell, born Westminster, Vt., March 26, 1797; died Springfield, Vt., Oct. 4, 1852–55; married, Aug. 18, 1822, Eliza Williams, who was born March 15, 1803; she resides, a widow, in Charlestown, N. H., and from a family of nine children she lost six in infancy. Although she has seen affliction, she says that she knows that her Heavenly Father is very merciful and kind, and does not willingly afflict. Children:

383. 1. Russell Williams, born July 5, 1825; died at Saratoga, June 19, 1826.

384. 2. Russell Williams, born April 3, 1827; married Elizabeth R. Parker of Ludlow, Nov. 12, 1851, and resides at Pittsburg, Penn., and has children: 1. Edward Parker. 2. A daughter.

387. 3. John Westfield, born Sept. 4, 1829; died Springfield, Vt., July 26, 1830, aged 10 months, 22 days.

388. 4. John Westfield, born June 2, 1831; died Springfield, Vt., April 20, 1832, aged 10 months, 21 days.

389. 5. Harriet Eliza, born March 2, 1833; died Springfield, Vt., March 16, 1833, aged 14 days.

390. 6. Harriet Eliza, born May 14, 1834; died Springfield, Vt., April 14, 1838, aged 3 years, 11 months, 9 days.

391. 7. George Henry, born Feb. 23, 1837; died Springfield, Vt., Aug. 6, 1839, aged 2 years, 5 months, 13 days.

392. 8. George Henry, born June 5, 1839.

393. 9. Charles Clinton, born Oct. 26, 1842.

394. Rhoda, born Westminster, Vt., June 25, 1799; died Westminster, Vt., March 18, 1818.

395. Elijah, born Westminster, Vt., March 31, 1802; died August, 1804.

396. George Emery, born Westminster, Oct. 27, 1803; died August, 1842.

397. Udney, born Sept. 1, 1806; married, Jan. 1, 1833, Mary McRinstry. She was born Aug. 17, 1812, and was the daughter of Alexander and Mary (Chaplin) McRinstry, and granddaughter of William of Scotland. Mr. Burke resides in Springfield, Vt., and is successfully engaged in Scythe Sneath manufactory. Children:

398. 1. Edmund Chaplin, born Oct. 5, 1833; married, Jan. 15, 1857, Elnora Mason, born Aug. 23, 1827, and had Arthur Udney, born March 23, 1859.

400. 2. Olivia Adelaide, born Feb. 4, 1835; married, Oct. 5, 1857, Lieut. Henry W. Closson, born June 6, 1833, who was the son of the Hon. Henry and Emily (Whitney) Closson, Judge of Probate.
Children: 1, Henry Burke Closson, born Newport, R. I., Aug. 12, 1858; 2, Olivia Texita Closson, born Texas, Jan. 2, 1860.

403. 3. Ellen Adell, born June 29, 1839; died Feb. 15, 1846.

404. Edmund, born Westminster, Jan. 23, 1809. "He was educated in the common schools of the village in which he was born, and resided, until the age of thirteen years, when he received from private tutors sufficient instruction in the classics to qualify him for the study of law, for which profession he was designed by his parents. At the age of sixteen years he was entered as a student at law, in the office of Hon. William C. Bradley of Westminster, Vt., at that time the most eminent of his profession in that State, and a man of great ability, eloquence, and literary as well as legal attainments.

He remained in the office of Mr. Bradley as a student, nearly five years, when he was admitted to the Bar of Windham County, on the September term of the Court in 1829; and, in the winter following, he was admitted to the Bar in Cheshire Co., N. H. In the spring of 1830 he removed to the northern part of New Hampshire, and first commenced the practice of law in the town of Colebrook, Coos Co. Subsequently, during the same year, he removed to Whitefield, in the same county; where he continued in the practice of his profession until the autumn of 1833, when he removed to Claremont, Sullivan Co., in the same State. There, in connection with his profession, he assumed the editorial control of the New Hampshire Argus, a democratic newspaper, then published in that place, of which he also was part proprietor. He continued to reside in Claremont until Oct. 1834, when he removed to Newport, the shire town of the same county, and there established himself in his profession, at the same time continuing his connection with the Argus, which was removed to Newport. He continued his editorial connection with the Argus, (afterwards united with the New Hampshire Spectator, and published under the title of the New Hampshire Argus and Spectator), until the spring of 1839, when he was elected by the Democratic party a member of the House of Representatives in the Congress of the United States. He filled the office six years, having been re-elected to the same office; his last election being contrary to the customary practice of his party, which was to give to their representatives, ordinarily, two elections only.

On the accession of Mr. Polk to the Presidency of the United States, he was tendered by the President the office of Commissioner of Patents. He held the office during the Presidency of Mr. Polk, a period of four years.

He then became joint editor with the celebrated Thomas Ritchie of the Washington Union, then the central organ of the National Democratic Party. He continued editor of the Union for one year, when he retired from that journal and returned to Newport, N. H., his former residence, where he resumed and still continues the practice of his profession. He has, since his return to New Hampshire, engaged actively in political affairs; and has written, at all times, much for the political press, having since his return been the editor of the "Old Guard," and the Democratic Standard, both democratic papers, and both published in Concord, N. H. He was editor of the Standard at the time of its destruction by the mob, in the summer of 1861.

In addition to his editorial labors, he delivered several speeches in Congress, namely, upon the Sub-Treasury, in the first term of the XXVIth Congress; in defence of New Hampshire against the assaults of Hon. Thomas D. Arnold of Kentucky, in the first session of the XXVIIth Congress, and on the Tariff, during the same session. He was a member of several important committees, and among others, chairman of the Select Committee to investigate the facts concerning the Suffrage movement in Rhode Island, and in that capacity made a long and elaborate report.

He was also the author of the "Bundelcome Essays" upon the tariff policy of the country, taking the free-trade view of that subject. These Essays were written while Mr. Burke was Commissioner of Patents, and originally published in the Washington Union. An edition of the same work was subsequently published at Washington, of which about 20,000 copies were taken and circulated by members of Congress, and other persons. It was in whole, or in part, re-published in nearly every democratic newspaper in the United States.

Mr. Burke has also delivered several elaborate political addresses, prepared Congressional documents, and also delivered addresses on agriculture and other topics, besides diligently laboring in his profession.

So far his life has been one of activity and industry. Mr. Burke was married, Dec. 1, 1840, to Ann Matson, who was born Stoddård, N. H., June 20, 1823, and died Newport, N. H., Jan. 28, 1857, aged 33 years, 7 months, 5 days. She was the only daughter and child of Francis and Susan (Gilson) Matson, who was the only son and child of the Hon. Aaron and Frances (Carpenter) Matson, formerly a member of Congress from New Hampshire. He moved from Connecticut to Stoddard, N. H. Frances Carpenter, wife of Aaron Matson, was a resident of Charlestown, N. H. The tradition of the family is, that she was a direct lineal descendant of Peregrine White, who was born in the Mayflower, on its passage with the Pilgrims from England.

Mr. Burke's daughter has now preserved for her, as an heir loom, a copper tea-kettle, which is said to have been brought over in the Mayflower, by the family of Whites, was then the property of Peregrine, and from him has been handed down in the direct line of descent to Miss Burke, who is the only lineal descendant of the Matson family, through the Aaron Matson branch.

Child of Edmund Burke:

405. 1. Frances Matson Burke, born Washington, D. C., Oct. 7, 1847.

406. Thales, born Westminster, Vt., Jan. 31, 1811; resides in Eau Galla, Dunn Co., Wis. He married, Oct. 30, 1834, Margaret Cascaden, born Donegal, Donegal Co., Ireland, Sept. 18, 1814, and had children:

407. 1. Gratia Eleanor, born Hemingford, Canada East, Jan. 31, 1837; married, Feb. 23, 1854, John McGilton, and had children: 1, Emily Justina, born Hemingford, Canada East, April 5, 1855;

2, Edmund George, born Eau Galla, Dunn Co., Wis., Feb. 10, 1859; 3, Thomas Wesley, born Eau Galla, Dunn Co., Wis., Dec. 10, 1861; 4, Maggy Belle, born Eau Galla, Dunn Co., Wis., Jan. 19, 1863.

412. 2. Martha Isabella, born Hemingford, C. E., Dec. 22, 1843; married, Feb. 3, 1863, Rev. Horace A. Wentz.

413. Gratia, born March 22, 1815; resides at Newport, N. H., with her mother and brother.

414. Catharine, born May 5, 1817; married, Oct. 27, 1845, Thomas Pratt, and had children: 1, Grace Marion; 2, Helen Burke; 3, Ellen Alice; 4, Rosamond; 5, Edmund Burke; 6, Frederika; 7, Lilian; 8, Harriet Newell.

V. 68. David Burke,

Born Jan. 26, 1772; died April 28, 1844. He was the son of Isaiah and Ann (Mason) Burke, who was the son of Jonathan and Thankful (Wait) Burke, who was the son of Richard and Abigail (Sawtell) Burke, who was the son of Richard and Mary (Parmenter) Burke.

He resided in Hartland and in Bridgewater, Vt., and married

Olive Short.

Born July 28, 1776, and resides with her son, Alonzo Burke, in Sherborn, Vt.

Children—

423. Levi, born March 18, 1798; married Margaret Haffed.

424. Belinda, born March 14, 1800; married Charles Brown.

425. Lavinia, born March 16, 1803; died Sept. 1856.

426. David, born Nov. 22, 1805; married Maria Cheesman.

427. Siloam, born Feb. 23, 1807.

428. Daniel, born Oct. 8, 1809.

429. Olive, born July 8, 1817; single.

430. Alonzo, born Feb. 25, 1819; single.

V. 71. Ezra Burke,

Born April 4, 1776, died in Ludlow, March, 1862. Son of Isaiah and Ann (Mason) Burke, who was the son of Jonathan and Thankful (Wait) Burke, who was the son of Richard and Abigail (Sawtell) Burke, who was the son of Richard and Mary (Parmenter) Burke. He resided in Mount Holley and in Ludlow. He married, 1, Sally White, born ——; died in Mount Holley; 2, Widow ——. He had children.

V. 72. Anna Burke,

Born June, 1778; died in Bridgewater, Vt., Aug. 1856. She was the daughter of Isaiah and Ann (Mason) Burke; who was the son of Jonathan and Thankful (Wait) Burke, who was the son of Richard and Abigail (Sawtell) Burke, who was the son of Richard and Mary (Parmenter) Burke. She married

Abel Farwell.

They resided in various places, (Vermont, Wisconsin,) and left children.

431. Mason S., born in Hartland, Vt.; married, 1, Mary Danforth; 2. Sarah Hawkins.

Children by first wife:

432. 1. Mason Danforth, married Marinda Tinkham.
433. 2. Infant, born ——.
434. 3. Leonard Warren, born ——; married Phebe McMaster
435. 4. Mary Ann, born ——; married Cyrus Kneeland.
436. 5. Edwin Perkins, born ——, and married ——.
437. 6. Ellen, born ——; married, 1, ——; 2, Mr. Carpenter.
438. 7. Amanda ——.

Children by Sarah Hawkins:

439. 1. J. Morton, single, and lives in Wisconsin.
440. 2. Dunbar, single, and lives in Wisconsin.

441. Martha, born ——, in Hartland; married William Dodge.
442. Susan, born ——, in Hartland; was an actress.

443. Betsey, (?) born ——; married Lyman Spaulding.
444. Mariette, born ——; was an actress; married, 1, —— 2, ——.

V. 74. Capt. Caleb Burke,

Born Windsor, Vt., May 1 or 7, 1773; died Columbus, Wis., April 26, 1854, aged 80 years, 11 months, 26 days. He was the son of Solomon and Keziah (Benjamin) Burke, who was the son of Jonathan and Thankful (Wait) Burke, who was the son of Richard and Abigail (Sawtell) Burke, who was the son of Richard and Mary (Parmenter) Burke.

He was universally respected, and was a natural mechanic, and his work, place of business, and everything about him, showed that he was a person of neatness and of order. He was celebrated as a "Last maker."

He resided in Windsor and Dorchester, Vt., and in Columbus, Wisconsin. Aug. 5, 1799, his father conveys land to him in Windsor, Vt., and in Hartland, Vt. In 1807 he conveys land in Windsor, Vt., to Alvan Marcy. He was dismissed from the church in Windsor, Vt., and recommended to the church at Dorchester, Vt.

He married, 1st, Aug. 28, 1797,

Celia Stowell,

Born ——, 1772; died Windsor, Vt., Oct. 19, 1799, aged 27 years.

> "In memory of Mrs Celia Consort of Capt. Caleb Burke, who died Oct. 19th, 1799 in her 27 year."

[Windsor, Vt., burial-ground.

He married, 2d, Feb. 4, 1807,

Charlotte Comins,

Born ——, 1783; died Windsor, Vt., Sept. 16, 1820, aged 38 years.

> "Mrs. Charlotte Burke died Sept. 16, 1820 aged 38 years, Consort of Capt Caleb Burke."

[Windsor, Vt., burial-ground.

Capt. Caleb Burke married, 3d, Nov. 12, 1820,

Lois Knight,

Born Rockingham, Vt., May 12, 1793; resides at Columbus, Wisconsin.

Child of Capt. Caleb and Celia Burke—

445. Cyril Stowell, born Windsor, Vt., Dec. 18, 1798; died Brooklyn, N. Y., Sept. 22, 1851; married, Dec. 28, 1829, Julia Nearing, born Windsor, Conn., Dec. 14, 1810, and had children:

446. 1. Helen Burke, born Hartford, Conn., Dec. 31, 1830; married, Jan. 18, 1858, Richard R. Morris of Pottsville, Penn., and have children: 1, Richard L. Morris, born Pottsville, Penn., Nov. 5, 1858; 2, Robert R. Morris, born Pottsville, Penn., April 18, 1861; 3, Helen Burke Morris, born Pottsville, Penn., March 24, 1863.

450. 2. Pascal Caleb Burke, born Windsor, Conn., July 24, 1836; married, May 21, 1860, Jane A. Swalm of Brooklyn, N. Y.; no children.

Children of Capt. Caleb and Charlotte Burke:

451. Leonard Comins, born Windsor, Vt., Aug. 21, 1808; died Aug. 31, 1808, aged 10 days.

452. Maria, born Windsor, Vt., July 6, 1811; died Oct. 3, 1811, aged 3 months. [Windsor, Vt., burial-ground.

Children of Capt. Caleb and Lois Burke:

453. Celia, born Windsor, Vt., March 16, 1823; died March 16, 1823.

454. Jared Wait, born Windsor, Vt., Aug. 29, 1826; resides at Columbus, Wis. He settled in Wisconsin in the year 1850, and is a farmer by occupation. He married, Wisconsin, Nov. 5, 1854, Mrs. Mary Walker of Westminster, Vt., born 1819, and had one child, viz.:

455. 1. Celia Maria Burke, born Columbus, Wis., March 23, 1855. Mrs. Burke had one child by her former husband, John Walker, viz.: Mary Amelia Walker, born Westminster, Vt., Aug. 21, 1850.

V. 75. Benjamin Burke,

Born Windsor, Vt., Feb. 21, 1775; died Nashua, N. H., Sept. 28, 1855, aged 80 years, 7 months, 7 days. Son of Solomon and Keziah (Benjamin) Burke, who was the son of Jonathan and Thankful (Wait) Burke, who was the son of Richard and Abigail (Sawtell) Burke, who was the son of Richard and Mary (Parmenter) Burke. Mr. Burke resided at Windsor, Vt., until May, 1826, when he removed to Nashua, N. H., where he died. "The first Tuesday in July, Benjamin Burke was examined for admittance to the church, and be propounded next Sabbath."—[Church Records of Windsor, 1801?]. Mr. Burke was often appointed by the church to attend as a delegate to ordinations, &c. He was dismissed to the first church in Dunstable, N. H. He lived to be feeble and aged, but gave evidence of strong faith, as a devoted christian, in his Lord and Master. (See Appendix D.)

He married, Woodstock, Vt., Oct. 10, 1798,

Roxana Alvord,

Born Charlestown, N. H., Dec. 6, 1775; died Nashua, N. H., March 9, 1859. She was the daughter of Stephen and Abigail (Davis) Alvord. (See Alvord Genealogy.) She, with her older brother and sisters, were baptized at Charlestown, N. H., July 26, 1778. She united with the church at Windsor, Vt., Dec. 2, 1810. "Mrs. Rocksalana Burke, having previously given satisfactory evidence to the church of her gracious state & been duly propounded, was received to the communion and fellowship of the church." (See Records of the First Church of Windsor, Vt.) She died, as above, viz.: March 9, 1859, at 10 o'clock in the evening, aged 83 years, 4 months, and 3 days. The infirmities of old age had afflicted her for some years. The immediate cause of her death appeared to be inflammation of the lungs, or a kind of lung fever.

Children—

455. S[illegible] born Windsor, Vt., Aug. 19, 1799; died Windsor, Vt., Aug. 11, 1800, aged 11 months, 22 days.

456. Lucia, born Windsor, Vt., Feb. 4, 1802; died North Chelmsford, Oct. 12, 1828. She was dismissed from the church in Windsor, Vt., and recommended to the Second Church in Chelmsford in 1828. (See Church Records.) She married, Feb. 8, 1826, John R. Holmes, and had:

457. 1. Lucia Burke Holmes, born June 19, 1828; died at Nashua, N. H., Jan. 15, 1829.

458. Pascal Benjamin, born Windsor, Vt., Dec. 19, 1803; died Boston, Mass., Aug. 7, 1858, aged 54 years, 8 months, 28 days, of marasmus or dropsical consumption, and was buried at Nashua, N. H., according to his request, beside his father. He was married, at Boston, Mass., by the Rev. Hubbard Winslow, Oct. 21, 1838, to Esther Prentiss, who was born at Boston, Mass., July 23, 1806.

459. William Alvord, born Windsor, Vt., July 7, 1811. His early education was obtained principally at the Academy of Josiah Dunham, Esq., in Windsor, Vt., and with a view to a collegiate course, but circumstances not favoring such a plan, upon the removal of his parents to Nashua, (then Dunstable,) N. H., in 1826, he entered the machine shop of the Nashua Manufacturing Company in December of that year, as an apprentice to learn the machinists' trade. Excepting a part of the years 1829 and 1830, when he labored in the machine shop of the Locks and Canals in Lowell, Mass., he worked at his calling in Nashua until January, 1834, when he went to North Chelmsford, Mass., and had charge of a machine shop at that place, owned by Messrs. Ira Gay & Co. of Nashua, N. H. Here he remained till March, 1836, when he became master mechanic at the Boott Cotton Mills in Lowell, B. F. French, Esq., then being the agent. In October, 1839, he left the Boott Cotton Mills and took the agency of the Amoskeag Manufacturing Company's machine shop at Manchester, N. H., which had just been erected. He put in operation and had the direction and charge of these works until April,

1845, when he returned to Lowell and became the superintendent of the Lowell Machine Shop, a corporation that had been just organized, and had purchased the machine shop and some other property owned by the "Proprietors of Locks and Canals on Merrimack River." He held this situation for seventeen years, until April, 1862, when he became the agent of the Boott Cotton Mills (in Lowell) where he now (1864) remains.

He was married at Bedford, N. H., by the Rev. Thomas Savage, June 6, 1837, to Catharine French, born Bedford, N. H., April 28, 1819. She was the daughter of John and Amy (Nevins) French. Her father was born at Bedford, N. H., Dec. 31, 1781; died May 25, 1861, at Bedford, N. H. Her mother was born at Hollis, N. H., March 23, 1789, and died at Bedford, N. H., Oct. 28, 1838, aged 49 years, 7 months, and 4 days.

Children of W. A. and Catharine (French) Burke:

460. 1. Ellen Maria, born Lowell, Mass., March 19, 1838; died April 9, 1838, aged 3 weeks.

461. 2. Catharine Elizabeth, born Manchester, N. H., Feb. 9, 1843.

462. 3. William French, born Lowell, Mass., Aug. 31, 1848; died Lowell, Mass., May 18, 1857, aged 8 years, 9 months, and 18 days, of whooping cough, and of a disease of the spine, from which he had suffered for four years. "We shall go to him but he will not return to us."

463. 4. Annie Alvord, born Lowell, Mass., Dec. 6, 1850.

464. 5. Edward Nevins, born Lowell, Mass., Jan. 19, 1854.

V. 76. Rachel Burke,

Born Windsor, Vt., March 5, 1778; died at Barnard, Vt. She was the daughter of Solomon and Keziah (Benjamin) Burke, who was the son of Jonathan and Thankful (Wait) Burke, who was the son of Richard and Abigail (Sawtell)

Burke, who was the son of Richard and Mary (Parmenter) Burke. She married

Zebulon Lee.

Children—

465. Mary, married Hiram Aiken.
466. Rosamond, married Alvin Wood.
467. Christiana, married twice; resided at the West.
468. Martha, married —— Fitch.
469. Rinaldo Leland, born Jan. 6, 1823; married Emily Smith, and had, 1, Carrie E. Lee, born Nov. 19, 1859.
471. Son, died young.
472. Amanda.

V. 77. Jonathan Burke,

Born Windsor, Vt., July 7, 1780. Son of Solomon and Keziah (Benjamin) Burke, who was the son of Jonathan and Thankful (Wait) Burke, who was the son of Richard and Abigail (Sawtell) Burke, who was the son of Richard and Mary (Parmenter) Burke. He resided in Windsor, Vt., on his father's place, and afterwards became a pedler, and went to New Orleans, where it is said he died.

He married

Gratia Cady,

Born ——; died Claremont, N. H.

Children—

473. Susan, born ——; married —— Bartholomew, and went out West.
474. Hannah, born ——; married —— Vannorwan; went to Canada.
475. Franklin, born ——; married and settled in Cornish, N. H.; removed to Vermont, and from thence to Wisconsin.
476. Henry, born ——; settled in Canada.
477. Nahum, born ——; moved out West.
478. Edmund, born ——.

V. 78. Solomon Wait Burke,

Born Windsor, Vt., June 11, 1782; died Woodstock, Vt., Feb. 3, 1820. He was the son of Solomon and Keziah (Benjamin) Burke, who was the son of Jonathan and Thankful (Wait) Burke, who was the son of Richard and Abigail (Sawtell) Burke, who was the son of Richard and Mary (Parmenter) Burke. He was a High Sheriff of Windsor County, Vermont; also, a Brigadier General of the Vermont State Militia, both of which offices he held at the time of his death. He was buried under arms in the new burial-ground, at Woodstock, Vt., and his tombstone has the following inscription:

> "Erected to the memory of Gen. Solomon W. Burke,
> who died Feby. 3d, 1820, aged 38."

He was married at Westminster, Feb. 26, 1805, to

Mary Craige,

Born Northampton, Mass., June 26, 1782; died at Hanover, N. H., Nov. 21, 1840. Daughter of Major Thomas and Elizabeth (Allen) Craige. She was dismissed from the church at Windsor, Vt., to the church at North Woodstock, Vt., Oct. 26, 1810. She died at Hanover, N. H., and her remains were carried to Woodstock, Vt., and buried beside her husband. The inscription on her tombstone is

> "Mary Relict of Gen. Solomon Wait Burke died at
> Hanover N. H. Nov. 21, 1840 aged 59."
>
> "Faith is swallowed up in sight."
> "Her children arise up and call her blessed."

Children—

479. Frederick Wait, born Woodstock, Vt., Feb. 14, 1806; Sept. 1, 1820, was sent alone, when between 14 and 15 years of age, from Woodstock, Vt., to Brunswick, Me., and upon examination was admitted to Bowdoin College; graduated in 1824; came to the city of New York in 1825, where he studied law, and was admitted to full practice in 1830, and has ever since practised his profession in the city of New York. Married Miss

Ann Caroline Potter, in the city of New York, Sept. 10, 1833; removed his residence to the city of Brooklyn in 1844, where he has since resided. Children:

480. 1. Frederick Allen, born New York, Sept. 23, 1834; died New York, March 13, 1836.

481. 2. Mary Agnes, born New York, April 30, 1837; married Brooklyn, N. Y., Sept. 29, 1857, William Stewart, and had: 1, Frederick Burke Stewart, born Brooklyn, N. Y., Aug. 19, 1861; 2, —— Stewart, born Brooklyn, N. Y., Oct. 19, 1863.

484. 3. Elizabeth Elmer, born New York, Aug. 2, 1839.

485. 4. Ellis Potter, born New York, Oct. 8, 1842.

486. Mary Lucretia, born Woodstock, Vt., Jan. 19, 1808; married at Hanover, N. H., May, 1835, Rev. John Thalheimer; resides at Brooklyn, N. Y., and had children:

487. 1. Mary Elsie, born Knowlesville, N. Y., April 20, 1836.

488. 2. Emma, born Cambria, N. Y., Jan. 11, 1839; died Sept. 20, 1842.

489. 3. William Burke, born Strykersville, N. Y., Jan. 29, 1842.

490. 4. Henry Bernard, born Strykersville, N. Y., April 7, 1844.

491. Elizabeth Ann, born Woodstock, Vt., May 27, 1810; died Barnard, Vt., March 16, 1849; married, May 27, 1834, Dr. Samuel P. Danforth of Barnard, Vt., and had children:

492. 1. Samuel, born Barnard, Vt., Feb. 1838.

493. 2. Frederic, born ——; died Royalston, Vt., in 1862.

494. 3. Mary Elizabeth, born Barnard, Vt., Sept. 25, 1845.

495. 4. William Burke, born Barnard, Vt.

496. William Craige, born Woodstock, Vt., Feb. 19, 1812; graduated at Dartmouth College in 1833; graduated at Andover Theological Seminary in 1838; graduated at

the University of New York, Medical Department, in 1844; practised the profession of medicine in the city of New York till 1856. He resided six years in Skeneateles, N. Y, and two years at Norwalk, Conn. He married, May 16, 1848, Sarah Elizabeth Farrar, second daughter of Hon. Timothy Farrar of Boston, and had children:

497. 1. William Craige Burke, born New York, Oct. 13, 1851.

498. 2. Farrar Burke, born New York, Feb. 27, 1855.

499. 3. Anna Farrar Burke, born Skeneateles, N. Y., Dec. 28, 1857.

500. 4. Frederic Waite Burke, born Norwalk, Conn., Sept. 13, 1863.

501. Sarah, born Woodstock, Vt., Sept. 10, 1814; died Newton Centre, Mass., June 1, 1852, aged 37 years, 8 months, 20 days; married Lynn, Oct. 22, 1844, Bartholomew Wood, born Newburyport, Mass., May 31, 1813; son of Bartholomew and Anna (Todd) Wood, and had children:

502. 1. William Burke Wood, born Newton, Mass., May 10, 1847.

503. 2. Mary Elizabeth Wood, born Newton, Mass., June 2, 1849; died Newton, Oct. 4, 1855, aged 6 years, 4 months, 2 days.

504. 3. Sarah Janette Wood, born Newton, Mass., May 23, 1852.

505. Abel Benjamin, born Woodstock, Vt., Feb. 13, 1816; died at Alexander, Burke Co., Georgia, May 11, 1847; he married Miss Emma Pillsbury of Boscawen, N. H., and left no children.

506. Jennette, born Woodstock, Vt., March 1, 1819; married Brooklyn, N. Y., Nov. 3, 1853, Bartholomew Wood of Newton, Mass., born May 31, 1813, and had children:

507. 1. Maria Furber Wood, born Newton, Mass., March 3, 1855.

508. 2. Allen Titcomb Wood, born Milford, Mass., July 6, 1857; died Milford, Mass., July 31, 1863, aged 6 years, 25 days. "He was killed by laudanum, put up by an apothecary, for tincture of rhubarb."

509. 3. Susan Cushing Wood, born Milford, Mass., March 15, 1861.

V. 79. Alice Burke,

Born Windsor, Vt., Jan. 21, 1785. She now resides at West Windsor, Vt., (1863). She is the daughter of Solomon and Keziah (Benjamin) Burke, who was the son of Jonathan and Thankful (Wait) Burke, who was the son of Richard and Abigail (Sawtell) Burke, who was the son of Richard and Mary (Parmenter) Burke. She was admitted to the church at Windsor, Vt., on the profession of her faith in Christ, April 7, 1822, and in August following some of her children were consecrated in baptism. She is a consistent christian, and lives an exemplary life. She was married, Dec. 6, 1810, to

Josiah Perkins,

Born April 11, 1788; died West Windsor, Vt., Jan. 18, 1858. He was the son of Nathaniel and Hannah (Sturtevant) Perkins, and was admitted to the church at Windsor, Vt., by letter, April 2, 1820.

Children:

510. Moses Burke, born Dec. 6, 1811; married, Dec. 22, 1833, Clarissa M. Washburn, born Dec. 15, 1814; daughter of Reuben Washburn. He resides at West Windsor, Vt., and manufactures machine-knit stockings, and has children:

511. 1. Frances W. Perkins, born Nov. 26, 1834; died June 28, 1839.

512. 2. Infant son, born ——; died Sept. 5, 1836.

513. 3. Infant son, born ——; died June. 12, 1840.

514. 4. Infant son, born ——; died Jan. 21, 1845(?).

515. 5. Norman Eugene Elliott, born Oct. 28, 1841; a volunteer in the 12th Vermont Regiment of nine months' men.

516. Josiah Sturtevant, born Dec. 11, 1814. Manufactures corn brooms. He has lost the use of his sight. He married, 1, June 21, 1841, Miss Maria H. Hubbard, who was born Jan. 12, 1815, and died Sept. 15, 1858. He married, 2, Feb. 23, 1862, Miss Joanna Paulina Thomas, born Windsor, Vt., July 22, 1823. She was the daughter of Nehemiah and Drusilla (Thompson) Thomas.

Children by the first wife:

517. 1. Augustus Edward, born April 22, 1842; a volunteer in Company F, Vermont Volunteers, three months' men.

518. 2. Edgar Freeland, born Feb. 20, 1845; a volunteer in the 12th Vermont Regiment nine months' men.

519. 3. Edwin Tracy, born April 23, 1847.

520. 4. Emma Adelaide, born Nov. 2, 1849.

521. 5. Vileroy, born ——; died in infancy.

522. 6. Alice Maria, born Aug. 23, 1853.

523. Solomon Wait, born March 4, 1817; resides at West Windsor, Vt., and manufactures machine-knit stockings. He married, June 26, 1843, Miss Rhoda Pilsbury Story, born April 26, 1818. She was the daughter of Asa and Rhoda (Pilsbury) Story, who was the son of Zechariah and Susan (Lowe) Story. Children:

524. 1. Estella Emugene, born Sept. 1, 1845.

525. 2. Willie Story, born May 24, 1854.

526. Leonard Cummings, born Dec. 14, 1818; married Jan. 30, 1850, Adeline M. Gibson, who was born Aug. 9, 1813. No children.

527. Edwin Eugene, born July 9, 1821; died Lowell, Sept. 14, 1847.

528. Norman Elliott, born Nov. 19, 1823: married, Dec. 15, 1845 Catharine Savage, who was born June 16, 1823, children:

529. 1. Alma Alice, born Jan. 8, 1847; died Sept. 18, 1849.

530. 2. Ella Susan, born June 4, 1849.

531. 3. Charles Henry, born Oct. 12, 1850.
532. 4. Alva Kate, born Aug. 21, 1852.
533. 5. Clara Hulett, born Aug. 11, 1854.

534. Edward Homer, born March 8, 1826; married, Oct. 1, 1849, Persis Chamberlain Stevens, born Stow, Me., July 19, 1823, and had children:
535. 1. Orra Amanda, born Windsor, Vt., July 6, 1850.
536. 2. Mary Jane, born West Windsor, June 23, 1852.
537. 3. George Homer, born West Windsor, April 24, 1854.
538. 4. Luella Adelaide, born West Windsor, April 5, 1856.
539. 5. Charles Dudley, born West Windsor, July 19, 1858.
540. 6. Jennie Wyman, born West Windsor, Sept. 13, 1860.
541. 7. Lottie Wight, born West Windsor, Vt., March 10, 1863.

V. 80. Moses Burke,

Born Windsor, Vt., Jan. 21, 1785. Son of Solomon and Keziah (Benjamin) Burke, who was the son of Jonathan and Thankful (Wait) Burke, who was the son of Richard and Abigail (Sawtell) Burke, who was the son of Richard and Mary (Parmenter) Burke. He resided in Windsor, Vt., on the estate of his father. (See Solomon Burke, IV., No. 40.) He now resides at Otsego, Columbia Co., Wisconsin.

He married

Laura Lull.

Children:

542. Joel Lull, born ——. He and his father's family moved to Wisconsin, with the exception of his sister Mary.
543. Mary, born ——; married Mr. Vannorman, and moved to Canada.
544. Eveline, born ——; married Dr. Alonzo Knap, and resides at Otsego, Wisconsin.

545. Sarah, born ——; married John Pulver.
546. Laura, born ——.
547. Emily.
548. Marcus.

V. 81. Nahum Burke,

Born Windsor, Vt., July 13, 1789. Son of Solomon and Keziah (Benjamin) Burke, who was the son of Jonathan and Thankful (Wait) Burke, who was the son of Richard and Abigail (Sawtell) Burke, who was the son of Richard and Mary (Parmenter) Burke. He resided in Windsor, Vt., on his father's estate, Woodstock, Vt., Anson, Me., "out West," and at Nashua, N. H., where he now resides.

He was married, 1, at Woodstock, Vt., April 19, 1818, to

Evelina Philomitta English Taylor,

Born May 13, 1799; died at Nashua, N. H., April 29, 1844.

He was married, 2, at Nashville, N. H., March 5, 1848, to

Mary Smith Bailey,

Born Chelmsford, Mass., Sept. 29, 1807.

Children by first wife:

549. George Eliphalet, born Woodstock, Vt., March 18, 1819; resides at Chelsea, Mass., and his place of business is in Boston. He was married in Nashua, N. H., Feb. 9, 1840, to Jennett Allen Thompson, born in Hebron, Me., Sept. 21, 1821, and had children:
550. 1. Abby Ann, born Nashua, N. H., Nov. 17, 1840; died Nashua, N. H., Aug. 9, 1858.
551. 2. George Wallace, born Nashua, N. H., Dec. 12, 1842.
552. 3. Leonard Orcutt Fairbanks, born Nashua, N. H., June 25, 1844.
553. 4. Lewis Crebasa Brown, born Nashville, N. H., March 28, 1846.
554. 5. Mary Eveline, born Nashville, N. H., Nov. 14, 1847.
555. 6. Alice Arabelle, born Nashville, N. H., May 20, 1849; died Nashua, N. H., Aug. 18, 1852.

556. 7. Jennett Maria, born Nashville, N. H., Jan. 30, 1851.

557. 8. Frank Pierce, born Nashville, N. H., Oct. 18, 1852; drowned Chelsea, Mass., Aug. 19, 1861.

558. 9. Arabelle Blanch, born Nashville, N. H., May 21, 1855.

559. 10. Henry Nahum, born Nashua, N. H., June 8, 1858; died Chelsea, Aug. 5, 1860.

560. 11. Charles Albert, born Chelsea, Mass., Sept. 13, 1861.

561. Sarah Taylor, born Windsor, Vt., Jan. 20, 1821; died Windsor, Vt., Sept. 22, 1822.

562. Helen Isabella, born Windsor, Vt., May 1, 1823; died Windsor, Vt., Aug. 28, 1824.

563. Nahum Wallace, born Anson, Me., May 14, 1825; resides on Elm street, Nashua, N. H. He was married at Nashville, N. H., Oct. 14, 1847, by Rev. Austin Richards, to Maria Lewis, born Francistown, N. H., July 23, 1828. Children:

564. 1. Ann Maria, born Milford, N. H., July 5, 1848; died Milford, N. H., Aug. 7, 1848.

565. 2. Charles Lewis, born Milford, N. H., Oct. 31, 1849: died Milford, N. H., Aug. 9, 1850.

566. 3. Charles Horace, born Milford, N. H., Dec. 14, 1850.

567. 4. Hattie Bell, born Milford, N. H., Aug. 24, 1852.

568. 5. Frederic Taylor, born Nashua, N. H., July 5, 1857.

569. 6. Helen Maria, born Nashua, N. H., July 1, 1859.

570. Arabella Evelina, born Anson, Me., Feb. 20, 1827. She was married at Nashua, N. H., Oct. 5, 1853, by Rev. Mr. Fay to Charles G. Saxton. No children.

571. Mary Barstow, born Anson, Me., March 15, 1829. She was married at Nashua, N. H., July 18, 1852, by Rev. L. C. Brown, to Oliver Henry Phillips, born Meredith Bridge, N. H., June 2, 1828. He was the son of John and Sarah (Sanborn) Phillips. Children:

572. 1. Mary Ida, born Nashua, N. H., June 17, 1853.

573. 2. John Henry, born Nashua, N. H., April, 22, 1856.

574. Edgar Bruce, born Anson, Me., April 22, 1831; married, Nashua, N. H., March 20, 1853, Sabra M. Watson, born New Boston, N. H., Sept. 11, 1833, daughter of Levi H. and Alice Watson, and had children:

575. 1. Willis Edgar, born Nashua, N. H., Nov. 12, 1853; died Sept. 1, 1858.

576. 2. Alice Hadley, born Nashua, N. H., Nov. 9, 1860; died Oct. 6, 1862.

3. Ella Francis, born Nashua, N. H., Jan. 9, 1863; died Aug. 14, 1863.

577. Franklin Fayette, born Anson, Me., Aug. 6, 1833.

578. Georgianna Lucinda, born Anson, Me., Jan. 20, 1836; married John Day.

579. Betsey Taylor, born Nashua, N. H., March 30, 1839.

580. Lucius Marcellus, born Nashua, N. H., Sept. 17, 1841.

THE BURKE FAMILY OF BERNARDSTON.

I. 1. Richard Burke,

Of Northampton, Mass.

We do not know when he came to Northampton. On Northampton Proprietors' Book, in the year 1700, page 162, on a list of men's estates, according to which the commons were divided, we find the name of Richard Burk. We find no grant to him, but he had property, and accordingly had six rods in length and eight rods in breadth, as his division. These divisions were according to each man's lot. As we find no grant to him, perhaps he received the above division in right of his wife's thirds, &c., (which she received as widow of Nehemiah Allen).

From the Hampshire County Records, (*Clerk of Courts*,) *page* 121.—"Whereas in the distribution of Nehemiah Alline, deceased, his estate, there was a distribution to the children, one of wh^{h} is since dead viz. Silence Allyne, who being young w^{n} she died, and Richard Birkes, who married the widow, requires pay for her keeping wth her one yeer & halfe, & soe likewise his wife for keeping her, one yeer & halfe or thereabouts."

"This Courte Judge meete to allow them twelve pound a piece, in County pay, the sd Birke's having engaged to leave the dispose of this estate to be disposed by his wife, for the good of her children. March 1690."

"Richard Birk's appearing in this Corte and shewing his dissatisfaction in^{t} w^{t} as at the Co^{r}te in march Last, the Court allowed him and his wife Twelve pound a peice out of the estate, or portion, belonging to Silence Allyne, deceased, for bringing her up, & it being put all to her dispose of his wife (be?) pleaded Right to the Twelve pounds wch was expended in his time, to be at his disposal wch this cor^{te} Granted, & the distribution, and further settlem^{t} of those conveyance as follows.

An account of the distribution of the estate of Nehemiah Allyne:

The Honoured Corte ordered that the Eldest son Sam Allyne should have an hundred pound, & the 2nd son fifty pound, & the four daughters, forty pound a piece, and the remainder of the estate was given to the widow, she quitting the third of the land &c.

Accordingly, I, being Stated, Administrator to said estate, have ordered as to the paym^ts^ of the 4 children their portions as followeth, only It is to be noted that the youngest child being since dead, the honoured Court have allowed to ye sd widow, and her now husband, twenty four pound, out of that Child's portion, and the remainder of her portion, to be equally divided amongst the surviving children.

And accordingly, I have ordered that as to the Eldest son Son Samuel, his portion, being an hundred pounds, and his share out of the childs portion wch is dead being three pound four shillings, & also y^t^ being due to him for money paid towards the finishing the house, ye sum of three pounds fifteen shillings, so that the whole due, is one hundred six pounds nineteen shillings.

For his portion he is to have out of the homestead		41. 19 00	lb s 106. 19.
To one Lot at the Lower end of Manham at		26 10 00	
To three acres & halfe in the nooke at		16 00 00	
To Earles Lot at		13 00 00	
To an house 4lb. 10s. joiners tools 5lb.		09 10 00	
ffor Nehemiah Allyns Portion it being fifty pound & he is to have out of his sisters portion—Three pound four shillings			the whole being 53lb. 4.
And for his portion is set out to him in the homestead the sum of		25 05 03	53. 04. 00
To Woodford Lot in Manham	21 ; 05,09	21 05 09	
To what he is indebted by agreement given to learn a trade	03,00,00		
To one acre of land & sixteen Rod in Alexanders Lot	03.13,00		
Sarah Allynes Portion being wth her share of her sisters, wch died forty three pounds four shillings			
to her part in the homestead		23; 06, 03	43. 04 3
Smith Lot		19; 18 00	

To Hannah Allyne her portion being	43;£ 4	
to her part in the homestead	23: 06: 03	43. 06 3
Mr Mays Lot	15. 00: 00	
to one acre out of Hanchet's Lot	05: 00 00	

To Ruth Allyne her portion being the sum of 43:£ 4.		
to her part of the homestead	23: 06 03	
halfe raine bow Lot,	10: 00 00	42. 14 0
& out of Hanchets Lot she is to have 4. 18. 0. per acre so much as comes to the sum of	09. 07. 09	

And for the Remainder of the Estate, it is ordered that Sarah Birks shall have at her own dispose, the Remainder of Alexander's Lot wch is about, or near two acres at 9$^{£.}$ 5$^{s.}$ & 2$^{£,}$ 15, more out of the moveables for satisfaction for what the honoured Corte allowed to her for bringing up the youngest child, & for the remainder of the lands wch is about one acre and a quarter in Rainbow, and what is in Hanchet's Lot wch is an acre & halfe more or Lesse & the pasture above Isaac Sheldings, that being about four acres this to be and remain in the Custody and free improvement of Richd Birks, (who married the mother of the aforesaid children) til the children Redeem it;

Onely, it is to be considered, y^{t} w^{r} as ye children or some of y^{m} haveing taken some moveables in pt of y^{r} Portions as Samuel the Eldest hath taken nine pounds ten shillings to his satisfaction in moveables;

And Nehemiah indebted three pound, & the honored Corte, having granted him, about twelve pounds as compensation for bringing up the youngest child while it lived the whole w^{r} of being twenty four pounds ten shillings, that so much land be made over to him as his own proper estate giving the sons seven years to Redeem it."

The above sd allowed of in Corte.

He was married at Northampton, Sept. 1, 1687, to

Sarah (Woodford) Allen,

Born Hartford, Sept. 2, 1649; died ——, 1712. She was the widow of Nehemiah Allen of Northampton, and daughter of Thomas and Mary (Blott) Woodford.

Mr. Thomas Woodford, in 1632, came from London, in the William and Francis, with Edward Winslow, in which voyage, as from the History of Winthrop is learned, "that there were about sixty passengers, when the custom house records proves that the names of only sixteen were made known to the government, among whom was neither that of Rev Stephen Bachiler, or of Rev. Thomas James, or of Rev Thomas Weld, though each was then on board, to elude the malignant feebleness of Archbishop Laud." Mr. Woodford came to Roxbury, Mass. He removed early to Hartford, and about 1656 to Northampton. Sarah married Nehemiah Allen, Sept. 4, 1664, when she was two days more than 15 years old. She married Mr. Burke in 1687, and after his death, married, July 11, 1706, Judah Wright.

Child of Richard and Sarah Burke:

2. †John, born Northampton, July 19, 1689; died Hatfield, Mass.; married, 1, Northampton, Nov. 25, 1714, Mehitable Hastings; married, 2, Sarah ——.

II. 2. John Burke,

Born Northampton, July 19, 1689; died Hatfield previous to March, 1736–7. Son of Richard and Sarah (Allen) Burke. He resided at Hatfield. March 8, 1736–7, Sarah Burk, relict of John Burke, late of Hatfield, appointed Adm. Mary Gillet, guardian to Mehitable Burke; —— of Hatfield, to Elisha Burk, a minor, over 14 years; Sarah to Ruth Burke; Obadiah Dickinson to John Burk, over 14 years. Feb. 14, 1737–8, Settlement of the estate of John Burke, late of Hatfield, deceased; Widow Sarah Burke—Eldest son, John Burke, the other son, Elisha Burke—Mehitable Burke eldest daughter, Ruth Burke the other daughter. He married, 1, Hatfield, Nov. 25, 1714,

Mehitable Hastings,

Born Hatfield, June 23, 1684; died Hatfield. She was the daughter of Dr. Thomas and Anna (Hawkes) Hastings of Hatfield, who, at one time, was the only doctor for Northampton, Hadley, Hatfield, and Deerfield. Dr. Hastings was the son of Dea. Thomas Hastings, (by his second wife, Margaret Cheney,) who embarked at Ipswich, England, April 10, 1634, aged 29, in the Elizabeth, William Andrews, master, and settled in Watertown, where he was often selectman, town clerk, and in 1673, was a representative, &c.

Mr. Burke married, 2,

Sarah ——.

Children of John and Mehitable Burke:

3. Eddy, born Hatfield, Sept. 11, 1715; probably died young.
4. †John, born Hatfield, Nov. 28, 1717; died Deerfield, Oct. 27, 1784; married Deerfield, Dec. 6, 1740, Sarah Hoyt.
5. Mehitable, twin, born Hatfield, Aug. 3, 1722; married Deerfield, May 28, 1742, Remembrance Sheldon.
6. Elisha, twin, born Hatfield, Aug. 3, 1722. Administration of his estate was granted July 24, 1746, unto John Burke and Mehitable Sheldon, both of Fall Town. In the settlement of the estate, May 10, 1748, John Burke, Mehitable Sheldon, wife of Remembrance Sheldon, alias Mehitable Burke, and Ruth Burke, are mentioned.

Child of John and Sarah Burke:

7. Ruth, born Hatfield, Feb. 2, 1735–6, at 9 o'clock at night.

III. 4. Major John Burke,

Born Hatfield, Nov. 28, 1717; died at Deerfield, Oct. 27, 1784, aged 67, while attending the public service. He was the son of John and Mehitable (Hastings) Burke, and grandson of Richard and Sarah (Allen) Burke.

April 18, 1737, Robert Blare of Deerfield, for the sum of eighteen pounds, paid by John Burke of Hatfield, weaver, convey all my right and title in a Township, granted by y[e] General Court to y[e] officers and soldiers that were in y[e] Fall fight, together with an additional grant that shall, and may hereafter be made to sd. Company of officers and soldiers, on y[e] account of sd. Falls fight.

June 16, 1749, John Norton, of East Hampton, in Middletown, in the county of Hartford and Colony of Connecticutt, Clerk, for thirty pounds, old Tenor, paid by John Burke of

Fall Town, in the county of Hampshire, gentleman, conveys one parcel of land lying within the bounds of the Township of Fall Town. The lot numbers Forty Three, in the second division. There are various other transactions, which will be omitted.

Jan. 16, 1766. He was assessor and collector of Bernardston under the General (Covenant?).

His will, dated Bernardston, May 10, 1783, probate Nov. 2, 1784, mentions wife Sarah, son John, male heirs of my daughter Sarah, viz., Joe, Edde, Israel, Solomon, and Oliver, daughter Lydia, daughter Mehitable, and son John executor. Vol. 13, 48.

"Hon. Major John Burke, was one of the first settlers of Bernardston and quite a distinguished man in that section of the state, for thirty years, before the Revolutionary war, both in civil and military affairs. He was first commissioned by Gov. Shirley, under King George II., March 1$^{st.}$ 1747, as 'Ensign of a company of Volunteers raised for his Majestie's service for the defence of the western frontiers.'

He was, subsequently, commissioned as lieutenant, then captain, and finally as major, by Gov. Pownal, in 1760, in the thirty-third year of the reign of King George II.

He was in active service in the French and Indian War, and was at the surrender of Fort William Henry, Aug. 10, 1757, at which time he narrowly escaped from massacre, losing all his clothes except his deerskin breeches and his silver watch."

During the French and Indian war, the settlers of Bernardston suffered severely, and (1755) "while it continued the people lived mostly in Burk's fort."

The following is the inscription on his grave-stone in the old burying-ground in Bernardston:

"[illegible]mory of the Hon. Maj^{r} John Burke who died
Octr 27th, 1784 in ye sixty seventh year of his age."

"Were I so tall to reach the pole
Or grasp the ocean with my span,
I must be measured by my soul;—
The Mind's the standard of the man."

He married Deerfield, Dec. 6, 1740,

Sarah Hoyt.

Children :

8. Sarah, born Hatfield; married Joel Chapin of Bernardston, son of Caleb and Catharine (Dickinson) Chapin, and was born April 22, 1732. Joel Chapin was in the old French and Indian war, and saw his father after he was killed, Sept. 8, 1755, by the Indians in battle at Bloody Pond, near Lake George. His father said to him, and to his brother Hezekiah, "Boys, they are too hard for us, you must run, I am wounded and cannot." That was the last they saw of him alive.

Children of Joel and Sarah (Burke) Chapin:

9. 1. Joel, married Alice Penfield, and died at Bernardston, of consumption.

10. 2. Israel, married Esther Webster, and died at Bernardston.

11. 3. Eddy, married Ruth Parmenter, and moved to Guilford, Vt., and died there.

12. 4. Solomon, married Rebecca Porter, and moved to Guilford, Vt., and died there.

13. 5. Gratia, married Joel Warner, in Bernardston, and died there.

14. 6. Oliver, died at Thompson, Conn.

15. Ruth, bapt. Deerfield, May 31, 1752.

16. Mehitable, born Bernardston, July 15, 1753.

17. Lydia, born Bernardston, April 4, 1755.

18. †John, born Bernardston, Sept. 15, 1760; died Bernardston, July 17, 1796; married Lavinia ——.

IV. 18. John Burke,

Born Bernardston, Sept. 15, 1760; died Bernardston, July 17, 1796. Son of Major John and Sarah (Hoyt) Burke, who was the son of John and Mehitable (Hastings) Burke, who was the son of Richard and Sarah (Allen) Burke of Northampton.

He resided in Bernardston, and married

Lavinia ——.

Nov. 22, 1796, Lavinia Burke appointed adm. of the estate of John Burke late of Bernardston deceased. Vol. 20 : 33.

Children :

19. †John, born Bernardston, May 8, 1785; died Bernardston, June 17, 1813; married Roxsey Morley of Gill, Sept. 27, 1806.
20. †Horace, born Bernardston, Oct. 25, 1788; died Bernardston, Nov. 26, 1815; married, Oct. 22, 1812, Lavinia F. Hale.
21. Daniel Loomis, born Bernardston, Nov. 9, 1791; died aged about 30.
22. Lavinia, born Bernardston, Oct. 6, 1794.

V. 19. John Burke,

Born Bernardston, May 8, 1785; died Bernardston, June 17, 1813. Son of John and Lavinia (——) Burke, who was the son of Major John and Sarah (Hoyt) Burke, who was the son of John and Mehitable (Hastings) Burke, who was the son of Richard and Sarah (Allen) Burke of Northampton.

Will, dated Bernardston, March 30, 1813, mentions wife Roxsey; daughter Lavinia, with provision with regard to the expense of her schooling, &c.; son John Erie Burke. In presence of Horace Burke, Daniel L. Burke, Amasa L. Rogers. [Greenfield, Franklin Co., Vol. 1 : 274.

He resided in Bernardston, and married, Sept. 27, 1806,

Roxsey Morley,

Children :

23. Lavinia, born Bernardston, Aug. 19, 1807.
24. †John Erie, born Bernardston, Oct. 1809; married Elvira L. Parmenter.

V. 20. Horace Burke,

Born Bernardston, Oct. 25, 1788; died Bernardston, Nov. 26, 1815. Son of John and Lavinia (——) Burke, who was the son of Major John and Sarah (Hoyt) Burke, who was the son of John and Mehitable (Hastings) Burke, who was the son of Richard and Sarah (Allen) Burke of Northampton.

His will, dated Nov. 25, 1815, mentions wife Lavinia Burke, father-in-law Israel Hale, daughter Priscilla H. Burke, daughter Lavinia H. Burke. In naming certain bounds, Loomis Burke and Daniel Loomis are mentioned. Elizabeth Hale has property bequeathed to her, but she is not called daughter.

He resided in Bernardston, and married, Oct. 22, 1812,

Lavinia F. Hale.

Children:

25. Priscilla H., born Bernardston.
26. Lavinia H., born Bernardston.

VI. 24. Dea. John Eric Burke,

Born Bernardston, Oct. 1809; died Bernardston, March 23, 1858. Son of John and Roxsey (Morley) Burke, who was the son of John and Lavinia (——) Burke, who was the son of Major John and Sarah (Hoyt) Burke, who was the son of John and Mehitable (Hastings) Burke, who was the son of Richard and Sarah (Allen) Burke of Northampton. He resided in Bernardston.

Dea. John Burke "is the last male descendant from his distinguished ancestor the Hon. Major Burke."

Dea. Burke was ever esteemed and trusted in the community in which he lived. For many years he was a deacon of the Baptist church in Bernardston, a selectman of that town in 1850, a representative in the Legislature, a justice of the peace, and on the first Monday of March, 1858, was elected by the town one of the trustees of Power's Institute." See N. E. G. R., Vol. 12, p. 282.

He married, (Int. of mar. May 2, 1829,)

Elvira L. Parmenter.

She is now living (his widow) in Bernardston, in a pleasant cottage, which she purchased since the death of her husband, a part of which she rents. The place which her husband owned and resided upon she sold, as the care of it was too much for her.

Child:

27. Corisana Elvira, only daughter of Dea. John E. Burke; died Dec. 11, 1841, aged three years.

THE

BURKE AND ALVORD

Memorial:

A GENEALOGICAL ACCOUNT

OF THE

DESCENDANTS OF ALEXANDER ALVORD,

OF WINDSOR, CONN.

COMPILED BY JOHN A. BOUTELLE,

FOR

WILLIAM A. BURKE.

Alford.

BOSTON:

PRINTED BY H. W. DUTTON AND SON,

90 & 92 WASHINGTON STREET.

1864.

THE ALVORD MEMORIAL.

WE find upon our public records that the above name (even the descendants of Alexander and Benedict), has been variously written, even for the same person. We find it written Alluard, Alluerd, Alvard, Alford, Alvord, Allord, Alved, Alfort, Allford, &c.

In this work, we intend to give a brief genealogy of some of the descendants of Alexander Alvord, who moved from Windsor, Conn., about the year 1661, and settled in Northampton, Mass.; and we shall likewise give a very brief genealogy of some of the descendants of Benedict, who remained at Windsor, Conn.

There were others of this name, who early settled in New England, besides Alexander and Benedict Alvord, whom, we suppose, might originally have been of the same family.

There was a William Alford, who came from London, about the year 1634, and settled in Salem, Mass., who was a member of Skinner's company. His wife Mary joined the church in 1636, and had Nathaniel, baptized 19 March, 1637; Samuel, 17 Feb. 1639; Bethia, 26 June, 1642; he had also Elisha, Mary, and Elizabeth. Savage says: "He had favored the party of Wheelwright, and under the name of Mr. Alfoot on the record in 1637, was disarmed by the General Court, and thereupon removed for a season to New Haven, and there had, probably, two or more of his children born before 1654. He came back to Massachusetts, but settled in Boston, was a merchant, and by another wife, Ann, had John, born 29 Nov. 1658, who died aged two months. He died Jan. 1677. His will was dated 13 April, with a codicil, 9 July, 1676.

We find upon the early records of the county of Essex, that there was an Abraham Alved.

"Gent men & honest freinds pray be pleased to paye vnto my frend Edward Joanes the severall sums of Suger which you owe me which each Gentleman's sume is heare vnder neath mentioned & directed to you & every of you severally for ye each p ticular sum or sums, taking the said Joanes his receipt for any sume you for my acct: & in for soe doeing you will oblige him

Yo[rs] to serve you to his power

ABRAHAM ALVED.

To Coll Timothy Cornhill y	45	74	
To ditto for one tunn of cask	3	60	
To Thomas Hart for	1	55	
To Elizabeth Smale	1	74	for accot of Thomas Webb
To Mr John Bawden	15	74	bill
To Mr John Cates (or Gates)	2	25	bill
To John Seddon for	10	00	bill paid by accot
To William Bragg for 2 Barrells of tar	6	00	bill
	84	37	

A coppy of this Acco[t] or order I have received of Mr Abram Alveds and am to be accoumptable to him or order; for what I shall receive of it.

Witness my hand this 25 January 1666–7.

EDWARD JOANES.

We also find a Benjamin Alford upon the early record of the county of Essex at Salem. "Benjamin Alford. Whereas there was an obligation und[r] y[e] hands of John Ruck, Bartholomew Gedny, John Price, John Higginson & Hilliard Veren bearing date Nov. 26, 1674 for three hundred forty eight pounds starl. payably to John ffoott or assigns, the saith ffoott sending over power to me whoose name is under written for receiving of ye same I doe by these presents acknowledge to have received of y[e] above named p sons y[e] full sum of three hundred forty eight pounds in marchantable fish in tyme as was expressed in said bond & do acquit & discharge y[e] said persons above named from al or any pt of said sum haveing received full satisfaction, as witness my hand dated Aug 9, 1675. BENJAMIN ALVORD.

[See Reg. Deeds, Vol. 4 : 98.

John ffoott of Bristol merchant now in London late resident in Boston N. E. constitutes Benjamin Alford of Boston aforesaid Merchant his true and lawfull Attorney. May 10. 1675.

Recorded Vol. 4 : 120.

There are two documents upon Court files where Benj. Alford, Oct. 31, 1676, as an attorney of John Sweeting of London, gave his deposition with regard to the payment of a bill to John Shepheard, master of the Thomas and Mary.

Benjamin Alford was a merchant of Boston, and was a member of the artillery company in 1671. Savage says that he was probably son of William. He married Mary, daughter of James Richards, Esq., of Hartford, and had Mary, born 15 Sept., bapt. 14 Oct. 1683; John, bapt. (at third or O. S. church) 5 July, 1685; Benjamin, born 5, bapt. 10 Oct. 1686; Judith, bapt. 16 Sept. 1688; James, born 19, bapt. 26 July, 1691; Sarah, born 17, bapt. 18 March, 1694; and Thomas, whose date is not found. "He had been a prisoner in Barbary and after his return was a man of importance in Boston. His will of Feb. 19, 1697, (probate thirteen years after,) provides for his children and widow. His widow, with his brother-in-law Benj. Davis, he makes Excors. His eldest son, Hon. Col. John, of Charlestown, was a member of the Ancient and Honorable Artillery Company in 1714; was one of the King's Councillors, and was distinguished as founder of the Alford Prof. of Nat. Theology, &c., at Harvard, and for giving a large sum to the Society for Propagating the Gospel among the Indians, &c., in North America. Hon. John Alford married Margaret, daughter of Col. Thomas Savage, merchant of Boston, 12 Nov. 1713, and died in Charlestown, Sept. 1761, aged 76, highly respected for his moral worth, and left no children.

There was a Henry Alvord, or Alford, very early in New England, according to Plymouth Colony Records.

April 20, 1679, John Alford of Salem, seaman, conveys his now dwelling-house in Salem to Edmond Batter of Salem, merchant. He was in Salem in 1668. Col. Remain Alford of New London died Aug. 12, 1709, aged 63.

Historians seem to agree that Alexander and Benedict, of Windsor, Conn., were brothers, and that Alexander's sister, Joan Alvord, married May 26, 1646, Ambrose Fowler.

Many of the names of the original members of the First Church who went with their pastor, Rev. John Warham, as a body, from Dorchester, Mass., to Windsor, Conn., in 1635, are obliterated, and we do not know whether Alexander and Benedict are of that number.

We suppose, from what records we are in possession of, that Alexander and Benedict Alvord emigrated from the county of Somerset, England, and that Benedict after coming over and patriotically volunteering to assist in defending the Connecticut colony from the Pequots, returned to England after his espoused, Joan Newton (Nurton). For, in 1637, "Brave Sergeant Alvord was one of the thirty who went from Windsor, Conn., to make an offensive war against the Pequots," [See Benedict Alvord,] and the 20th of Feb. 1639, he must have been in Broadwaye, county of Somerset, England; the 25th of August, 1640, he had returned to Massachusetts, and Nov. 26, 1640, he was married in Windsor to Joan Newton.

"The third of Septembe[r.] 1640. The Record of the Deede shewed in Court betwixt Richard Standerwick & Nicholas Nurton."

"Know all men by these p[r]nts, that I Richard Standerwick of Broadwaye, in the county of Som'sett, in Old England, clothyer, for and in consideracon of the sum of twelve pounds of lawfull money of England, payd vnto me by Nicholas Nurton of Waimouth, in New England haue graunted, bargained, & sould, and by these p[r]nts do freely and absolutly graunt, bargaine, and sell vnto the said Nicholas Nurton all the cattell, whether cowes, steeres or calues whatsoeũ I have with Mr Hull in New England.

In witnes whereof, I the said Richard Standerwick have herevnto set my hand and seale the twentyeth day of February in the year 1639." "RICHARD STANDERWICK." [His Seal.]

"Sealed in the p^rnts of us.
John Hawkins,
Peter Pinny,
John Dwelly ⋈ signe,
Benedict ⋈ Alford,
John Purchase."

Benedict Alford & John Purchase, two of these witness, haue taken thire oaths before me, Thomas Dudley, Goūn^r of Massachusetts that they saw Richard Standerwick aboue named, seale & deliuer this bill to the use of th aboue named Nicholas Nurton, & subscribed theire names or markes as witnes^s thereof. Their oathes were taken the XXVth day of August 1640.

Before me, Thom. Dudley Goū.

I. 1. Alexander Alvord,

Born Somerset County, (?) England, probably about 1620; died Northampton, Mass., Oct. 3, 1683.

He was an early resident of Windsor, Conn., and moved to Northampton, Mass., about the year 1661, where he died. Some of the names on the earliest records of Windsor, Conn., being obliterated, we cannot tell whether he was among the very first or not. Still later we find the following upon the church records: Aug. 17, 1639. "Mr. Ephraim Hewett & Diverse others came up from the Bay to settle here."

From what records we have examined we suppose that he came from the county of Somerset, England, to this country. We find by the early records of deeds that he was an early proprietor in Windsor, Conn.

"Alexander Alford [Alvord] hath granted by virtue of purchase his home Lott six acres more or Less, ye bredth is Eighteen rods, bound west and norwest by John Warham & is there in length fifty Two rod, bounds East South East by Thomas Barber, and is there in length Sixty six rod, and North, North East bounded by John Helier."

"Also six acres of Swamp on the Mill Brook in length by y[e] bank (threscoore) : [blotted] rods, in bredth at the South— twelve rods in y[e] midst twenty rod, bounds south by John Drake."

"Also by Gift from his Father Richard Voar, in the woods forty Two acres, in length six scoore rod, in bredth fifty seven rod—Bounded South by Jonathan Gillet North by Thomas Bascomb." (No date.)

The question may be asked, Where did Alexander Alvord reside?

"The road to Poquonnoc above the old mill at just about the place where the present road from the bridge near the 1st Congregational Meeting house comes in, was anciently intersected at right angles by a highway running about South West from the Rivulet. On this highway we find the residence of Alexander Alvord," who sold to Josiah Ellsworth in 1654, and he sold to Cornelius Gillett in 1658. "This is the present Oliver S. Gillett place." Some of his neighbors, were Thomas Barber, Humphrey Hyde, Jonathan Gillett, Nathan Gillett.

"Alexander Alford of Windsor unto Humphrey Hide." "Know all men by these presents that I Allexander Alford of Windsor in Conn. have sold and upon good Considerations to me Secured, do Allienate &c. unto Humphrey Hide of Windsor aforesaid, one parcell of land, Containing four acres more or Less being in bredth sixteen rod more or Less as it lyes Bounded East by the Land of Nathan Gillett, North by a highway, South by the mill brook," &c. Signed May 27, 1645.

Witness, Bray Rosseter, Daniel Clark.

From the Town Records of Northampton.—"At a Legal Town meeting Feb[y]. 20, 1661. Voted & agreed the day and year above written that Alexander Alvord was granted that portion of land that lieth in the Little Rainbow which was sometime George Alexander's & was upon a public[k] consideration given to Mr. Mather, did surrender it up to the Town, & the Town granted it to Alexander Alvord," &c.

His land in the First Division was No. 57.—Second Division, No. 16.

The Record of Alexander Alvord's Land which he hath purchased and which was granted to him by the Town of Northampton which was given to him and to his heirs and assigns to have And to hould forever. ffeb: 1 : 1661. Proprietors' Record viz.

"Imp^r^ A parcell of Land with a house upon it which the sd Alexander Alverd Bought of Zachariah ffeild, Lying within the Co̅mon fence which is thus bounded, the ends butting on the fence, westerly and on the wett swamp, easterly, the sides Lying against the Lands of Samuel Wright Jun, Northerly, and A brushy swamp southerly containing five Acres More or Lesse."

More Another p cell Bought of Lieut wilton Lying at the vpper end of Little Rainbow which is thus bounded Lying Against the great River Northerly And Butting on the highway westerly and Agnst. ye Lands of sd Alexander Alluerd southerly and running to A point easterly containing one Acre more or Lesse.

More Another pr cell of vpland which the sd Alluerd Bought of Zachariah field sen[r] which is thus Bounded, the ends butting Against William Jones' land Westerly and against his owne easterly & Against Samll. wright's land Northerly, the side Lying Against the Land of Zachariah feild and Thomas Bascom Southerly containing two Acres.

"More another p[r]cell Lying at the vpper end of Little Rainbow wch I y[e] sd. Aluerd had given him by the Towne as is Abue expressed which is thus bounded the ends Butting Against the high way westerly and the Great river Easterly the sides lying against the Lands of David Wilton Northerly and Nathaniel Dickerson Southerly containing three Acres & one rood & seven rods more or Lesse."

"More Another p[r]cell of vpland at the easterly end of Thomas Bascom Sen his Lot which is thus Bounded, the ends Butting on y[e] Lot of sd Thomas Bascom westerly, And Allexander Aluerd and easterly Lying Against the Land of Samuel wright Jun[r] northerly and Robert Lyman and sd Allverd's Land Southerly" &c.

"More a Little piece of Land wch sd Alverd had of James Bridgeman at the easterly end of his Lot three rods deep," &c.

"More Another Litle parcell of Land that the sd Aluerd had of Robert Liman," &c., &c., &c.

"More Another small peice of Land which was granted to the said Allex Ander Aluerd By the towne of Northampton in the time of the Indian warr which began in the year 1675 granted as is Above expressed, and laid out by a comittee appointed there vnto which land Lies on the westerly side of the street opposite to the hom Lots which was some times John Brottons and Joseph fiches their Land and is bounded viz. fronting on the street or high way westerly And the breadth there six rods & $\frac{3}{4}$; southerly bordering on the land of Nehemiah Allyn: the west^{r}ly on the land of John Weller."

"More another pr cell of Land with a house on it which the sd Allexander Aluerd Bought of Increase Turner As Apears by a deede baring date Agust 10, 1684 which is thus bounded Butting on the high way or street westerly And on the Land of said Alex Ander Alluard Easterly Bordering on the Land of Thomas bascom Southerly An the Land of John brotton northerly containing one Acre more or Lesse with the house which is on it and every appurtenance thereunto belonging."

April 13, 1680, An agreement was made between Thomas Lyman, John Bridgman and Alexander Alvord for the maintaining the Common fence at the rear of their home lots. [See Northampton town records.

In 1682 Alexander Alvord had the largest number of rods of fence to be built except John Stebbins: "A List of each man's Proportion of fence which they now possess & own according as it was measured in 1679."

For Alexander Alvord's will, see Appendix E.

He was married, according to Windsor, Conn., Church Records, Oct. 29, 1646, to

Mary Vore,

Born ——; died Northampton, Mass., previous to 1683. She was the daughter of Richard and Ann (——) Vore, or Voar, of Windsor, Conn. Mr. Vore came to Dorchester, Mass., perhaps in 1630, with Rev. John Warham, where he was a member in full communion with Mr. Warham's church, and in 1635 accompanied him with the body of his church to Windsor, Conn.

He resided in Windsor, Conn, south of the rivulet, or little river in the vicinity of the mill; between that and the foot of Stony Hill, and in his immediate neighborhood, were located Rev. John Warham, &c., &c.

"He also owned meadow land between the Rivulet and Mill Brook, where the latter empties into the former, called upon the records Vore's Point." Rev. Mr. Warham requested the privilege to build a little house upon his land for Mary Jones, "Whereas Richard Vore upon Mr. John Warham's request, formerly gave him liberty to build a little house upon his land joining the north end of his [Vore's] then and now dwelling house for the use of his kinswoman Mary Jones to dwell in during her life, and at her death to give it to the said Richard; and the said Mary Jones being now deceased; this is to testify that I John Warham do hereby alienate assign and set over the said house I builded as aforesaid to Richard Vore of Windsor in the County of Hartford Conn. &c., &c., Dated Dec. 15, 1666."

Mrs. Mary (Vore) Alvord had sisters, viz.: Lydia, who married Nathaniel Cook, June 29, 1649; Sarah, who married Benjamin Parsons, Oct. 6, 1653; and Abigail, who married Timothy Buckland, March 27, 1662. The father died Nov. 22, 1683, and the mother, "Ann," "relict of Richard Vore died in Windsor, Dec. 7, 1683."

Mrs. Mary Alvord was one of the original members of the first church in Northampton, Mass.

Children:

2. Abigail, born Windsor, Conn., Oct. 6, 1647; married Northampton, Mass., 1666, Thomas Root of Northampton, son of Thomas Root, who was of Salem, Mass., in 1637, when he had a grant of land, and moved to Hartford, Conn., as early as 1639, and was a weaver by occupation, and removed to Northampton about the year 1659, "where he was one of the seven pillars for

foundation of the church in 1661," and died at a great age, July 17, 1694.

They had children:

1. Thomas, born Northampton, 1667.
2. Abigail, born Northampton, 1668.
3. Samuel, born Northampton, 1673.
4. Hezekiah, born Northampton, 1676, who died young.

After 1700 they probably removed to Coventry.

7. †John, born Windsor, Conn., Aug. 12, 1649; died Northampton. Will dated April 18, 1721, Prob. Dec. 8, 1727; married Abigail Phelps.

8. Mary, born Windsor, Conn., July 6, 1651; married Northampton, March 24, 1669–70, John Weller of Northampton, who moved to Deerfield about 1683. Children:

    1. John, born Northampton, Feb. 14, 1671; settled in New Milford.
    2. Mary, born Northampton, Sept. 11, 1672.
    3. Hannah, born Northampton, May 14, 1674.
    4. Elizabeth, born Northampton, Feb. 12, 1676.
    5. Sarah, born Northampton, April 15, 1678.
    6. Thomas, born Northampton, Aug. 1680; settled in New Milford.
    7. Experience, born Northampton, Dec. 4, 1682.

    Perhaps others.

16. †Thomas, born Windsor, Conn., Oct. 27, 1653; died Northampton, Mass., July 22, 1688; married Northampton, March 22, 1681, Joanna Taylor.

17. Elizabeth, born Windsor, Conn., Nov. 12, 1655; married Northampton, 1684, Henry Burt of Northampton, who was the son of David and Mary (Holton) Burt, born in England, and one of the first settlers in Northampton, who was the son of Henry Burt, early of Roxbury, afterwards of Springfield, where he was clerk of the writs, and died April 30, 1662. A tradition is preserved that Ulalia, wife of Henry Burt, who was clerk of the

writs, was laid out for dead in England, put into a coffin, but signs of life appearing at her funeral, she recovered, came to New England, and settled in Springfield, Mass., and had there nineteen children, where she died a widow, Aug. 29, 1690. Children of Henry and Elizabeth (Alvord) Burt:

1. Joseph, born Northampton, Dec. 1, 1685; an only son of his mother.
2. Elizabeth, born Northampton, May 2, 1687. The mother and daughter died soon.

20. †Benjamin, born Windsor, Conn., Feb. 11, 1658; died Northampton, 1715. He married Northampton, 1690, Deborah Stebbens.

21. Sarah, born Windsor, Conn., June 24, 1660; died Springfield, Mass., May 16, 1704; married July 10, 1687, as his second wife, James Warriner of Springfield, eldest son of William and Joanna Warriner, and had children:

1. Sarah, born Springfield, Mass., 1690.
2. Jonathan, born Springfield, Mass., 1692.
3. John, born Springfield, Mass., Nov. 29, 1694; died in a few months.
4. Benjamin, born Springfield, April 15, 1698.
5. David, born Springfield, Oct. 8, 1701.

27. †Jeremiah, born Northampton, Mass., May 9, 1663; married, 1, Mehitable, widow of Hezekiah Root; married, 2, Mary Gull.

28. †Ebenezer, born Northampton, Dec. 23, 1665; died Northampton, Nov. 29, 1738; married, 1, in 1691, Ruth Baker; married, 2, Elizabeth ——.

29. †Jonathan, born Northampton, April 6, 1669; died Northampton, Aug. 13, 1727; married Northampton, Jan. 12, 1693, Thankful Miller.

II. 7. John Alvord,

Born Windsor, Conn., Aug. 12, 1649; died in Northampton.

At a legal Town meeting in Northampton, July 23, 1675, "The Town granted John Alvord a lot of six acres for a home lot in some convenient place, we say, where it may not prejudice The Town, provided he dwell in the Town four years and build on that or some other and possess it four years."

The following is an abstract of a deed now in the possession of a connection:

Jan. 20, 1693–4. William Hulberd & Mary his wife for twenty pounds sterling, convey unto John Alvord of Northampton, within the Common field or meadow land, called the Last *Demison*, five acres be it more or less, and is bounded "Butting on the high waies westerly; bordering on the land of Wm. Miller Northerly; on Isaac Sheldon southerly, &c.

In presence, &c.	William Hulburd
Medad Pumry	The mark of ⋊
Jonathan Alvard	Mary Hulberd."

For grants of land to him see Proprietors' Book, Northampton, page 81.

In his will, dated April 18, 1721, prob. Dec. 8, 1727, he bequeaths all his property to his widow, Abigail Alvord.

He was married in Northampton, to

Abigail Phelps,

Born Windsor, Conn., April 5, 1655; died Northampton, Aug. 26, 1756. Daughter of Nathaniel and Elizabeth (——) Phelps of Northampton, who was the son of William Phelps, who probably came in the Mary and John from Plymouth in 1630, and settled in Dorchester, Mass. Mr. William Phelps, grandfather of Mrs. Alvord, was a person of much note in his day. In 1634 he was a representative and selectman; and in 1635 he moved with Rev. John Warham to Windsor, Conn., where he was for many years one of the Governor's "Assistants."

Mrs. Alvord was considered a lady of dignity.

"Abigail Alvord wife to John Alvord of Northampton being presented by the Grand Jury to this Court for wearing silk contrary to law & it being found the witnesses were sometime mistaken she was dismissed." [County Court Records, March 26, 1678.

She conveyed her property to her nephew, Joseph Alvord. See Joseph Alvord, No. 49.

Abstract from an original deed, now in the possession of a descendant of Joseph Alvord:

Abigail Alvord relict of John Alvord dec, of my own free will, as also upon the account of ye love and affection I have unto my kingsman Joseph Alvord son unto Ebenezer Alvord as alsoe for and upon ye Consideration of my sd kingsman Joseph Alvord taking care of mee and my estate during my natural Life; therefore I ye sd Abigail Alvord having by my sd. husband John Alvord's *last will* . . . all his estate of all sorts both Real & Personal; now upon ye Considerations aforesaid of ye sd Abigail Alvord; doe for myself &c give unto my sd kingsman all ye whole of my sd estate both Real & Personal, descending or given to mee by said *husbands will* or belonging to mee or descending to mee by any other ways or means.

Provided this conveyance is to be understood with this limitation, that it is not to take effect till after my decease; only my sd kingsman is to use and improve my estate out of which I am to have a Comfortable and honorable maintenance according to my degree, which if my said kingsman should fail in, then I doe Reserve to my self a Liberty, to Lease out any of my Real Estate or sell any of my personal estate for my support and maintenance. Signed Jan. 8, 1727–8.

She died at the house of Joseph Alvord. The town records say, "1756 Aug 26 Died the aged Wid^o^ Abigail Alvord said to be about one hundred and two years, said to have been born in the same year this town was first planted." Savage says, "She was the oldest person that ever died in Northampton; but exact truth, after the correction of old style, makes her age 101 years, 4 mos. and 11 days."

No children.

II. 16. Thomas Alvord,

Born Windsor, Conn., Oct. 27, 1653; died Northampton, July 22, 1688. Son of Alexander and Mary (Vore) Alvord. He resided in Northampton, Mass.

The town of Northampton granted to Thomas Alvord "In prim[r] a home Lot which is thus bounded; on the south on Mr Hawleys land being in length 26 rods, bounded on the commons on the north butting on the Round Hill on the (sequestered land?) westerly in breadth at this end 16 rods and 5½ feet butting on a high way easterly in breadth 26 rods and 5½ feet, &c."

His Inventory was presented by Lieut. John Taylor, Aug. 10, 1688. See Hampshire Prob. Rec., Vol. 2 : 48.

He was married at Northampton, March 22, 1681, to

Joanna Taylor,

Born September 27, 1665. She was the daughter of John and Thankful (Woodward) Taylor, who may have been the son of John Taylor of Windsor. She outlived her husband, and married, 2, Northampton, 1690, Samuel King (son of John,) whom she outlived; and, in 1702, married Deliverance Bridgman.

Children:

30. John, born Northampton, Aug. 10, 1682; died Northampton, Aug. 25, 1682.
31. †Thomas, born Northampton, Aug. 28, 1683; died Chatham, Conn.; married, 1, Jan. 3, 1705–6, Esther Parsons; married, 2, Mary ——.
32. †John, born Northampton, Oct. 19, 1685; died South Hadley, Mass., Nov. 21, 1757; married Northampton, Dec. 29, 1708, Dorcas Lyman.
33. Josiah, born Northampton, Feb. 7, 1688; died Northampton, Dec. 13, 1691.

II. 20. Benjamin Alvord,

Born Windsor, Conn., Feb. 11, 1658; died Northampton, Mass., 1715. Son of Alexander and Mary (Vore) Alvord. He resided in Northampton.

The inventory of his estate was presented March 9, 1715–16, by Deborah Alvord, William Southwell, and Benjamin Alvord.

He was married Northampton, in 1690, to

Deborah Stebbens,

Born Northampton, March 5, 1672. She was the daughter of John and Abigail (Bartlett) Stebbens, born in England, 1626, and resided in Springfield and in Northampton, and granddaughter of Rowland Stebbens, who came from Ipswich Co., Suffolk, England, in the Francis, in 1634, aged, according to the custom-house records, 40, and settled in Springfield, Mass. She outlived her husband, and, April 4, 1816, married Henry Burt of Springfield.

Children:

34. Abigail, born Northampton, 1691. Named in the settlement of her father's estate as having her share previous to his death. Married, Aug. 19, 1714, Samuel Judd.(?)
35. Elizabeth, born Northampton, Sept. 1693. Named in the settlement of her father's estate as having her share previous to his death. She married Preserved Bartlett, Jan. 24, 1712.(?)
36. †Benjamin, born Northampton, Sept. 1695. Named in the settlement of his father's estate as eldest son, and to have a double share. He married, 1, Eunice ——; 2, Ruth Alexander, Jan. 17, 1733.
37. Deborah, born Northampton, May, 1698. Named in the settlement of her father's estate.
38. Experience, born Northampton, Oct. 5, 1700. Named in the settlement of her father's estate.
39. Josiah, born Northampton, April 13, 1704. Named in the settlement of his father's estate.
40. Sarah, born Northampton, May 28, 1707. Named in the settlement of her father's estate.

II. 27. Jeremiah Alvord,

Born Northampton, Mass., May 9, 1663; died Hatfield, Mass.(?) Son of Alexander and Mary (Vore) Alvord. He resided at Northampton, Deerfield, and Hatfield.

He was married in Deerfield, in 1691, to

Mehitable (Frary) Root,

Born Hadley; died Deerfield, Mass., Nov. 7, 1698. She was the widow of Hezekiah Root of Northampton, by whom she had children; the youngest of whom was killed by the Indians at Deerfield, at the same time her own father, Sampson Frary, was killed.

She was the daughter of Sampson and Mary (——) Frary, who resided in Hadley, on the west side of the river, which afterwards became Hatfield, and moved to Deerfield, where he was killed, Feb. 29, 1704, by the French and Indians, who took his wife Mary captive, and killed her before they reached Canada.

Mr. Alvord moved to Hatfield, and married

Mercy Gull,

Born Hadley, Mass., June 27, 1688. She was the daughter of William and Elizabeth Gull, who was of Wethersfield, Conn., in 1649, and moved to Hadley, Mass., in 1663. Her mother, Elizabeth, was the daughter of Lieut. Samuel Smith of Wethersfield, Conn., and married, 1st, Nathaniel Foot.

Mrs. Mercy Alvord's grandfather, Lieut. Samuel Smith, came from Ipswich, England, in the Elizabeth, in 1634, aged 32, and probably resided a short time in Watertown; for most of the passengers went to Watertown, Mass., some of whom removed to the banks of the Connecticut with him.

He settled in Wethersfield, Conn., where he was elected a representative more than any other man.

In 1659 he removed to Hadley, Mass., with many of Rev. Henry Smith's opponents (who supported his successor, Rev. John Russell's side of the Hartford controversy), where he was in very high repute, and was often elected there as a representative;

and was lieutenant in command of the militia from 1663 to 1678, when he was honorably discharged, and his son Philip made a lieutenant, and a captain was appointed for the first time.

Children of Jeremiah and Mehitable Alvord:

41. Jeremiah, born Deerfield, Mass., Feb. 17, 1692; died in infancy, at Deerfield.
42. Jeremiah, born Deerfield, March 31, 1694; drowned at Hatfield, July 10, 1718.
43. Nancy, born Deerfield, Aug. 15, 1696.

Children of Jeremiah and Mercy Alvord:

44. Elizabeth, born Hatfield, Mass., April 1, 1703; died in Hatfield, in infancy.
45. Elizabeth, born Hatfield, Mass., June 14, 1705; died.
46. Hannah, born Hatfield, Mass., 1707.
47. Ebenezer, born Hatfield, Mass., Nov. 11, 1710.

II. 28. Ebenezer Alvord,

Born Northampton, Dec. 23, 1665; died Northampton, Mass., Nov 29, 1738. Son of Alexander and Mary (Vore) Alvord; resided in Northampton.

A home lot was granted to him by the town of Northampton, "23 March 1702–3, wch land lye on this side timber swamp toward Hatfield. And is bounded; Butting on the highway easterly, and to the Rocky Hill westerly, and to the highway northerly, and to Benjamin Carpenter's land."

Abstract from original deeds from Ebenezer Alvord, husbandman, to his son Joseph Alvord, weaver; said deeds now in possession of a descendant of said Joseph Alvord:

Ebenezer Alvord of Northampton, for the sum of forty pounds paid by my son Joseph Alvord, conveys several tracts of land in Northampton bounded as follows viz:

One piece containing one acre and a quarter, bounded northerly by the Grantor's land, eastwardly by ye Meadow Hill, southwardly by Thomas Bridgman's & Benj. Stebben's Home Lots, out of which a high way is reserved by the Grantor sufficient for him to pass an repass to his land beyond.

Also another tract of land, lying under sd Meadow Hill being one half of sd Grantor's land there viz, the lower or southerly half; containing about six acres; bounded northerly by the Grantor's land, eastwardly by Venturers' Field, so called, southerly by the whole side, or the Bushy Swamp, (so called) and westerly by the Meadow Hill.

Also a piece of land in Young Rainbow, bounded north by the river; eastwardly by the land of Samuel Lankton, and southerly by the highway on Young Rainbow Hill; lying in a triangle containing one and a half acres.

Also a lot in the Long Division outlands being thirteen rods wide; bounded northerly by Samuel Wright's land and southwardly by the lot which formerly belonged to Joseph Hawley Esq deceased.

Also all my right or proportion of land, as I am proprietor with others in that tract of land, known by the name of the Inward Commons lying at the eastwardly end of Long Division lots—and also in all other parts of the town except that on the south side of Manhan river and west of Westfield road.

Signed March 1st. 1732. EBENEZER His ⋈ mark. ALVORD.

He married, 1, in Northampton, in 1691,

Ruth Baker,

Born Northampton, May 6, 1668; died Northampton, March 4, 1706. She was the daughter of Joseph and Ruth (Holton) Baker, who was killed by the Indians, Oct. 29, 1675, with her brother, Joseph Baker.

Edward Baker, her grandfather, was of Lynn, Mass., in 1630, moved to Northampton, where he lived many years, and returned to Lynn, where he died, March, 1687. Mrs. Alvord's mother was the daughter of William Holton, who came in the Francis, from Ipswich, England, in 1634, aged 23, and was an original proprietor of Hartford, Conn., moved to Northampton, where he was ordained the first deacon, May 13, 1663, and was representative in 1664, '67, '69–71, and once for the town of

Hadley. Mrs. Alvord's uncle, Thomas Holton, was killed by the Indians, March 14, 1676.

Mr. Ebenezer Alvord married, 2,

Elizabeth ——.

She outlived her husband, and with her son, Joseph Alvord, administered on her husband's estate, and was guardian unto her sons, Ebenezer and Thomas Alvord, minors, under 14 years of age.

Children of Ebenezer and Ruth Alvord:

48. Ebenezer, born Northampton, Aug. 24, 1693; died Northampton, in infancy.
49. †Joseph, born Northampton, March, 1697; died Jan. 1 or 9, 1786, at Northampton; married Northampton, July 30, 1730, Clemence Wright.
50. Mary, born Northampton, June 24, 1699.
51. †Noah, born Northampton, June 27, 1701; married, Feb. 9, 1726, Hannah Burt. He settled in Springfield, Mass.

Children of Ebenezer and Elizabeth Alvord:

52. Ruth, born Northampton, Aug. 24, 1710.
53. James, born Northampton, July 22, 1712; died Northampton, July 28, 1712.
54. Elizabeth, born Northampton, Sept. 7, 1713.
55. Rebecca, born Northampton, Oct. 25, 1716; died Northampton, Nov. 29, 1716.

55a. Rebecca, born Northampton, Feb. 10, 1718.

56. †Ebenezer, born Northampton, Dec. 17, 1720; married Northampton, Dec. 19, 1754, Catharine Strong.
57. Sarah, born Northampton, 1725; probably died young.
58. Thomas, born Northampton; his mother was his guardian.

II. 29. Jonathan Alvord,

Born Northampton, April 6, 1669; died Northampton, Aug. 13, 1727. Son of Alexander and Mary (Vore) Alvord. He was by occupation a tailor, and resided in Northampton. He had a grant of land in 1695, another in 1704, another in 1709, another in 1714.

The power of administration was granted to his widow, Thankful Alvord.

He married, at Northampton, Jan. 12, 1693,

Thankful Miller,

Born Northampton, April 25, 1669;(?) died Northampton, March 30, 1738. Daughter of William and Patience Miller.(?)

Her will is upon record at the Probate Office, Hampshire Co., dated March 25, 1737–8, in which she names sons John and Jonathan, and daughters Patience and Thankful Alvord.

Children :

59. Jonathan, born Northampton, April 9, 1694; died Northampton, March 4, 1701.
60. †John, born Northampton, Mass., June 28, 1696; married, Aug. 4, 1721, Prudence Baker.
61. Jonathan, born Northampton; died Northampton, April 11, 1706.
62. Patience, born Northampton, June 22, 1701.
63. Zebadiah, born Northampton, Oct. 30, 1705.
64. Mary, born Northampton, July 21, 1707.
65. Thankful, born Northampton, Aug. 10. 1709; died Aug. 7, 1747. Her will, dated March 7, 1745, makes her brother, Jonathan Alvord, and friend Jonathan Rust, sole executors.
66. †Jonathan, born Northampton; married Elizabeth ——.

III. 31. Thomas Alvord,

Born Northampton, Aug. 28, 1683; died Chatham, Conn. Son of Thomas and Joanna (Taylor) Alvord, and grandson of Alexander and Mary (Vore) Alvord. He resided in Northampton, Mass., Middletown, Conn., and Chatham, Conn.

A conveyance by his heirs. Thomas Alvord of Middletown, Seth Alvord, Jabez Woods and Mary his wife of Chatham in the county of Hartford and Jonathan Alvord of Winchester in the county of Litchfield all in the state of Connecticut and Asahel Alvord of Litchfield Conn, and Mary Alvord, and David Nichols & Hannah his wife all in the state of Conn, being heirs of Thomas Alvord late of sd Middletown now of Chatham deceased, convey land in Belchertown County of Hampshire Inn Holder, Oct. 2, 1780. [Reg. of Deeds at Springfield, Mass., Vol. 17, 268.

He married, 1, at Northampton, Jan. 3, 1705–6,

Esther Parsons.

Esther Alvord was drowned Oct. 3, 1707.

He married, 2,

Mary ——.

Children of Thomas and Mary Alvord:

67. Thomas, born Northampton, May 18, 1710; settled in Middletown, Conn., where he was in 1780.
68. †Jonathan, born Northampton, Nov. 16, 1711;(?) died in Winchester, in 1784; he resided in Chatham and in Winchester, Conn.
69. Aaron, born Northampton, July 16, 1713.
70. Seth, born Northampton, Nov. 13, 1714; was of Chatham in 1780.
71. Elisha, born Northampton, June 19, 1727.
72. Asahel, born Northampton, Dec. 16, 1720.
73. Mary, born Northampton, Sept. 3, 1724; married Jabez Woods. They were of Chatham in 1780.
74. Hannah, born Northampton; married David Nichols.

III. 32. John Alvord,

Born Northampton, Oct. 19, 1685; died South Hadley, Nov. 21, 1757. Son of Thomas and Joanna (Taylor) Alvord; and grandson of Alexander and Mary (Vore) Alvord. He resided in Northampton and in South Hadley.

"At a meeting of the Precinct (afterwards South Hadley) 10 August 1733;" "voted that the day for the ordination of Mr Grindell Rawson shall be the third day of October next with the concurrence of Mr Grindell Rawson." "Voted that Ebenezer Moody, Nathan^{ll} White John Alverd Dan^{ll} Nash and John Smith be a comitte to send for ye assistance of such ministers and messengers of Churches as they shall think best for ye ordination, &c."

John Alvord, March 12, 1733, was one of the first assessors of South Precinct Hadley.

He married Northampton, Dec. 29, 1708,

Dorcas Lyman,

Born Northampton, 1688;(?) died South Hadley, Nov. 15, 1770, aged 82.

Children:

75. †John, born Northampton, Oct. 29, 1711; died South Hadley, July 8, 1758; resided in South Hadley, and married Abigail White.
76. Mindwell, born Northampton, Aug. 4, 1713.
77. †Saul, born Northampton, April 23, 1717; he married Martha.
78. †Elijah, born Northampton, Jan. 17, 1718–9; died Greenfield, Mass. He married Hannah (Huntington?).
79. Dorcas, born Northampton, March 28, 1720.
80. †Job, born 1729; died Jan. 30, 1789, aged 60; married, Jan. 5, 1762, Rebecca Smith of South Hadley.
81. †Gad, born ——; died at Wilmington, Vt.; he married, 1, Lydia Smith; 2, Widow Holland.(?)
82. †Nathan, born South Hadley; (?) married South Hadley, Jan. 15, 1756, Lydia White.
83. Esther, born ——.
84. †Gideon, born South Hadley, June 12, 1734; died South Hadley;(?) married Sarah (Montague?).

III. 36. Benjamin Alvord,

Born Northampton, Sept. 1695.

"Mr Benjamin Alvord died in his chair suddenly and alone Oct. 22, 1772." [Northampton Town Records.

He was the son of Benjamin and Deborah (Stebbens) Alvord, and grandson of Alexander and Mary (Vore) Alvord. He resided at Northampton.

Will of Benjamin Alvord of Northampton, being arrived at an advanced age: Item son Noah Edwards & my daughter Jerusha Edwards. Item grandchildren—children to Bela

Strong and my daughter Eunice Strong late deceased. Item son Nathaniel Edwards and my daughter Margaret Edwards. Item grandchildren Amasa Strong; Eunice Strong; Ruth Strong; Naomi Strong; Belah Strong; children and heirs of my son Belah and Eunice Strong; said Belah Strong some time since died. Dated Jan. 8, 1771. Prob. Dec. 1, 1772.

In presence of Moses Alvord, Medad Alvord, Elisha Alvord.

He married, 1, Northampton,

Eunice ——,

Died Northampton, Oct. 8, 1732.

He was married, 2, at Northampton, Jan. 17, 1733, to

Ruth Alexander,

Died Northampton, June 6, 1770.

Children:

85. Eunice, born Northampton, June 14, 1727; married Bela Strong, and had children: 1, Amasa; 2, Eunice; 3, Ruth; 4, Thankful; 5, Naomi; and 6, Bela.

92. Infant child; died Nov. 3, 1732.
93. Jerusha, born Northampton; married Noah Edwards.
94. Margaret, born Northampton; married Nathaniel Edwards.

III. 49. Joseph Alvord,

Born Northampton, March, 1697; died Northampton, Jan. 1 or 9, 1786–89. Son of Ebenezer and Ruth (Baker) Alvord, and grandson of Alexander and Mary (Vore) Alvord.

For his will and codicil, see Appendix F.

Mr. Alvord resided in Northampton, on the estate he bought of Joseph Clesson, situated on the road to Hadley, about one-half mile from the bridge across the Connecticut river.

Abstract of a deed now in possession of a descendant:

"Joseph Clesson lately of Northampton now of Deerfield, husbandman in consideration of the sum of two hundred and sixty five pounds paid by Joseph Alvord March 26, 1730, conveys a certain homelot in the town of Hampton wt a dwelling house and barn standing thereon which home lot is bound as follows, viz: upon the highway northerly and upon Ebenezer Wright's Jun. lot, or the heirs of Judah Wright deceased lot; southerly upon the highway eastwardly and on the land of Moses Lyman and Gideon Lyman Westwardly, which lot contains five acres and a half or there about be it more or less.

JOSEPH CLESSON."

On the above lot Joseph Alvord lived and died; here all his children were born; here resided his son, Medad Alvord, also his granddaughter, Eunice Alvord, who married Luther Hunt. Mr. Joseph Alvord here carried on the business of a weaver, and employed a number of hands. His shop was east of his house, nearer to the road, and almost on the corner of a street. The old house he bought of Joseph Clesson he tore down, and erected a large, substantial mansion instead of it. His aunt Abigail, widow of John Alvord, (see wife of John Alvord, No. 7,) resided with him in the old house, and a room in the new house was furnished in a superior manner for her.

Tradition says, that Mr. Joseph Alvord was so faithful, kind, and attentive to the comforts of his aunt in her advanced age in life (over 101 years) that it would be an unrighteous act for any one to use him unkindly.

Nathan Clarke of Northampton, has lately purchased this homestead, and has moved the house a few rods in the rear, on a cross street, and has a new building in the course of erection, partly on the same foundation.

As you travel from Hadley towards Northampton Court House, you cross the river of the Connecticut, after which, in about one-half of a mile at your right, on the further corner of the second street on the same road, you come to the beautiful site, once the residence of Joseph Alvord and some of his descendants, soon to be the residence of Nathan Clark, Esq.

Mr. Alvord owned other estates.

May 5, 1758. Elisha Pomeroy of Northampton for forty pounds, conveys to Joseph Alvord a tract of land, lying in the meadow or common field in sd Northampton in that division commonly called Walnut Tree Division bounded as follows, viz easterly on a high way and northerly on Capt. Jonathan Hunt's land and westerly on the highway and southerly on Eleazer Burts land.

Jan. 21, 1744–5. William Hannum of Northampton in consideration of thirty seven pounds conveys to Joseph Alvord weaver, a certain parcel of land in the common field, bounded easterly on the Great River, westerly upon the high way, northerly upon Jonathan Strong's land & southwardly upon Hezekiah Roots land.

May 20, 1752. Samuel Sheldon of New Marlborough in consideration of the sum of thirty two pounds, conveys to Joseph Alvord weaver, land lying in the commonfield in Northampton (commonly called Venturers Field) bounded easterly by a high way, westerly by Ebenezer Alvord's land and Southerly by William Bartlett's land, &c.

March 30, 1754. Samuel Allen conveys to Joseph Alvord, a parcel of land lying in that part of the common field commonly called Old Rainbow; bounded west by Old Rainbow Hill northward by my brother Joseph Allen's land, easterly by the Great River and southward by land belonging to Reuben Wright and Aaron Wright.

May 18, 1761. Joseph Allen conveys a parcel of land called Old Rainbow, bounded, &c.

Timothy Mather to Joseph Alvord, land in Young Rainbow.

He was buried in the Northampton ancient burial-ground.

> "In memory of Mr Joseph Alvord who died
> Jany 1. 1786 in the 89 year of his age."

He married at Northampton, July 30, 1730,

Clemence Wright,

Born Northampton, Nov. 1703; died Northampton, March 25, 1776–73. She was the daughter of Dea. Ebenezer and Hannah (Hunt) Wright, who was the son of Samuel and Elizabeth (Burt) Wright, who was a soldier on service at Northfield, where he was slain by the Indians, Sept. 2, 1675, who was the son of Dea. Samuel Wright of Springfield, who was appointed by the town (after the return of Rev. Mr. Moxon, the first minister of Springfield, to his native land, in 1653) "to dispense the word of God for the present;" but about the year 1656 he removed to Northampton.

She was buried in the ancient burial-ground in Northampton.

"In memory of Mrs. Clemens wife of Mr. Joseph
Alvord who died March 25, 1776 in the 73 year of her age."

Children:

95. †Elisha, born Northampton, March 15, 1731; resided in Northampton; he married, Oct. 27, 1757, Mary Hamilton.
96. †Joseph, born Northampton, May 12, 1733; married, Dec. 29, 1759, Sarah Knight.
97. †Stephen, born Northampton, Aug. 18, 1735; died Canada, March, 1812; married Abigail Davis.
98. †Medad, born Northampton, Jan. 6, 1738; died May 15, 1798, aged 61; married, 1, Northampton, Sarah Baker; married, 2, May 10, 1791, Betsey (Lane) Partridge.
99. Lucy, born Northampton, Jan. 12, 1740; married Elisha Parsons, March 22, 1770.
100. †Simeon, born Northampton, May 14, 1742; died Hartland, Vt.; married, 1, April 14, 1768, Prudence Stevens; married, 2, Widow Susannah Page; married, 3, Widow (Speedy?) Bramble.
101. Infant child; died Northampton, Sept. 19, 1748.

III. 51. Noah Alvord,

Born Northampton, June 27, 1701; resided in Springfield, Mass. He was the son of Ebenezer and Ruth (Baker) Alvord, and grandson of Alexander and Mary (Vore) Alvord.

June 7, 1745. Noah Alvord of Springfield in the county of Hampshire, blacksmith, for six pounds, conveys to my brother Joseph Alvord of Northampton all the lands which I have in Northampton whether divided or undivided as I am an heir to my Hon^rd father Mr. Ebenezer Alvord late of Northampton deces[d]; as also as I am an heir to the estate of my grandfather Mr. Joseph Baker formerly of Northampton deces[d], both by my Hon[d] mother who was daughter to sd Joseph Baker and also by my brother Ebenezer Alvord dec'd an heir to the sd Ruth my Honoured mother and grandfather aforesaid.

NOAH ALVARD.

[Abstract of an original deed.]

He married Springfield, Mass., Feb. 9, 1726,

Hannah Burt.

Children:

102. Hannah, born Springfield, March 5, 1727–8.
103. Moses, born Springfield, March 20, 1730–1.
104. Aaron, born Springfield, July 29, 1734.
105. Elizabeth, born Springfield, July 22, 1738.

III. 56. Ebenezer Alvord,

Born Northampton, Dec. 17, 1720; resided in Northampton. Son of Ebenezer and Elizabeth (——) Alvord, and grandson of Alexander and Mary (Vore) Alvord.

He married Northampton, Dec. 19, 1754,

Catharine Strong.

She was buried in the ancient burial-ground in Northampton.

"Mrs. Catharine Alvord wife of Ebenezer Alvord
died Sept 11 1773 in the 45 year of her age."

Children:

106. Eliab, born Northampton, Sept. 4, bapt. 7, 1755.
107. Elizabeth, born Northampton, Feb. 15, bapt. 20, 1757.
108. Thomas, bapt. Northampton, March 25, 1759.
109. Jerusha, bapt. Northampton, Dec. 27, 1761.
110. Catharine, bapt. Northampton, April 24, 1768.
111. Rhoda, bapt. Northampton, July 14, 1771.
112. Infant, born ——; "died the same day its mother, Sept. 12, 1773."

III. 60. John Alvord,

Born Northampton, June 28, 1696; resided in Northampton. Son of Jonathan and Thankful (Miller) Alvord, who was the son of Alexander and Mary (Vore) Alvord. He resided in Northampton.

His will is on file in the Probate Office at Northampton, but was never recorded. He mentions sons Zebadiah and John Alvord. Item dau. Sarah wife of Ebenezer Malloon of Amherst. Item Sarah Malloon and Eleazer Malloon children of my daughter Sarah. Item dau. Mary Alvord.

Will dated July 20, 1765—addition, Aug. 8, 1768.

Witness, Ebenezer Hunt. JOHN ALVORD.
Mary Alvord, Elisha Alvord.

April 4, 1780. Zebadiah Alvord & John Alvord Executors.

He married Northampton, Aug. 4, 1721,

Prudence Baker.

Died Northampton, Aug. 1752.

Children:

113. Zebadiah, born Northampton, April 20, 1722; died young.
114. †Zebadiah, born Northampton, Feb. 14, 1724; died Easthampton; married Rebecca.
115. Sarah, born Northampton, March 2, 1726; married in 1759, Ebenezer Mattoon (for his second wife), son of Dea. Eleazar Mattoon, and had children:
116. 1. Sarah, born about 1761; died April 11, 1803, aged 42.
117. 2. Eleazar, born ——, bapt. Aug. 19, 1764; died unmarried.
118. 3. Roxana, born Aug. 31, 1766; married, 1785, John Kellogg of Amherst, Mass., and died Sept. 2, 1804, aged 37.
119. 4. Lovisa, born about 1770; married Eli Dickinson of Amherst, and died Jan. 31, 1845, aged 75.
120. John, born Northampton, Jan. 16, 1728; married, 1, ——; 2, ——.

121. Rachel, born Northampton, March 26, 1730; died Aug. 22, 1748.

122. Mary, born Northampton, Feb. 19, 1734.

III. 66. Jonathan Alvord,

Born Northampton. Son of Jonathan and Thankful (Miller) Alvord, and grandson of Alexander and Mary (Vore) Alvord. Thankful Alvord, daughter of Jonathan and Thankful Alvord, in her will of March 7, 1745, makes her brother Jonathan Alvord, and friend Jonathan Rust, sole executors.

He married

Elizabeth ——.

Children:

123. Thankful, born Northampton, Jan. 16, 1749.

124. †Jonathan, born Northampton, Nov. 29. 1751 (married Freelove?).

125. Beriah, born Northampton, Feb. bapt. 10, 1754.

126. †Jehiel, born Northampton, Jan. 7, bapt. 11, 1756; married Northampton, June 11, 1778, Dorothy French.

IV. 68. Jonathan Alvord,

Born Northampton, Nov. 16, 1711;(?) died Winchester, Conn., 1784, aged 73. Son of Thomas and Mary (——) Alvord, who was the son of Thomas and Joanna (Taylor) Alvord, who was the son of Alexander and Mary (Vore) Alvord. He was called Capt. Jonathan Alvord. Oct. 2, 1780, he was of Winchester, Conn., and as one of the heirs of Thomas Alvord conveys land in Belchertown to Ebenezer Warner. See Register of Deeds, Hampshire Co., Vol. 17, 268.

Children:

127. †Eliphaz, born Jan. 13, 1742; married, Nov. 27, 1764, Esther Hart.

128. David, born June 14, 1753; married ——. "Moved to Vernon, N. Y., about 1800."

IV. 75. John Alvord,

Born Northampton, Oct. 29, 1711; died South Hadley, July 8, 1758. Son of John and Dorcas (Lyman) Alvord, who was the son of Thomas and Joanna (Taylor) Alvord, who was the son of Alexander and Mary (Vore) Alvord. He resided in South Hadley. For his will, see Appendix G.

He married

Abigail White,

Born Hadley, Aug. 20, 1713; died Nov. 19, 1757, aged 44. She was the daughter of Dea. Joseph and Abigail (Craft) White, who was the son of Dea. Nathaniel and Elizabeth (Savage) White, who was the son of Capt. Nathaniel and Elizabeth (——) White, (who was born about 1629, and resided in Middletown, Conn.,) who was the son of John and Mary (——) White, who came in the Lion, and arrived at Boston, Mass., from London, England, Sept. 16, 1632, and probably tarried a few years in Cambridge, then Newtown, and then moved to Hartford, Conn.

Children:

129. †Moses, born Aug. 26, 1735; married Percés ——, and resided in South Hadley.
130. †Azariah, born Jan. 20, 1738; resided in Springfield and in West Springfield; he married, 1, Abigail Nash, Jan. 5, 1768; he married, 2, March 5, 1789, Lucy Nash of Granby.
131. Abigail, born Sept. 23, 1739. Named in father's will.
132. Jerusha, born Sept. 27, 1741. Named in father's will.
133. Dorcas, born South Hadley, Nov. 4, 1743. Named in father's will.
134. Rachel, born South Hadley, April 15, 1747. Named in father's will.
135. Phineas, born South Hadley, June 26, 1750. Named in father's will.
136. †Luther, born South Hadley, March 4, 1753; married Elizabeth Ingram.
137. Rebecca, born South Hadley, April 14, 1756.

IV. 77. Saul Alvord,

Born Northampton, April 23, 1717. Son of John and Dorcas (Lyman) Alvord, who was the son of Thomas and Joanna (Taylor) Alvord, who was the son of Alexander and Mary (Vore) Alvord.

Dec. 20, 1743, John Alvord conveyed to his son, Saul Alvord, a certain parcel of land. Nov. 20, 1751, he received of his father, John Alvord, a deed of land in Hadley Precinct. April 17, 1754, Saul Alvord of Northampton, conveys land in South Hadley to Gideon Alvord of South Hadley. He was a barber and hair-dresser by occupation, and resided in Northampton and in Bolton, Conn.

He married

Martha ——.

Children:

138. Saul, born Northampton; died Northampton, July 5, 1753.
139. Martha, born Northampton, June 29, 1747; died June 28, 1748.
140. Lydia, born Northampton, Sept. 7, 1748; died Northampton, June 22, 1750.
141. Ann, born Northampton, Oct. 7, bapt. 12, 1755.
142. Eunice, born Northampton, Jan. 2, bapt. 7, 1759.

IV. 78. Elijah Alvord,

Born Northampton, Jan. 17, 1718–19; died at Greenfield, Mass. Son of John and Dorcas (Lyman) Alvord, who was the son of Thomas and Joanna (Taylor) Alvord, who was the son of Alexander and Mary (Vore) Alvord. He resided in South Hadley, where he owned a warehouse, situated near what is now called Smith's Ferry, then Alvord's Ferry, and tended by Gideon Alvord.

Mr. Alvord was a prominent man in town and church affairs, and was often appointed on committees.

March 9, 1761, he was elected to the office of selectman.

He, with Nathaniel White, Jr., was appointed a committee to prosecute certain persons who cut down and drew away part of the meeting-house. He removed to Greenfield. May 15, 1788, power of administration on the estate of Elijah Alvord, late of Greenfield, was granted to Caleb Alvord of Greenfield, who declared the estate insolvent.

He married

Hannah (Huntington?).

She outlived her husband.

Children:

143. †Caleb, born Oct. 5, 1751; died Greenfield, Mass., Dec. 22, 1819, aged 68 years, two months; married, Dec. 26, 1776, Mary Murdock.
144. †Hannah, born 1754; died Greenfield, Mass., Sept. 22, 1811, aged 57; married Abner Smead.

IV. 80. Lieut. Job Alvord,

Born 1729; died Jan. 30, 1789, aged 60. Son of John and Dorcas (Lyman) Alvord, who was the son of Thomas and Joanna (Taylor) Alvord, who was the son of Alexander and Mary (Vore) Alvord. He resided in South Hadley and in Springfield.

He received a grant of land from his father, John Alvord of South Hadley. Aug. 21, 1789, Justin Alvord of South Hadley administrator on the estate of Job Alvord, late of South Hadley.

Lieut. Job Alvord of Springfield married, Jan. 5, 1762,

Rebecca Smith,

Born South Hadley,(?) 1740; died, a widow, Jan. 19, 1832, aged 92.

Children:

145. †Justin, born Springfield, Nov. 30, 1763; died South Hadley,(?) Oct. 1852, aged 89; married South Hadley, 1788, Jerusha Wait.
146. Lucina, born Springfield, Oct. 20, 1771; married South Hadley, July 4, 1794, Solomon Lyman.

IV. 81. Gad Alvord,

Born 1729; died Wilmington, Vt. Son of John and Dorcas (Lyman) Alvord, who was the son of Thomas and Joanna (Taylor) Alvord, who was the son of Alexander and Mary (Vore) Alvord.

He resided in South Hadley, on the bank of the Connecticut river. March 20, 1752, he received of his father a tract of land in the South Precinct of Hadley; and Sept. 2, of the same year, his brother, Nathan Alvord, conveyed to him a parcel of land. He removed to Wilmington, Vt.

He married, 1, Nov. 17, 1750,

Lydia Smith,

Born April 7, 1728; died prior to 1786. She was the daughter of Samuel and Lydia (Smith?) Smith, who was the son of Capt. Luke and Mary (Crow) Smith, who was the son of Chiliab and Hannah (Hitchcock) Smith, who was the son of Lieut. Samuel Smith, who sailed for New England, April 30, 1634, aged 32, in the Elizabeth, Ipswich. Lieut. Samuel Smith settled in Wethersfield, Conn., but subsequently moved to Hadley, where he held important offices both of Church and State.

He married, 2,

Widow Holland.

Children of Gad and Lydia Alvord:

147. †Samuel, born South Hadley, Nov. 27, 1751; died South Hadley, July 9, 1814, aged 63; married Meriam White.
148. Rhoda, born South Hadley, Aug. 26, 1753.
149. Lucina, born South Hadley, April ye 15, 1755; died South Hadley, Feb. 12, 1763.
150. †Sibyl, born South Hadley, March 23, 1757.
151. †Gad, born South Hadley, June ye 27, 1759; resided in Granby, Mass.; married Phebe White.
152. †Asher, born South Hadley, June 9, or 4, 1761; died Wilmington, Vt., Nov. 12, 1837; married Martha Ayres, and moved to Wilmington, Vt.

153. †Zerah, born South Hadley, Nov. 10, 1765; died Shelburne, Mass., June 17, 1845; married, 1, Greenfield, Mass., Nov. 11, 1790, Hannah Nims; married, 2, Sarah Foster.

154. †Seth, born South Hadley, June 29, 1763; died Wilmington, Vt., May 17, 1835; married Ruth Taylor, and moved to Wilmington, Vt.

155. Enos, born South Hadley, Aug. 15, 1768; married Anna Smith.

IV. 82. Nathan Alvord,

Born South Hadley. Son of John and Dorcas (Lyman) Alvord, who was the son of Thomas and Joanna (Taylor) Alvord, who was the son of Alexander and Mary (Vore) Alvord.

March 20, 1752, he received from his father, John Alvord, a grant of land in South Hadley. He conveys, Sept. 2, 1752, to his brother, Gad Alvord, land in South Hadley, and says in the deed, "My hon[d] father John Alvord." He married South Hadley, Jan. 15, 1756,

Lydia White.

Children:

156. Selah, born Aug. 17, 1756; married Miss Lewis, from Norwich. They moved to Indiana, where they died, leaving children, Levi and Elvira.

159. Lois, born Aug. 8, 1758; married David Nash, (born South Hadley, Feb. 10, 1755; died Watervliet, N. Y., Oct. 6, 1832,) son of Dea. David and Elizabeth (Smith) Nash, who was the son of Dea. John and Hannah (Ingram) Nash, who was the son of Lieut. John and Elizabeth (Kellogg) Nash, who was the son of Lieut. Timothy and Rebecca (Stone) Nash, born in England, or Leyden in Holland, in 1626, who was the son of Thomas Nash of New Haven, Conn. David Nash, who married Lois Alvord, resided in Granby, Mass., Bolton, N. Y., and in Watervliet, N. Y. He outlived all of his children. His direct line of ancestors of the

first four generations in this country, were either gunsmiths or blacksmiths. Children:

160. 1. Levi, born Granby, Mass., Jan. 17, 1787; died, unmarried, at Warrensburg, N. Y.

161. 2. David, born Granby, Mass., May 2, 1790; died Granby, Mass., Jan. 17, 1792.

162. 3. David, born Granby, Mass., March 13, 1792; married, Sept. 3, 1818, Hannah Payne. "He kept what used to be called the Half-way House, in Watervliet, N. Y., between Albany and Troy."

163. 4. Lydia, born Granby, Mass., Nov. 24, 1793; married Daniel Howard; died in Warrensburg.

164. 5. Lois, born Granby, Mass., Feb. 3, 1796; died, unmarried, in Bolton, N. Y.

165. 6. Erastus, born Granby, Mass., Aug. 24, 1797; married Lucy Yeomans, and resided in Troy, N. Y., where he died in 1830, leaving one child, who died the same year.

166. 7. Alvin, born ——; died, unmarried, in Albany, N. Y., aged 24 years.

167. †John, born July 13, 1760; married, 1, Abigail Smead; married, 2, Rhoda Mather of Shelburne, Mass.

168. Lydia, born April 25, 1762; married Enos Kellogg of South Hadley, and had Pliny and Lydia.

169. Nathan, born Aug. 21, 1764; died Jan. 3, 1766.

170. Nathan, born Sept. 5, 1766; died Oct. 2, 1766.

171. Nathan, born April 3, 1768; married Rebecca Damon of Williamstown, Vt., and moved to the State of Pennsylvania about the year 1818. They had children: 1, John; 2, Nathan; 3, Polly; 4, Justin; 5, Cheny; 6. Adaline; 7, Royal; 8. Lois.

180. †Elijah, born Sept. 3, 1770; married, 1, Greenfield, Mass., Jan. 16, 1791, Anna Bascom; married, 2, Lucretia Clarke of Colchester, Conn.

IV. 84. Gideon Alvord,

Born South Hadley, June 12, 1734; died South Hadley. Son of John and Dorcas (Lyman) Alvord, who was the son of Thomas and Joanna (Taylor) Alvord, who was the son of Alexander and Mary (Vore) Alvord. He resided in South Hadley, where he tended the ferry, then called Alvord's Ferry.

We infer, by a deed of Nov. 2, 1756, that Gideon Alvord lived on the homestead of his father, John Alvord, who reserved a life-lease for himself and Dorcas, his wife, with sundry privileges for their maintenance. [See Vol. W, p. 318, Reg. Deeds.

He married

Sarah (Montague ?).

Children:

181. Naomi, born South Hadley, Oct. 20, 1761; married, 1, South Hadley, July 2, 1783, Frederic Howard of Northampton; married, 2, Samuel Dickinson.
182. Jemima, born South Hadley, Dec. y[e] 3, 1762.
183. Dorcas, born South Hadley, March 23, 1765.
184. Sarah, born South Hadley, March 14, 1767; married South Hadley, Jan. 21, 1801, Stephen Tyler of Wilmington, Vt.
185. Tamsin, born South Hadley, July 14, 1769; died South Hadley, Jan. 27, 1770.
186. Ebenezer, born South Hadley, April 26, 1770; settled in Wilmington, Vt., where he died.

IV. 95. Elisha Alvord,

Born Northampton, March 15, 1731. Son of Joseph and Clemence (Wright) Alvord, who was the son of Ebenezer and Ruth (Baker) Alvord, who was the son of Alexander and Mary (Vore) Alvord.

He held the office of clerk for the Proprietors of Northampton, from Oct. 25, 1763, when he took the oath, until Nov. 2, 1768, and perhaps later. He wrote an elegant hand.

His house stood near where the present Court House now is, in Northampton, and the well is now under the hardware store of Mr. George D. Eames. The water was excellent, and the well not deep, but it is not now used.

Oct. 6, 1767, his lot of land was deeded to Ebenezer Hunt and others, for the public use of erecting a Court House, &c., thereon. [See Appendix H.

He married Northampton, Oct. 27, 1757,

Mary Hamilton.

Children:

187. Daniel, bapt. Northampton, May 28, 1758. Named in his grandfather's (Joseph Alvord) will.
188. ———, bapt. Northampton, Sept. 23, 1761.
189. Eleazer. Named in his grandfather's (Joseph Alvord) will.
190. Elisha, bapt. Northampton, Oct. 21, 1764. Named in his grandfather's (Joseph Alvord) will.
191. William, bapt. Northampton, April 6, 1766. Named in his grandfather's (Joseph Alvord) will.
192. Luther, bapt. Northampton, July 13, 1777.

1. Elisha, son of Elisha Alvord, Jr., bapt. Dec. 5, 1779;
2. Seth, son of Elisha of ye Fenno, bapt. May 12, 1782;
3. Solomon, son to Elisha, bapt. Feb. 22, 1784;
4. Eleazer, son to Eleazer, bapt. Nov. 3, 1782;
5. Eunice, daughter of Eleazer, bapt. Oct. 2, 1788.

Who are these?

IV. 96. Joseph Alvord,

Born Northampton, May 12, 1733. Son of Joseph and Clemence (Wright) Alvord, who was the son of Ebenezer and Ruth Baker Alvord, who was the son of Alexander and Mary (Vore) Alvord. He resided in Northampton and in Bernardston.

April 16, 1787, Joseph Alvord of Bernardston, conveys to his brother, Medad Alvord, a parcel of land situated in Northampton, in the upper end of Young Rainbow, bounded on the Great River, &c.

In presence of Cornelius Lyman, Elisha Alvord.

[Abstract of an original deed.] JOSEPH ALVORD.

He married, 1, Northampton, Dec. 29, 1759,

Sarah Knight,

Born ——; died Northampton, Jan. 21, 1766.

He married, 2,

Submit Chapin.

Children:

198. Phineas, bapt. Northampton, April 20, 1760. A Phineas Alvord married, 1, Northampton, July 5, 1782, Rachel Judd; married, 2,(?) Northampton, Feb. 27, 1794, Salome Judd, and had children:

199. 1. Rachel, born Northampton, Sept. 28, 1783.
200. 2. "Child of Phineas Alvord died March 25, 1786."
201. 3. Naomi, born Northampton, Aug. 10, 1789.
202. 4. Samuel, born Northampton, Jan. 5, 1792.
203. 5. "Phineas Alvord's daughter died Aug. 16, 1803."
204. 6. Timothy, born Northampton, Oct. 1804.
205. 7. Lewis, born Northampton, April 11, 1807.

206. Seth, bapt. Northampton, Jan. 26, 1766.
207. Sarah, bapt. Jan. 26, 1766; married Northampton, Dec. 28, 1790, Israel Bridgman. She was adopted by her uncle, Medad Alvord, who gave her a marriage portion.

IV. 97. Stephen Alvord,

Born Northampton, Aug. 18, 1735; died Canada, March, 1812. Son of Joseph and Clemence (Wright) Alvord, who was the son of Ebenezer and Ruth (Baker) Alvord, who was the son of Alexander and Mary (Vore) Alvord. He was a hatter by occupation. He lived in Charlestown, N. H., before he was married. He also resided in Windsor, Vt., and in Woodstock, Vt., but died in Canada.

"Charlestown, N. H., Lord's day, June 1, 1777, Stephen Alvord and wife were admitted to our communion." [Charlestown First Cong. Church.

Their five eldest children were baptized July 26, 1778.

Mrs. Gibbs says that her father became an Episcopalian. He was in the war of the Revolution.

Feb. 25, 1804, Stephen Alvord was formerly guardian to Elihu and Josiah Taylor, heirs of the estate of Robert D. Taylor, late of Woodstock.

He married

Abigail Davis,

Born Chesterfield,(?) 1747;(?) died Windsor, Vt., June 3, 1820, aged 73. She was the daughter of Simon and Mary (Powers) Davis, and had brothers, Elias, Simon, Phineas, and Sampson.

Mr. Davis came up from Chesterfield, so says Mrs. Gibbs, and settled in Woodstock, Vt., where he died.

Mrs. Alvord, after the death of her husband, returned from Canada to Vermont, and resided in Windsor, where she died.

"The widow Abigail Alvord having been recommended to our Christian fellowship by the church of Christ in Woodstock, Vt., and having satisfied the church of her religious experience, and been propounded the usual time—no objection; was received to the communion and fellowship of the church." [See Windsor Church Records.

Children:

208. †Pathenia, born Charlestown, N. H., July 4, 1767; died Enosburg, Vt., Jan. 26, 1798. Upon the Church Records she is called Triphena. She married, 1, Robert Dennison Taylor; 2, Joseph Waller.

209. Stephen Washington, born Charlestown, N. H., bapt. July 26, 1778; married Polly Thomas.

210. Abigail, born Charlestown, N. H., bapt. July 26, 1778; married Zacheus Ellis.

211. Lucy Wright, born Charlestown, Nov. 6, 1774, bapt. July 26, 1778; married, Feb. 17, 1805, Josiah Gibbs, born Dec. 25, 1761; died Dec. 29, 1839.

Children of Josiah and Lucy (Wright) Gibbs:

212. 1. Lyman, born April 16, 1806; married —— Huggins.
213. 2. Abial, born Feb. 11, 1808; living in 1863.
214. 3. Roxanna, born March 14, 1810; never married.
215. 4. Clarinda, born March 10, 1812; married Anson Danes; living in 1863.

216. 5. Matilda, born April 20, 1814; married Charles Bell.

217. 6. Oliver Alvord, born July 25, 1817; living in 1863; married, 1, Betsey Perkins; 2, ——.

218. Roxana, born Charlestown, N. H., Dec. 6, 1775, bapt. July 26, 1778; died Nashua, N. H., March 9, 1859; married, Oct. 10, 1798, Benjamin Burke. [See Burke Genealogy, No. 75.

219. Isaac, bapt. Charlestown, N. H., July 3, 1779; married Abigail Bald.

220. Clemence, bapt. Charlestown, N. H., April, 1781; never married.

IV. 98. Medad Alvord,

Born Northampton, Jan. 6, 1738; died Northampton, May 15, 1798. Son of Joseph and Clemence (Wright) Alvord, who was the son of Ebenezer and Ruth (Baker) Alvord, who was the son of Alexander and Mary (Vore) Alvord.

He resided on Bridge street, Northampton, on the homestead of his father, Joseph Alvord. His father sold to him, March 21, 1781, for twenty pounds in silver, fifty acres of woodland, situated in that part of Northampton called Inner Commons, lying over Boggy Meadow, bounded, &c.

June 21, 1773, Samuel Bodman and William Bodman of Hatfield, convey to Medad Alvord 96 acres of land, situated in Williamsburg, in that part called "Hatfield Three Mile Addition."

Medad Alvord's bond unto Isaac Johnson of Williamsburg, in the sum of two hundred pounds. Said Johnson has agreed to cut down and carry off, the wood timber, of 16 acres of land of sd Medad Alvord's farm in Williamsburg; on which the said Johnson lives; on the north east side of the road as it now runs; and fit and prepare the sd 16 acres for the plow or drag within five years, &c. but he is to leave all the green chestnut trees.

If the sd Johnson does not fail then the sd Alvord is to give a warranty deed of a certain part of Medad Alvord's farm in Williamsburg containing 31 a. 32 r. 21.

Mr. Medad Alvord was a man of common sense, strong mind, and good judgment, and a philanthropist.

His will, dated March 2, 1797, mentions wife Betsey Alvord, the household goods she brought with her. Item, dau. Eunice, wife of Luther Hunt.

In memory of Mr. Medad Alvord who died
May 15, 1798 in the 61st year of his age.

[Northampton Burial-ground.

Mr. Medad Alvord married, 1,

Sarah Baker,

Born Northampton,(?) 1741;(?) died Northampton, April 8, 1790, aged 49. She was the daughter of Samuel and Sarah (Langdon) Baker, and was buried in Northampton ancient burial-place.

"Here lies the body of Mrs Sarah Alvord the wife of
Mr Medad Alvord who died April 8, 1790 in the 49th year of her age."

"Let virtue guard the narrow bed
Where virtue's image rests her head,
Religion shed a rich perfume,
And Angels watch around the tomb."

He married, 2, Northampton, May 10, 1791,

Widow Betsey (Lane) Partridge,

Children of Medad and Sarah Alvord:

221. Sarah, born Northampton; died in infancy, 1778.
222. †Eunice, born Northampton, April 18, 1776; died Northampton, June 23, 1860, aged 84; married, June 19, 1796, Luther Hunt.
223. Infant, born June 5, 1782; lived only three hours; died June 5, 1782.

IV. 100. Simeon Alvord,

Born Northampton, May 14, 1742; died Hartland, Vt. Son of Joseph and Clemence (Wright) Alvord, who was the son of Ebenezer and Ruth (Baker) Alvord, who was the son of Alexander and Mary (Vore) Alvord.

He resided in Windsor, Vt., in Charlestown, N. H., and in Hartland, Vt. He was a man of property. He owned real estate in Windsor, Hartland, and in Hartford, Vt. He owned in Windsor, a house, shop, bark mill, mill stones, vats for tanning, &c., &c.

An aged christian lady of Hartland, who was acquainted with him when she was a child, says, "Mr. Simeon Alvord was a good, candid christian, and was much esteemed for his counsel. He was naturally very cheerful, and was very good company; but he would often censure himself for being so lively. He often, with tears, would say how much he regretted the manner of spending his life in his younger days. He was uncommonly gifted in prayer. I not only loved to hear him talk but I loved to hear him pray." He left no children, but his property fell to the children of his last wife by a former husband.

He married, 1, April 14, 1768,

Prudence Stevens.

They lived together but a short time. He married, 2,

Widow Susannah Page.

She was a sincere christian. She died Hartland, Sept. 12, 1783. He married, 3,

Widow (Speedy?) Bramble.

She was the widow of Abel Bramble of Hartland, and was a member of the Baptist church. She had a large family by a former husband.

IV. 113. Zebadiah Alvord,

Born Northampton, Feb. 14, 1724; died Easthampton. Son of John and Prudence (Baker) Alvórd, and grandson of Jonathan and Thankful (Miller) Alvord, and great-grandson of Alexander and Mary (Vore) Alvord. He resided in Northampton and in Easthampton.

His will is upon record at Northampton, dated May 11, 1802. He married

Rebecca ——.

Children:

224. Caleb, born Northampton.(?) Named in his father's will.
225. Timothy, born Northampton.(?) Named in his father's will.
226. Elisha, born Northampton.(?) Named in his father's will.
227. Seth, born Northampton, bapt. July 11, 1756; died Oct. 17, 1756. Not named in will.
228. Perez, born Northampton, bapt. April 2, 1758; died Nov. 7, 1758. Not named in will.
229. Phineas, born Northampton, bapt. 1760. Named in his father's will.
230. Esther, born Northampton, bapt. 1762. Named in her father's will.
231. Noadiah, born Northampton. Named in his father's will.
232. Rebecca, born Northampton. Named in her father's will.
233. Two children of Zebadiah Alvord died Northampton, April 28, 1767.
234. Daughter, baptized July 14, 1771.

IV. 120. John Alvord,

Born Northampton, Jan. 16, 1728; died Easthampton. Son of John and Prudence (Baker) Alvord, who was the son of Jonathan and Thankful (Miller) Alvord, who was the son of Alexander and Mary (Vore) Alvord. He resided in Northampton and in Easthampton.

His will is on record at the Probate Office at Northampton, dated Sept. 9, 1802.

He married, 1, ——; 2, ——.

Children:

235. John, born Northampton. Named in his father's will.
236. Rachel, born Northampton. Named in her father's will. Married Samuel Pomeroy.
237. Prudence, born Northampton. Named in her father's will. Married James Farmer.
238. Elijah, bapt. Northampton 1758; was drowned. Named in will.
239. Jemima, bapt. Northampton, 1761. Named in will. Married Benjamin Strong.
240. Samuel, born Northampton; died in West Springfield; married Hannah Day, and had children:
241. 1. Sewall, born West Springfield; married Jemima Williams, and died at Chickopee Falls, and left no children.
242. 2. Eunice, born West Springfield; married Henry Stiles, and had children:
243. a. Henry, born ——; married Mary Granger.
244. b. Almira, born ——; married —— Stockbridge.
245. c. Eunice Ann, born ——.
246. d. William, born ——; moved off South.
247. 3. Polly, born West Springfield; married Francis Vanhorne. Children:
248. a. Hannah Vanhorne, born ——.
249. b. Francis Vanhorne, born ——.
250. c. Elizabeth Vanhorne, born ——.
251. 4. Ebenezer, born West Springfield, March 29, 1794, married Hope Ashley, and had children:
252. a. Wellington, born ——; married Rosanna Monson.
253. b. Jane, married John Jones.
254. c. Delia, married Edwin Granger.
255. d. Ebenezer, married —— Monson.
256. e. Mary, married Luther Stearns.
257. f. Eunice, married James Stebbens.
258. g. Edward, married Charlotte Allen.

259. Experience, daughter of John Alvord, was baptized Sept. 27, 1767.
260. A daughter of John, bapt. July 18, 1772.
261. Dolphus, son of John, bapt. June 10, 1787.
262. Achsa, daughter of John, bapt. Sept. 20, 1789.

IV. 124. Jonathan Alvord,

Born Northampton, Nov. 29, 1751; died West Hampton. Son of Jonathan and Elizabeth (——) Alvord, who was the son of Jonathan and Thankful (Miller) Alvord, who was the son of Alexander and Mary (Vore) Alvord.

We do not know whether the above Jonathan Alvord is the one who died in Westhampton, whose will of March 18, 1826, mentions wife

Freelove.

263. Item, daughter Cynthia, wife of Daniel Townsley.
264. Item, granddaughter Elizabeth, wife of Asa Church.
265. Item, heirs of daughter Dorcas, dec.
266. Item, daughter Thankful, wife of Joseph Chilson.
267. Item, daughter Anna, wife of Richard Clapp.

IV. 126. Jehiel Alvord,

Born Northampton, Jan. 7, bapt. 11, 1756; died West Hampton. Son of Jonathan and Elizabeth (——) Alvord, who was the son of Jonathan and Thankful (Miller) Alvord, who was the son of Alexander and Mary (Vore) Alvord. He resided at West Hampton. He was married at Northampton, by Rev. Solomon Williams, June 11, 1778, to

Dorothy French.

Children of Jehiel and Dorothy Alvord:

268. Isaac, born ——; married Sarah ——, and had children:
269. 1. Joseph, married Ruth Starkweather, and had children: 1. Willie; 2. Josephine; 3. Dana. Adopted Hattie and Allie.
273. 2. Jehiel, born ——. Single; lives out West.
274. 3. Thankful, born ——.

275. 4. Almeda, born ——; married Elnathan Phelps.
276. 5. Sarah, born ——; married Frank Ludden.

277. Jehiel, born ——; died at West Hampton, about the year 1859; married and had children:
278. 1. Nelson, resides at Leeds, Northampton; married Sarah Strong, and had children:
279. a. Frank Clark, born Dec. 21, 1836.
280. b. Emeline, born Feb. 7, 1838; married Joseph Warner, and died Jan. 5, 1863.
281. c. Sarah Jane, born ——; died young.
282. d. Susan Amelia, born June 1, 1846.
283. e. Fanny Jane, born Sept. 1, 1850.

284. 2. Seth, born ——; single; resides at West Hampton.
285. 3. Abiathar, born ——; single; resides at Northampton.
286. 4. Emeline, born March 31, 1821; married Archelaus Leonard, born Nov. 19, 1819; died June 15, 1850, and had children:
287. a. Chester Leonard, born Oct. 12, 1842.
288. b. Henry S. Leonard, born March 8, 1844.
289. c. Mary Elizabeth Leonard, born June 11, 1845.
290. d. Sarah Adelia Leonard, born July 1, 1846; died Aug. 5, 1862.
291. e. Alva Robbins Leonard, born July 29, 1848; died July 19, 1815.
292. f. Lucy Anna Leonard, born May 14, 1850.

293. 5. Sarah, born ——; married James M. Angel, and resides in Chesterfield, Mass.
294. 6. Eunice, born ——; married Zenas Judd, and resides in West Hampton. They have children:
a. Amelia Thankful. b. Henry Alva.

297. Dorothy, born ——; married —— Hayden. Named in her father's will.

V. 127. Eliphaz Alvord,

Born Chatham, Middleton,(?) Jan. 13, 1742; died Winchester, Ct., April 18, 1825. Son of Jonathan and Elizabeth (Sanford) Alvord, who was the son of Thomas and Mary (——) Alvord, who was the son of Thomas and Joanna (Taylor) Alvord, who was the son of Alexander and Mary (Vore) Alvord.

He was married to

Esther Hart,

Born Farmington, Conn., April, 1742; died Winchester, Nov. 18, 1818, and had a son,

298. John Alvord, who was father of

299. C. A. Alvord of New York City, who is a printer by occupation, and whose office is 15 Vandewater street, N. Y.

V. 129. Moses Alvord,

Born South Hadley, Aug. 26, 1735. Son of John and Abigail (White) Alvord, who was the son of John and Dorcas (Lyman) Alvord, who was the son of Thomas and Joanna (Taylor) Alvord, who was the son of Alexander and Mary (Vore) Alvord. He resided in South Hadley, and married

Perces ——.

Children:

300. Benjamin, born South Hadley, Jan. 5, 1762.

301. Rebecca, born South Hadley, March 24, 1764.

302. Lucy, born South Hadley, Feb. 18, 1766.

303. Caroline, born South Hadley, Jan. 18, 1768.

V. 130. Azariah Alvord,

Born South Hadley,(?) Jan. 20, 1738; died South Hadley, Jan. 11, 1819. Son of John and Abigail (White) Alvord, who was the son of John and Dorcas (Lyman) Alvord, who was the son of Thomas and Joanna (Taylor) Alvord, who was the son of Alexander and Mary (Vore) Alvord. He resided in Springfield, West Springfield, and in South Hadley.

His will, dated South Hadley, Sept. 1, 1808, mentions wife Lucy, grandson Helaz Alvord, son Bezaleel Alvord of South Hadley, Tirzah, wife of Nehemiah Day of South Hadley, Rachel, wife of Zenas Church of South Hadley, Zeruiah Alvord of North Haven, daughter of my son, Ariel Alvord, late of South Hadley, deceased.

He married, 1, Jan. 5, 1762,

Abigail Nash,

Born Feb. 17, 1740; died South Hadley, March 31, 1782. Supposed daughter of Daniel and Abigail Nash, who was the son of John and Elizabeth (Kellogg) Nash, who was the son of Timothy and Rebecca (Stone) Nash, who removed from Hartford, Conn., to Hadley in 1663, who was the son of Thomas and Margery (Baker) Nash.

He married, 2, March 5, 1789,

Lucy Nash,

Of Granby, born Sept. 18, 1750. She was the daughter of Eleazer and Phebe (Kellogg) Nash, who was the son of Ephraim and Joanna (Smith) Nash, who was the son of Timothy (born in England) and Rebecca (Stone) Nash, who was the son of Thomas and Margery Nash.

Children:

304. Bezaleel, born Springfield, Nov. 19, 1762; married Mary Goodman. Children:

305. 1. Chester, born South Hadley, Sept. 12, 1781; married Susannah Browning, and had children:

306. a. Tristram Browning, born South Hadley, Sept. 27, 1804; went out West.

307. b. Dolly, born South Hadley, Jan. 26, 1807; went out West.

308. c. Bezaleel, born South Hadley, June 4, 1809; went out West.

309. d. William Dwight, born South Hadley, March 25, 1812; went out West.

310. 2. Laura, born South Hadley, Jan. 30, 1784.

311. 3. Tristram, born South Hadley, Dec. 26, 1787; died April 11, 1812.

312. 4. Helez, born South Hadley, March 28, 1791; married Dolly Brainard. Was a physician.

313. 5. Melzar, born South Hadley, April 1, 1793.

314. 6. Polly, born South Hadley, March 10, 1796; died South Hadley, Feb. 17, 1814.

315. 7. Philoftus, born South Hadley, Sept. 21, 1798.

316. 8. Milton, born South Hadley, March 11, 1801.

317. 9. Philansa, born South Hadley, July 27, 1803.

318. 10. Ariel, born South Hadley, Sept. 6, 1807.

319. Tryphosa, born Springfield, Mass., Feb. 17, 1765; died South Hadley, May 22, 1784.

320. Ariel, born Springfield, Mass., Jan. 27, 1767; died South Hadley, May 25, 1776.

321. Tirzah, born South Hadley, Feb. 24, 1769, married Nehemiah Day. She died Aug. 5, 1826.

322. Helez, born South Hadley, May 15, 1772; died South Hadley, Feb. 3, 1775.

323. Phineas Porter, born South Hadley, Aug. 8, 1774; died South Hadley, May 28, 1779.

324. Ariel, born South Hadley, Nov. 16, 1776; married Lucretia ——, and had one daughter:

325. a. Zeruiah, born May 26, 1806. He died Sept. 28, 1807.

326. Rachel, born South Hadley, March 8, 1779; married Zenas Church.

V. 136. Luther Alvord,

Born South Hadley, March 4, 1753; resided in South Hadley. Son of John and Abigail (White) Alvord, who was the son of John and Dorcas (Lyman) Alvord, who was the son of Thomas and Joanna (Taylor) Alvord, who was the son of Alexander and Mary (Vore) Alvord.

Administration of Luther Alvord's estate of South Hadley granted to Nathaniel Ingram, Nov. 27, 1784. His estate was insolvent. Elizabeth Alvord was appointed guardian to Zerusha Alvord, aged four years, and Elizabeth Alvord, aged two years.

He married

Elizabeth Ingram.

Children:

327. Zerusha Alvord, born South Hadley, about 1780.
328. Elizabeth Alvord, born South Hadley, about 1782.

V. 143. Caleb Alvord,

Born Oct. 5, 1751; died Greenfield, Mass., Dec. 22, 1819, aged 68 years 2 months. Son of Elijah and Hannah (Huntington?) Alvord, who was the son of John and Dorcas (Lyman) Alvord, who was the son of Thomas and Joanna (Taylor) Alvord, who was the son of Alexander and Mary (Vore) Alvord.

He settled in Greenfield, Mass., and moved to Wilmington, Vt., where he resided a few years, and then returned to Greenfield, Mass., where he died.

He married, Dec. 26, 1776,

Mary Murdock,

Born Jan. 15, 1751; died March 26, 1836, aged over 84. She was the daughter of Samuel Murdock of Wilmington, Vt.

Children:

329. †Elijah, born Wilmington, Vt., Nov. 18, 1777; died Greenfield, Mass., Sept. 8, 1840; married, Nov. 12, 1805, Sabra Wells; resided in Greenfield, Mass.
330. †Caleb, born Wilmington, Vt., May 3, 1779; moved out West.
331. †Pliny, born Greenfield, Mass., March 13, 1781; died Dec. 5, 1859; married Sept. 1, 1808, Laurana Bardwell.
332. Melinda, twin, born Greenfield, Mass., June 12, 1783; died Greenfield, July 4, 1784.
333. Lucinda, twin, born Greenfield, Mass., June 12, 1783. Single. Living in Boston.

334. Melinda, born Greenfield, Mass., May 13, 1785; died Cambridge, Dec. 15, 1846. She died after a long and painful illness. The remains were deposited in the receiving tomb at Mount Auburn, Sunday, Dec. 20, and in May following buried in the family lot, (No. 149). She was married July 28, 1805, to Joseph T. Buckingham. He was the son of Nehemiah and Mary Tinkham, and was born at Windham, Conn., Dec. 21, 1779. His name was changed by the General Court of Massachusetts, May, 1804, from Joseph Buckingham Tinker to Joseph T. Buckingham. Children:

335. 1. Joseph Huntington; married Eliza Willet.

336. 2. Melinda Alvord; married Samuel Edwin Robbins.

337. 3. Edwin; died a young man.

338. 4. Edgar, (a minister); married Sally Merritt Hart, and resides in Troy, N. Y.

339. 5. Caleb Alexander; died single.

340. 6. Charles Alfred; died in infancy.

341. 7. Charles Edward, (a physician); married Mary Elizabeth Marshall.

342. 8. Francis William; married Abby Sheldon Beecher.

343. 9. Ellen Maria; resides in Boston.

344. 10. Lucy Ann; resides in Boston.

345. 11. Lucius Henry; married Angelina Bradley Hyde.

346. 12. Frederick Alexander; single; in the Second Minnesota Volunteers.

347. †Alpheus, born Greenfield, Jan. 17, 1787; married, Sept. 13, 1821, Clara ——.

348. †Alfred, born Greenfield, Mass., Feb. 15, 1789; died Oct. 31, 1853; married July 12, 1824, Mary Allen of Wendell, Mass.

349. Mary, born Greenfield, Mass., April 17, 1791; died April 2, 1836;(?) married Jonathan White. Was a farmer by occupation. Children:

350. 1. Mary, married Dea. Dutton, Northfield, Mass.

351. 2. Hiram, (a physician); in the army.

352. 3. Jonathan, (a physician); in the army.
353. 4. Martha; married.
354. 5. Harriet; married. And perhaps others.
355. Fanny, born Bernardston, Mass., Sept. 12, 1793; married, April 3, 1817, Josiah White, born Heath Mass., March 2, 1791. She lives in Nashua, N. H., and has children:
357. 1. Fanny Alvord, born Bath, N. H., Feb. 5, 1818.
358. 2. Josiah Carleton, born Bath, N. H., April 8, 1820; died Brattleboro', Vt., July 4, 1828.
359. 3. Edwin Buckingham, born Bath, N. H., July 18, 1822; married, 1, Serena Bragg of Swanzey, Mass.; married, 2, Laurana Clement of Hudson.

Children of Edwin B. and Serena White:

360. a. Charles Henry; died aged about three years.
361. b. Willie E.; died in infancy.
362. c. Sereno Edwin.

Children of Edwin B. and Laurana White:

363. d. Charlie. f. Arthur. g. Infant daughter.

364. 4. Charles King, born Brattleboro', Vt., Oct. 9, 1825; married Sarah Elizabeth Barnard of Boston. He died in California; she died in Boston, and left no children.
365. 5. Josiah Clinton, born Brattleboro', Vt., July 9, 1828; married in Swanzey, Mass., Edna ——. He is in the army.
366. 6. Jane Elizabeth, born Brattleboro', Vt., July 31, 1831; married Isaac H. Marshall, and resides in Nashua, N. H. He is a merchant. They have children:

a. Kate Atherton. b. Frank. c. A daughter.

370. 7. Caleb Benjamin, born Brattleboro', Vt., Jan. 11, 1835.

V. 144. Hannah Alvord,

Born 1754; died Greenfield, Mass., Sept. 22, 1811, aged 57. Daughter of Elijah and Hannah (Huntington?) Alvord, who was the son of John and Dorcas (Lyman) Alvord, who was the son of Thomas and Joanna (Taylor) Alvord, who was the son of Alexander and Mary (Vore) Alvord.

She resided in Greenfield, Mass., and married

Abner Smead,

Born ——; died Greenfield, Mass., Feb. 2, 1797.

Children:

371. Elijah, born Greenfield, Oct. 8, 1774; died Greenfield, Sept. 1, 1777.
372. Lucinda, born Greenfield, Sept. 24, 1776; married Daniel Clay of New York.
373. Hannah, born Greenfield, Mass., Oct. 14, 1778; married Ozias Newton, son of Rev. (Roger?) Newton of Greenfield, Mass.
374. Elijah, born Greenfield, Mass., Aug. 24, 1780; died Milledgeville, Ga.; he married a southern lady.
375. Infant son, born Greenfield, Mass., Dec. 14, 1782; died Greenfield, Dec. 14, 1782.
376. Caroline, born Greenfield, Mass., Nov. 14, 1783; married Richard B. Callender.
377. Cyrus, born Greenfield, Mass., Dec. 23, 1785. Single.
378. Roxana, born Greenfield, Mass., Jan. 26, 1788; died Greenfield, July 25, 1788.
379. Abner, born Greenfield, July 25, 1789.
380. Roxana, born Greenfield, Mass., Sept. 18, 1791; died Boston, May, 1862; married Joel Thayer.
381. Infant son, born Greenfield, July 30, 1794; died Greenfield, July 30, 1794.

V. 145. Justin Alvord,

Born Springfield, Nov. 30, 1763; died of old age, Oct. 1852, aged 89. Son of Lieut. Job and Rebecca (Smith) Alvord, who was the son of John and Dorcas (Lyman) Alvord, who was the son of Thomas and Joanna (Taylor) Alvord, who was the son of Alexander and Mary (Vore) Alvord. He resided in South Hadley, where he was buried, and married, 1, 1788,

Jerusha Wait,

Born South Hadley, Feb. 6, 1767; died Feb. 3, 1803. She was the daughter of Martin and Jerusha Wait.

He married, 2,

Lois Chapin,

Born 1777; died South Hadley, May 20 or 29, 1860, aged 83. Daughter of Reuben and Mary (Mirrick) Chapin, who was the son of Samuel and Anna (Horton) Chapin, who was the son of Samuel and Hannah (Sheldon) Chapin, who was the son of Japhet and Abihenah (Cooley) Chapin, who was the son of Dea. Samuel and Cisily (——) Chapin, who settled in Springfield, Mass., in 1642.

Children of Justin and Jerusha Alvord:

382. Lowell, born South Hadley, July 2, 1795; died South Hadley, Nov. 10, 1806.
383. Clarissa, born South Hadley, Nov. 15, 1797; married Porter Taylor.
384. Jerusha, born South Hadley, March 6, 1801; married Pliny Dale of Chickopee Falls.

Children of Justin and Lois Alvord:

392. Justin, born South Hadley, June 5, 1805. Went West.
393. Lois, born South Hadley, Sept. 21, 1806; married Almanzer Clark of Great Barrington.
394. Abigail, born South Hadley, Feb. 14, 1808. Went off with the Mormons.
395. Lowell, born S. Hadley, Nov. 16, 1809; died a young man.
396. Lucina, born South Hadley, June 6, 1811; died of consumption, April 10, 1843.
397. Cornelia, born South Hadley, Nov. 19, 1812. Went off with the Mormons.
398. Job, born South Hadley, July 11, 1814; died South Hadley, Oct. 30, 1814.
399. Edwin, born South Hadley, Sept. 20, 1815.
400. Mary, born South Hadley, July 1, 1817.
401. Hiram, born South Hadley. Went out West.
402. Infant daughter, born Oct. 30, 1820; died Nov. 30, 1820.

It is said that there were 19 children belonging to the above family. Perhaps there were some born before any that I have here.

V. 145. Samuel Alvord,

Born South Hadley, Nov. 27, 1751; died South Hadley, July 9, 1814, aged 63. Son of Gad and Lydia (Smith) Alvord, who was the son of John and Dorcas (Lyman) Alvord, who was the son of Thomas and Joanna (Taylor) Alvord, who was the son of Alexander and Mary (Vore) Alvord. He resided in South Hadley, and married

Miriam White,

Born South Hadley, Aug. 2, 1758; died South Hadley, Feb. 25, 1844, aged 86. Daughter of Joseph and Editha (Moody) White, of South Hadley, who was the son of Dea. Joseph and Abigail (Craft) White of South Hadley, who was the son of Dea. Nathaniel and Elizabeth (Savage) White, born in Middletown, Upper Houses, Conn., now Cromwell, July 7, 1652, and settled in Hadley, upon the original home-lot of his grandfather, Elder John White, who was the son of Capt. Nathaniel and Elizabeth (——) White, born in England about 1629, and was one of the original proprietors and first settlers of Middletown, Conn., where he held various offices of trust, who was the son of Elder John White, who sailed from London, England, and arrived at Boston, Mass., Sept. 16, 1632. Elder John White was one of the first settlers of Cambridge, Mass., of Hartford, Conn., and of Hadley, Mass. Elder White's home-lot, with his dwelling-house in Cambridge, was on the street then called Cow-Yard Row. It is supposed that "Gore Hall," the beautiful library building of Harvard University, now graces this cow-yard.

Children:

403. Calvin, born South Hadley, Aug. 3, 1779; died Nov. 18, 1856, aged 78. A widower. He resided in South Hadley, and married Mary Brewster, Oct. 8, 1801, and had children:

404. 1. Broughton, born South Hadley, Jan. 14, 1802.

405. 2. Ruby, born South Hadley, Jan. 22, 1805; married Ellis Coney.

406. 3. Calvin, born South Hadley, March 14, 1810; died Feb. 11, 1835.

407. 4. Mary Ann, born South Hadley, Jan. 4, 1814; died single.

408. 5. Jesse Brewster, born South Hadley, Aug. 15, 1816; died Nov. 22, 1863, aged 47.

409. Orange, born South Hadley, Jan. 25, 1781; died Wilmington, Vt., March 15, 1862. He resided in South Hadley and in Wilmington, Vt. He married Sophia Taylor, and had children:

410. 1. Clarissa, born South Hadley, Jan. 5, 1803; died South Hadley, Oct. 14, 1803, aged 9 months.

411. 2. Sophia, born South Hadley, Dec. 24, 1805; died Wilmington, Vt., May 8, 1859, aged 53.

412. 3. Clarissa, born South Hadley, Sept. 6, 1808; died Wilmington, Vt., Jan. 16, 1837, aged 28.

413. 4. Stillman, born South Hadley, Dec. 10, 1811; was married by Theophilus Packard, at Shelburne, Mass., May 5, 1846, to Miss Lydia L. Alvord, born Oct. 26, 1823, daughter of Epephas and Hannah (Lufken) Alvord, who was the son of Zerah and Hannah (Nims) Alvord, who was the son of Gad and Lydia (Smith) Alvord, who was the son of John and Dorcas (Lyman) Alvord, who was the son of Thomas and Joanna (Taylor) Alvord, who was the son of Alexander and Mary (Vore) Alvord. They had:

414. a. Francis Albert, born March 7, 1852.

5. Fidelia, born Wilmington, Vt., Nov. 16, 1817; married Joseph Dickinson of Amherst, Mass., June, 1841.

415. Julius, born South Hadley, June 6, 1783; died Oct. 24, 1785, South Hadley.

416. Miriam, born South Hadley, May 26, 1785; married, March 13, 1806, Levi White, born South Hadley, Mass., Feb. 14, 1779; died East Hampton, Mass., Aug. 26, 1852, aged 73. He was the son of Nathaniel and

Huldah (Clark) White of East Hampton, (a Revolutionary soldier, was in the battle of Bunker Hill, and was present at Burgoyne's surrender,) who was the son of Nathaniel and Martha (Bascom) White of South Hadley, who was the son of Nathaniel and Esther (Strong) White, who was the son of Dea. Nathaniel and Elizabeth (Savage) White. [See Miriam White, wife of Samuel Alvord, V. 145.

Mr. Levi White was a painter by trade, and resided in East Hampton. Children:

417. 1. Julius, born July 16, 1808; resides in Southampton, Mass., and is a house-painter by trade; married, 1, Nov. 27, 1835, Elizabeth Sheldon; married, 2, Widow Almira Barron.

418. 2. Cecil, born June 8, 1810; died Sept. 18, 1810.

419. 3. Edson, born Nov. 27, 1811. Is a farmer and painter; married, Feb. 1, 1855, Frances (Parsons) White, widow of his brother Lysander.

420. 4. Lucena, born Nov. 17, 1814; married, May 18, 1843, Julius Pomeroy of East Hampton, and died Dec. 4, 1858, aged 44, and had children:

421. a. Herbert White, born Aug. 27, 1844.

422. b. Ella Lucena, born Dec. 15, 1849.

423. c. Miriam White, born Oct. 6, 1852.

424. 5. Lysander, born April 27, 1818; died May 8, 1852; he married, Nov. 5, 1839, Frances Parsons, born Dec. 21, 1817, daughter of Joel Parsons, and had no children. He was a painter by trade, and resided in East Hampton.

425. 6. Amanda, born June 1, 1821; married Augustine Munson, and has one daughter:

426. a. Lyander Munson, born Aug. 22, 1852.

427. Samuel, born South Hadley, Sept. 11, 1787; married, 1, South Hadley, Dec. 23, 1810, Sophia Day; married, 2, Delcena Lawton, and had children:

428. 1. Samuel, born ——; married ——; died without children.

429. 2. Sophia, born 1822; married Daniel Rice; resides Wilmington, Vt.

430. Cyrus, born South Hadley, Sept. 25, 1789; died Dec. 7, 1860, aged 71 years, 2 months; married, Nov. 27, 1816, Asenath Smith, and had children:

431. 1. Francis, born South Hadley, Mass., April 3, 1818. He transacts business for the Syracuse Salt Co.; now (March, 1864) at Blossburg, Pa., coal mines, and during the winter has two hundred men to look after, and in the summer twice that number. He married, June 10, 1847, Caroline Gleason of Liverpool, Onondaga Co., N. Y., where his family now resides, and has children:

432. arion F., born June 24, 1850.

433. b. Charles G., born Nov. 21, 1852.

434. 2. Hervey, born South Hadley, May 24, 1820; married, June 13, 1852, Eugenia Clementine Smith, and had children:

435. a. Ida Clementine, born March 14, 1855; died Sept. 16, 1855.

436. b. Luella Fidelia, born Oct. 9, 1856; died Sept. 3, 1863.

437. c. Francis Hervey, born Aug. 27, 1858.

438. d. Ellis Arthur, born Jan. 24, 1861; died South Hadley, of scarlet fever, June 13, 1864, aged 3 years, 4 months, and 20 days.

439. 3. Asenath, born South Hadley, Sept. 5, 1823. From Miss Asenath Alvord of South Hadley, I have received much valuable information with regard to the Alvord Genealogy. She resides with her mother, upon one of the old Alvord farms of South Hadley. Her uncle Luther resides with them.

440. 4. Miriam, born South Hadley, July 23, 1826; died March 26, 1836.

441. 5. Fidelia Smith, born South Hadley, Feb. 18, 1834; died April 11, 1856.

442. Luther, born South Hadley, Dec. 25, 1791; resides on the old place of John Alvord (who married Dorcas Lyman).
443. Editha, born South Hadley, Feb. 3, 1794; died Dec. 29, 1819, aged 26; married Eldad Smith.
444. Sophia, born South Hadley, Nov. 24, 1796; died South Hadley, Oct. 12, 1803.
445. Fidelia, born South Hadley, Dec. 10, 1799; died South Hadley, Jan. 30, 1833, aged 34; married Eldad Smith.

V. 150. Sybil Alvord,

Born South Hadley, March 23, 1757; died North Adams, Mass., Nov. 23, 1833. She was the daughter of Gad and Lydia (Smith) Alvord, who was the son of John and Dorcas (Lyman) Alvord, who was the son of Thomas and Joanna (Taylor) Alvord, who was the son of Alexander and Mary (Vore) Alvord.

She married

Shubael Nash,

Born South Hadley, Aug. 27, 1758; died Williamstown, Mass., Dec. 24, 1824. Son of Joseph and Abigail (Cooper) Nash, who was the son of Daniel and Abigail (——) Nash, who was the son of Lieut. John and Elizabeth (Kellogg) Nash, who was the son of Lieut. Timothy and Rebecca (Stone) Nash, who was the son of Thomas Nash, the emigrant. He settled in North Adams, Mass.

Children:

446. Azor, born Nov. 24, 1780; married, Jan. 25, 1804, Susannah Wright, and settled in North Adams, and had a large family.
447. Lydia, born April 4, 1782; married, March 17, 1813, Harris Arnold of North Adams, and had six children. She died July 14, 1846.
448. Abigail, born March 6, 1784; married, 1806, Miles Beach of New Ashford, Mass. She died Williamstown, Mass., Sept. 10, 1809.
449. Lewis, born May 23, 1786; married, Oct. 29, 1804, Jemima Bailey of Stephentown, N. Y., and had a large

family. He died in Williamstown, Mass., April 10, 1826.

450. Lucina, born Aug. 31, 1788, married, 1, Dec. 19, 1810, Fenner Briggs of North Adams; married, 2, 1836, Robert De Maranville. They reside in Cheshire, Mass.

451. Elihu, born Feb. 12, 1792; married, Dec. 8, 1831, Ermina D. Foster, and settled in Lima, Livingston Co., N. Y.

452. Maria, born April 14, 1794; married, Nov. 1812, Henry Beach, who settled in Otto, Cattaraugus Co., N. Y.

453. Melinda, born July 25, 1795; married, June 28, 1817, Atwater Beach, and settled in New Ashford, Mass.

454. Shubael Alvord, born Sept. 3, 1796; married Mary Ann Ford of Williamstown, Mass., and settled in North Adams, Mass.

455. Chauncey, born July 17, 1798; married, 1, 1824, Anna Youngs. Mrs. Nash lived a few years, and he married, 2, Dorothy Patterson. She died, and he married, 3, Sarah M. Board. He resides in Perry, Wyoming Co., N. Y.

456. Sybil, born May 13, 1802; died, unmarried, in Pittsfield, Mass., Aug. 12, 1852.

V. 151. Gad Alvord,

Born South Hadley, Mass., June ye 27, 1759. Son of Gad and Lydia (Smith) Alvord, who was the son of John and Dorcas (Lyman) Alvord, who was the son of Thomas and Joanna (Taylor) Alvord, who was the son of Alexander and Mary (Vore) Alvord. He resided in Granby, Mass., and married

Phebe White.

She was the daughter of Jonathan and Lydia (Rugg) White, who was the son of Nathaniel and Esther (Strong) White.

Children:

457. Theodocia, married Hezekiah Eastman.

458. Sewall.

459. Gaius, married Lydia Robinson.

460. Mary, married —— Gaiside.
461. Alvin.
462. Clarissa, married Azel Hubbard.
463. Electa.
464. Alanson, was a clergyman; died in 1862 or 1863.
465. Amanda, married Oliver Hooker.

V. 152. Asher Alvord,

Born South Hadley, June 9 or 4, 1761; died Wilmington, Vt., Nov. 12, 1837. Son of Gad and Lydia (Smith) Alvord, who was the son of John and Dorcas (Lyman) Alvord, who was the son of Thomas and Joanna (Taylor) Alvord, who was the son of Alexander and Mary (Vore) Alvord. He resided in Wilmington, Vt., and married, Jan. 19, 1786,

Martha Ayres,

Born Sept. 22, 1763; died March 27, 1846.

Children:

466. Lydia, born Aug. 11, 1787; died March 14, 1837.
467. Clarissa, born Jan. 14, 1793.
468. Horace, born Feb. 10, 1795; married, Sept. 15, 1819, Harriet Waldo Hamilton, born June 26, 1797; and had children:
469. 1. Calvin Thales, born Jan. 29, 1821; married, March 22, 1848, Catherine E. Crosby, born March 31, 1828, and had children:
470. a. Martha E. Alvord, born Feb. 5, 1849.
471. b. Mary F. Alvord, born Feb. 4, 1851; died Sept. 1, 1852.
472. c. Harriet M. Alvord, born Aug 20, 1855.
473. d. Mitta S. Alvord, born Sept. 22, 1858.
474. e. —— Alvord, a son, born Feb. 23, 1864; weighed 12½ lbs. at birth.
475. 2. Hervy Dwight, born Oct. 30, 1822.
476. 3. Nancy Maria, born April 16, 1827; died Oct. 4, 1828.

477. 4. Martha Maria, born Nov. 19, 1829; died Sept. 20, 1847.

478. 5. Edward Payson, born May 24, 1834; died Nov. 6, 1847.

479. 6. George Washington, born June 24, 1837; died March 2, 1839.

V. 153. Zerah Alvord,

Born South Hadley, Nov. ye 10, 1765; died Shelburne, Mass., June 17, 1845. Son of Gad and Lydia (Smith) Alvord, who was the son of John and Dorcas (Lyman) Alvord, who was the son of Thomas and Joanna (Taylor) Alvord, who was the son of Alexander and Mary (Vore) Alvord. He resided in Shelburne, Mass., and married, 1, Greenfield, Mass., Nov. 11, 1790,

Hannah Nims.

He married, 2d,

Sarah Foster.

Children by his first wife:

480. Adolphus, born Oct. 28, 1791; died Sept. 27, 1852; married Naomi Barnard, and had children:

481. 1. Sophia, born March 18, 1822.

482. 2. Eliza N., born April 29, 1824; married, Sept. 2, 1862, Martin L. Hubbard, who was born Aug. 15, 1816.

483. 3. Elisha B., born April 18, 1826; married, Oct. 5, 1859, Sarah E. Hawkes, who was born Nov. 7, 1830.

484. 4. Prudence H., born Aug. 3, 1831; married J. D. Newton of Greenfield, and had children:

485. a. Arthur E. Newton, born Sept. 18, 1854; died July 5, 1856.

486. b. Frank A. Newton, born Jan. 20, 1857.

487. c. Charles S. Newton, born Jan. 3, 1863.

488. Harriet, born Nov. 18, 1793.

489. Epephas, born June 10, 1796; died Aug. 15, 1862; married Hannah Lufkin, born June 12, 1798, and had children:

490. 1. Lucius Gad, born Shelburne, Mass., June 2, 1822; married, Sept. 5, 1849, Ellen Sherwin, and had children:

491. a. William M. Alvord, born April 15, 1851; died Feb. 9, 1853.

492. b. William S. Alvord, born Aug. 1853; died Jan. 28, 1854.

493. c. Arthur H. Alvord, born July 29, 1857.

494. 2. Lydia L., born Shelburne, Mass., Oct. 26, 1823; married, May 5, 1846, Stillman Alvord, (see No. 413,) and had—

495. a. Francis Albert Alvord, born March 7, 1852.

496. 3. Sarah F., born Shelburne, Mass., May 6, 1825; died May 24, 1842.

497. 4. Hannah L., born Wilmington, Vt., Feb. 28, 1828; married, Nov. 22, 1849, Levi Dole of Shelburne, and had children:

498. a. Ellen Amelia Dole, born Sept. 16, 1850.

499. b. Myron Abbot Dole, born Aug. 1, 1853.

500. c. Mary A. Dole, born Nov. 19, 1857.

501. 5. L. Amelia, born Wilmington, Vt., June 30, 1830; died Feb. 4, 1855; married, Nov. 24, 1851, Joseph Waite of East Hampton.

502. 6. Lucia A., born Wilmington, Vt., May 2, 1832; died Sept. 3, 1859; married, March 26, 1851, D. W. Jones.

503. 7. Alvan, born Shelburne, Mass., Dec. 2, 1833.

504. 8. Mary A., born Shelburne, Mass., March 13, 1837; married, April 24, 1860, John A. Franklin; now of the 10th Mass. Vols. (April 24, 1863).

505. Abigail, born March 5, 1799; married William Dole, who was born March 5, 1799, and had children:

506. 1. Hannah N., born Sept. 3, 1826; married, 1, Levi Forristall, who died Oct. 24, 1854; married, 2, A. P. Cooley. Children:

507. a. L. Abbie Forristall, born Nov. 14, 1849.

508. b. Acelia I. Forristall, born Aug. 25, 1852.

509. 2. Clarissa A., born Oct. 27, 1828; married, 1, D. W. Nims, born May 6, 1824, died April 9, 1851; married, 2d, Rufus L. Thayer, born July 3, 1839.

510. 3. Harriet A., born March 4, 1831; died March 6, 1853; married G. W. Hildreth, who was born Oct. 15, 1830.

511. 4. L. W., born June 30, 1833.

512. 5. Lydia S., born Feb. 7, 1836; married July 8, 1858, John W. Gurney, born Sept. 12, 1835, and had children:

513. a. Hattie R. Gurney, born June 26, 1859.

514. b. Carrie H. Gurney, born June 23, 1860.

515. Laura, born March 28, 1801.

516. Cephas, born Nov. 30, 1803; married Rachel B. Childs of Shelburne, and had children:

517. 1. Mercy C., born May 9, 1828; married, April 3, 1849; died Aug. 3, 1850.

518. 2. Zerah, born March 26, 1830.

519. 3. Sabra W., born Oct. 30, 1832.

520. 4. Henry B., born April 10, 1837.

521. 5. Sarah F., born July 10, 1844.

The above record is from Elisha B. Alvord of Shelburne, Mass.

V. 154. Seth Alvord,

Born South Hadley, June 29, 1763; died Wilmington, Vt., May 17, 1835. Son of Gad and Lydia (Smith) Alvord, who was the son of John and Dorcas (Lyman) Alvord, who was the son of Thomas and Joanna (Taylor) Alvord, who was the son of Alexander and Mary (Vore) Alvord. He resided in South Hadley, Dummerston, Vt., Shelburne, and Wilmington, Vt. He married

Ruth Taylor,

Born 1760; died May 10, 1838.

Children:

522. Ruth, born South Hadley, Aug. 27, 1786.
523. Julius, born South Hadley, Aug. 27, 1786; married, May 16, 1815, Sally Doty, and had children:
524. 1. Sarah Ann, born Dec. 22, 1817; married, May 28, 1843, John Robert Stearns, and had children:
525. a. Henry Clay Stearns, born June 5, 1845.
526. b. Josiah Stamford Stearns, born Jan. 16, 1849; died May 7, 1862.
527. c. Mary Ann Stearns, born Dec. 22, 1852.
528. d. John Robert Stearns, died March 7, 1860.

529. 2. Mary Loane, born Sept. 27, 1818; married, March 4, 1838, Erastus Cooley Hall, and had children:
530. a. Mary Augusta Hall, born Feb. 28, 1839; married, Oct. 29, 1862, William M. Arnold.
531. b. George Judson Hall, born Jan. 19, 1841.
532. c. Sarah Jane Hall, born Sept. 19, 1842; married Sylvester Hovey, July 20, 1862.
533. d. Julius Wesley Hall, born Aug. 21, 1845; died Sept. 11, 1849.
534. e. Sylvia Sears Hall, born June 16, 1848.
535. f. Clarissa Julia Hall, born Jan. 5, 1853.
536. g. Edith Viola Hall, born July 23, 1855.
537. h. Ernest Alvord Hall, born July 1, 1858.

538. 3. Julia Mondane, born March 11, 1820; married, Nov. 3, 1839, William Martin Hatch, and had children:
539. a. Margaret Lorinda Hatch.
540. b. Mary Hatch.
541. c. Sallie Hatch.
542. d. Martin Hatch.

543. 4. Alvin Wesley, born Oct. 25, 1822; married, Sept. 17, 1848, Electa Rowena Todd, and had children:

544. a. Julius Bela Alvord, born Nov. 10, 1849.
545. b. Augusta Albina Alvord, born Aug. 30, 1851.
546. c. Jessie Fremont Alvord, born May 15, 1856.

547. 5. John Quincy Adams, born June 9, 1828; died Sept. 3, 1832.

548. Otis, born Dummerston, Vt., Sept. 1, 1789; died Carol, N. Y., Aug. 7, 1854; married Jerusha (?) Doty, who died Oct. 4, 1856, and had children:
550. 1. Franklin Doty, born Oct. 12, 1817; died July, 1855; married, Nov. 3, 1839, Rebecca Louisa Hatch, and had
551. a. Harriet Emeline, born Oct. 12, 1843; died Jan. 13, 1857.

552. 2. Francis Milton, born Oct. 12, 1819; is a Methodist minister; he married, Sept. 18, 1844, Rebecca Pardee, and had children:
553. a. Ernest Henry Alvord, born June 15, 1847.
554. b. Merit Alvord, born Oct. 14, 1853; died Oct. 14, 1853.
555. c. Otis T. Alvord, born March 28, 1860.
556. d. Francis Martin, born Oct. 29, 1862.

557. 3. Frederick, born May 22, 1822; died May 5, 1823.
558. 4. Lorinda, born Oct. 22, 1824; died Oct. 5, 1825.
559. 5. Frederic Kilby, born Nov. 16, 1826; married Mary Ann Fenton, and had children:
560. a. Charles Alvord, born 1852, and died 1852.
561. b. Della Alvord, born June 2, 1860.

562. 6. Christiana, born July 25, 1830; married, 1, Lyman Price, who died in 1857. She married, 2, March 1, 1863, David Mason. She had two children by Mr. Price, but they died in infancy.

565. 7. Henry, born Dec. 22, 1834; died Aug. 25, 1836.
566. Spencer, born Shelburne, Oct. 3, 1791; died Wilmington, Vt., Sept. 23, 1855; married Clarissa Alvord, (?) born Wilmington, Vt., Feb. 4, 1792, and had children:

567. 1. Orpheus S., born Wilmington, Vt., March 11, 1816; married, 1, Oct. 15, 1839, Sophia H. Hastings, born Wilmington, Feb. 6, 1819; died Wilmington, Sept. 6, 1854; married, 2, Oct. 2, 1855, Clarissa A. Hastings, born Wilmington, March 23, 1821; sisters. Child by first wife:

568. a. Orsamus H. Alvord, born Wilmington, Vt., Nov. 27, 1843.

569. 2. Orsamus A., born Wilmington, April 1, 1819; married, April 10, 1844, Sarah I. Bissell.

570. 3. Clarissa F., born Wilmington, April 24, 1822.

571. 4. Rhoda M., born Wilmington, May 22, 1825.

572. 5. Barbara A., born Wilmington, Sept. 12, 1839.

573. Rhoda, born Shelburne, Oct. 3, 1791; died Wilmington, Vt., April 1, 1825.

574. Thankful, born Wilmington, Vt., May 16, 1796; died Wilmington, Vt., Sept. 26, 1696.

575. Barbara, born Wilmington, Vt., Dec. 27, 1797.

576. Thankful, born Wilmington, Vt., Oct. 19, 1801; died Eden, Illinois.

577. Seth, born Wilmington, Vt., June 10, 1804; died Adams, Mass., 1849.

578. Chester P., born Wilmington, Vt., Oct. 1, 1811; died Eden, Illinois, Jan. 25, 1856.

V. 167. John Alvord,

Born July 13, 1760; died Jan. 29, 1832, aged 72. Son of Nathan and Lydia (White) Alvord, who was the son of John and Dorcas (Lyman) Alvord, who was the son of Thomas and Joanna (Taylor) Alvord, who was the son of Alexander and Mary (Vore) Alvord.

He married, 1, Greenfield, Mass., Dec. 14, 1786,

Abigail Smead.

She died April 26, 1787, and he married, 2, Aug. 9, 1789,

Rhoda Mather

Of Shelburne, Mass. She died July 12, 1857, aged 90. Children:

579. Abigail, born Sept. 18, 1790; died Oct. 6, 1790.

580. William Mather, born Aug. 18, 1791; married, June 29, 1815, Talasha Bigelow of Brookfield, Vt. He resided in Brookfield, and had children:

581. 1. William Mather, born Aug. 13, 1818; married, May 1, 1849, Ann Edeston Adams of Randolph, Vt., and had children:

582. a. Edgar Duane Alvord, born March 11, 1850.

583. b. Emma Maria Alvord, born May 21, 1853.

584. c. Ann May Alvord, born Nov. 5, 1856.

585. d. John Willie Alvord, born June 27, 1859.

586. 2. John Milton Alvord, born Feb. 15, 1820; married Betsey Russell of Andover, N. H., Nov. 22, 1848, and resides in St. Johnsbury, Vt., and had children:

587. a. Addie Selma Alvord, born Aug. 7, 1850.

588. b. Fanny Alvord, born June 7, 1854; died Nov. 21, 1855.

589. c. Lucia Alvord, born Feb. 29, 1857.

590. d. George Russell, born Feb. 14, 1862.

591. 3. Orissel, born June 29, 1824; died July 9, 1824.

592. 4. Abigail Smead, born Nov. 8, 1829; died March 17, 1832.

593. 5. Abbie Annette, born April 4, 1833.

594. Cotton White, born April 12, 1797; resides Cabot, Vt.; married, 1, April 12, 1819, Deborah Bigelow of Brookfield, Vt., who died April 25, 1849. He married, 2, Clara F. Page of Plainfield, Vt., who died Dec. 30, 1861. Children:

595. 1. Daniel Bigelow, born May 25, 1820; died Hardwick, N. Y., 1842.

596. 2. Orissel Worthington, born March 4, 1826; resides at Northfield, Vt.; married Nov. 5, 1856, Augusta Maria Shaw of Northfield, Vt., who died Aug. 27, 1862.

V. 180. Elijah Alvord,

Born Sept. 3, 1770; died Greenfield, Mass. Son of Nathan and Lydia (White) Alvord, who was the son of John and Dorcas (Lyman) Alvord, who was the son of Thomas and Joanna (Taylor) Alvord, who was the son of Alexander and Mary (Vore) Alvord. He resided in Greenfield, Mass.

Administration of the estate of Elijah Alvord of Greenfield was granted to his widow, Lucretia Alvord.

He married, 1, Jan. 16, 1791,

Anna Bascom,

Who died Aug. 23, 1791, in her 22d year. He married, 2,

Lucretia Clarke.

She was of Colchester, Conn. They had children:

597. Anna, born Greenfield, Mass.(?), Dec. 7, 1793; married Bennet E. Phelps.

598. Nathaniel, born Greenfield, Mass., Jan. 27, 1795; died March 11, 1795.

599. Sarah, born Greenfield, Mass., Jan. 27, 1796; married Jesse Andrews.

600. George, born Greenfield, Mass., Sept. 31, 1798; died May 31, 1799.

601. George, born Greenfield, Mass., March 7, 1800.

602. Emily, born Greenfield, Mass., Feb. 4, 1802; married Job F. Howland of Harlem, N. Y.

603. Nathaniel Clarke, born Greenfield, Mass., Jan. 1, 1804; married, and resides at Trenton, Mich.

604. Elijah White, born Greenfield, Mass., Oct. 9, 1805.

605. Mary Ann, born Dec. 11, 1807; married Henry Raymond of Saginaw, Mich.

606. Henry Jones, born Montague, Mass., June 8, 1811. He is a physician, and resides at Washington, D. C.

Received assistance from W. M. Alvord.

V. 208. Pathenia Alvord,

Born Charlestown, N. H., July 4, 1767; died Enosburg, Vt., Sept. 24, 1852. Daughter of Stephen and Abigail (Davis) Alvord, who was the son of Joseph and Clemence (Wright) Alvord, who was the son of Ebenezer and Ruth (Baker) Alvord, who was the son of Alexander and Mary (Vore) Alvord.

Upon the church records, when she was baptized, her name was written Triphena. She was a sister of Roxana Alvord, who married Benjamin Burke. She married, 1,

Robert Dennison Taylor,

Born Mansfield, Conn., 1764; died Woodstock, Vt., Jan. 26, 1798. She married, for her second husband,

Joseph Waller.

Children by her first husband, Robert D. Taylor:

607. Abigail, born March 7, 1786; resides in Thetford, Vt. She married, June 21, 1807, Lake Robinson, born Jan. 20, 1782; died Sept. 25, 1854, and had children:

608. 1. Nancy, born March 6, 1808; died Chelmsford, Jan. 18, 1846; married Harvey Munger, Dec. 1828.

609. 2. Caroline, born Sept. 17, 1811; married, March 17, 1837, Royal Farnsworth.

610. 3. Noah H., born March 28, 1814; died April 13, 1815.

611. 4. Sarah, born July 6, 1816; married, July, 1843, Sewell K. Reed.

612. 5. Heman, born March 6, 1818; married, 1837, Marcy Coolbrooth.

613. 6. George L., born April 13, 1828; married, Oct. 10, 1852, Betsey B. Trissell.

614. Elisha, born Feb. 14, 1789; died Feb. 5, 1852, in New York; married Lucinda Waller, and had children:

615. 1. Lucinda Taylor, born Feb. 15, 1812; married David Stockwell, and resides at Two Rivers, Manitoowoc Co., Wisconsin.

616. 2. Carlos Taylor, born Dec. 29, 1814; married, Sept. 19, 1839, Hannah Wood, and had children:

617. a. Amelia Taylor, born Dec. 19, 1842.

618. b. Maria Taylor, born March 25, 1845.

619. c. Sheridan W. Taylor, born May 28, 1851.

620. 3. Caroline Taylor, born —— 29, 1814; married, May 11, 1837, Chauncy Child, and had children:

621. a. Edson Child, born May 28, 1838.

622. b. Cornelia C. Child, born Oct. 28, 1839.

623. c. Augusta C. Child, born July 22, 1845.

624. 4. Eliza Ann Taylor, born Dec. 18, 1816; married, Sept. 12, 1839, Henry D. Bostwick, and resides Waupaka, Wis.

625. 5. Robert D. Taylor, born March 8, 1819; resides Malone, N. Y.; married, Oct. 18, 1843, Caroline E. Wood, and had children:

626. a. Daphine Taylor, born April 10, 1847.

627. b. Albert D. Taylor, born March 5, 1852.

628. c. Newton W. Taylor, born April 21, 1857.

629. d. John E. Taylor, born Nov. 19, 1861.

630. 6. Joel C. Taylor, born July 18, 1824; married, June 1, 1848, Demise Hapgood, and had children:

631. a. Jennette Taylor, born June 10, 1849.

632. b. Herbert Taylor, born June 3, 1850.

633. c. Alice Taylor, born Feb. 16, 1862.

634. 7. Elisha D. Taylor, born July 10, 1822; married Caroline Shepard, Jan. 10, 1846, and had children:

635. a. Charles Taylor, born Oct. 1847.

636. b. Ellen Taylor, born Nov. 1851.

637. 8. L. Pathenia Taylor, born Sept. 2, 1827; single.
638. 9. Marshal W. Taylor, born Jan. 8, 1833.

639. Josiah, born April, 1792; married Deborah Waterman. Children:
640. 1. Mary Taylor.
641. 2. Fanny Taylor.

642. Pathenia, born July 22, 1794; married, Dec. 2, 1813, William Davis, born Oct. 27, 1790. He resides in South Richford, Vt., but his post office address is Montgomery, Vt. Children:
643. 1. Samuel Stillman Davis, born Oct. 12, 1814; married, Dec. 3, 1838, Lucy Davis.
644. 2. Bathsheba Davis, born Aug. 21, 1816; married, March 16, 1842, Daniel Henry Stevens.
645. 3. Joseph Willard Davis, born Dec. 8, 1818; married Melvina McAlister, Nov. 2, 1842; married, 2, Betsey Stevens—sisters.
646. 4. Timothy Elliot Davis, born Feb. 8, 1821; married, Aug. 19, 1846, Elizabeth Mills.
647. 5. Benjamin Burke Davis, born Jan. 16, 1823; married, March 24, 1854, Harriet Eliza Bean.
648. 6. William Alvord Davis, born Feb. 8, 1825; never married.
649. 7. Dennison Taylor Davis, born July 18, 1833; never married.
650. 8. Julia Lavina Davis, born June 17, 1836; never married.
651. 9. Celia Ann Davis, born Jan. 16, 1839; married, April 25, 1861, Sanford Allen.

652. Mary Dennison, born Woodstock, Vt., Aug. 15, 1796; resides with her son, Pashal Burke Simons, at Manchester, N. H. She married Lebanon, N. H., Aug. 18, 1822, John Simons, born Lebanon, N. H., Aug. 1, 1789; died Nov. 10, 1861, and had children:

653. 1. Mary Almira Simons, born Lebanon, N. H., July 9, 1823; resides at Nashua, N. H.; married, May 20, 1842, William Ambrose Swallow, and had children:

654. a. George Edwin Swallow; died in the army.

655. b. Henry Swallow.

656. c. Harriet Swallow.

657. d. Alfred Owen Swallow.

658. e. Addie Swallow.

659. 2. Alfred Gordon Simons, born Lebanon, N. H., April 5, 1825; married Manchester, N. H., Aug. 23, 1850, Mary Elizabeth Davis, who died at the Insane Hospital, at Brattleboro', Vt., and left an only child:

660. a. Ella Almira Simons, born Dec. 15, 1851.

661. 3. Paschal Burke Simons, born Lebanon, N. H., Aug. 22, 1826; married Goffstown, April 15, 1856, Amelia Henry, born March 13, 1832, and had one child:

662. a. George Paschal Simons, born Nov. 11, 1857; died July 22, 1859.

663. 4. John Dennison Simons, born Lebanon, N. H., May 29, 1828; died May 23, 1829.

664. 5. Hiram Dennison Simons, born Windsor, Vt., March 17, 1830; married Manchester, N. H., June 16, 1853, Marinda E. Johnson.

665. 6. John Taylor Simons, born Lebanon, N. H., July 12, 1833; died Aug. 12, 1834.

666. 7. Harriet Elizabeth Simons, born Lebanon, N. H., Sept. 1, 1835; died Oct. 20, 1837.

Children of Pathenia Alvord, by her second husband, Joseph Waller:

667. Dennison, born ——; married Eunice Lovey.

668. Octave, born Royalston, Vt., Jan. 2, 1804; married Enosburg, Vt., Harmon Wheeler, born April 21, 1828; died Fairfax, Vt., July 4, 1860, and left one child:

669. 1. Curtis Wheeler, born Enosburg, Vt., Dec. 19, 1828; married Berkshire, Feb. 24, 1852, Lavinia F. Chaffee, and had children:

670. a. Alice Octave Wheeler, born Enosburg, Vt., May 22, 1853.

671. b. Altha Viola Wheeler, born Fairfax, Vt., Aug. 19, 1858; died Jan. 4, 1863.

672. c. Henry Harmon Wheeler, born Fairfax, Vt., June 4, 1860; died Jan. 4, 1863.

673. Louisa, born Enosburg, Vt., March 16, 1808; died Fairfax, Vt., Sept. 30, 1858; married Enosburg, Vt., April 3, 1832, David Rowley. Children:

674. 1. Cordelia M. Rowley, born Enosburg, Vt., Jan. 2, 1833; married, May 7, 1858, Alburn M. Story; resides in Coventry, Vt., and has three children. (I have not the names.)

678. 2. Calvin J. Rowley, born Enosburg, Vt., Nov. 18, 1834.

679. 3. Marshall W. Rowley, born Enosburg, Nov. 27, 1836.

680. 4. Myron Rowley, born Enosburg, April 14, 1838; died March 27, 1839.

681. 5. Arvilla L. Rowley, born Fairfax, Vt., Feb. 21, 1846.

V. 223. Eunice Alvord,

Born Northampton, Mass., April 18, 1776; died Northampton, June 23, 1860. Daughter of Medad and Sarah (Baker) Alvord, who was the son of Joseph and Clemence (Wright) Alvord, who was the son of Ebenezer and Ruth (Baker) Alvord, who was the son of Alexander and Mary (Vore) Alvord.

She married, June 19, 1796,

Luther Hunt,

Born May 13, 1771; died Northampton, Mass., Aug. 28, 1817, aged 46. Son of Joel and Mary (Wright) Hunt, who was the son of Jonathan and Thankful (Strong) Hunt, who was the son of Jonathan and Martha (Williams) Hunt of Northampton, who was the son of Jonathan and Clemence (Hosmer) Hunt, who moved from Connecticut to Northampton about 1660, and was a man of note in his day.

Mr. Luther Hunt resided on Joseph Alvord's place, on Bridge street, Northampton. He learned his trade of David Saxon of Deerfield, Mass. His son, Medad Hunt, has now in his possession many papers formerly belonging to Joseph Alvord, grandfather of Eunice Alvord. Mr. Hunt and his wife were buried in the ancient burial-ground in Northampton.

"In remembrance of Luther Hunt who died
May 28, 1817 aged 46 years. Also of his wife
Eunice Alvord
who died June 23 1860, aged 84."

Children:

682. Frederic, born Northampton, Nov. 30, 1797; died Oct. 1831.

683. Medad, born Northampton, Nov. 24, 1799; died Sept. 16, 1802.

684. Twin children, born Northampton, Mass., Oct. 22, 1801; died Oct. 23, 1801.

686. Medad, born Northampton, Oct. 18, 1802; single; resides in Northampton, near the old Alvord place.

687. Roxana, born Northampton, Feb. 14, 1805; resides in Northampton; married, Dec. 3, 1840, Rosewell Hubbard, who is not living.

688. Eunice, born Northampton, Feb. 26, 1807; married, July 31, 1844, James Madison Ames.

689. Sarah Baker, born Northampton, March 3, 1809; married, Oct. 30, 1835, Elijah L. Smith of Hadley.

690. Joel, born Northampton, March 4, 1811; died April 28, 1853; married, Nov. 15, 1840, Chloe Bishop, born May 30, 1815. Children:

691. 1. Luther Hunt, born June 27, 1841; died Sept. 15, 1842.

692. 2. George Hunt, born April 29, 1843.

693. 3. Luther Hunt, born Nov. 3, 1845.

694. 4. Edward Hunt, born Dec. 15, 1848.

695. Susannah Hunt, born Northampton, May 7, 1813; died Dec. 28, 1832.

696. Luther Hunt, born Northampton, Sept. 3, 1815; died Dec. 4, 1826.

VI. 329. Elijah Alvord,

Born Wilmington, Vt., Nov. 18, 1777; died Greenfield, Mass., Sept. 8, 1840. Son of Caleb and Mary (Murdock) Alvord, who was the son of Elijah and Hannah (Huntington?) Alvord, who was the son of John and Dorcas (Lyman) Alvord, who was the son of Thomas and Joanna (Taylor) Alvord, who was the son of Alexander and Mary (Vore) Alvord. He resided in Greenfield, Mass., was a lawyer in full practice, and quite eminent in his profession. But he retired from practice early, and during the last twenty years of his life, held the offices of Clerk of the Courts and Register of Probate, for the county of Franklin; holding both at the time of his death. In early life he was in the Legislature more or less, and was a member of the Constitutional Convention of 1820.

He married, Nov. 12, 1805,

Sabra Wells,

Born Greenfield, Mass., Feb. 3, 1785; resides at Greenfield, Massachusetts.

Children:

697. Sarah Wells, born Greenfield, Mass., Aug. 23, 1806; died March 6, 1836; married Greenfield, Mass., Oct. 3, 1830, Joseph Warren Newcomb, born Greenfield, in 1802. He is still living. (He is a grandson, on his mother's side, of General Joseph Warren.) Children:

698. 1. Joseph Warren Newcomb, born at Salisbury, Mass., May 17, 1833; married, Oct. 20, 1858, Mary Sumner, and had one child:

699. a. Warren Putnam Newcomb, born at Hartford, July 20, 1859, who is a great-great-grandchild of Gen. Joseph Warren, and also a great-great-grandchild of Gen. Israel Putnam.

700. 2. Sarah Alvord Newcomb, born Worcester, July 19, 1835.

701. James Church, born Greenwich, Mass., April 14, 1808; died Sept. 27, 1839. He was elected to the State Legislature in 1836, to the State Senate in 1837, and to Congress in 1838. He died at the age of 31, before taking his seat in Congress. He married, Oct. 20, 1836, Anna Grew, born at Boston in 1811, and had a son who died in infancy.

702. Mary Upham, born Greenfield, Mass., Aug. 6, 1810; died young.

703. Martha, born Greenfield, Mass., Sept. 18, 1815; died in childhood.

704. Daniel Wells, born Greenfield, Mass., Oct. 21, 1816; he resides in Greenfield, Mass. He was Commissioner of Insolvency for the county of Franklin, from 1848 to 1853; was a member of the Constitutional Convention in 1853, of the State Senate in 1854; was elected District Attorney for the North East Judicial District in 1856, which office he held by re-election till July, 1863. In August, 1862, he was appointed Collector of the Internal Revenue for the 9th District, which office he still holds.

He married, 1, May 10, 1843, Caroline M. Clapp, born New York, Feb. 1, 1824; died Greenfield, Sept. 17, 1846. He married, 2, June 7, 1859, Caroline B. Dewey, born Northampton, March 26, 1827, who is a daughter of Judge Dewey, of the Supreme Court, and is also a granddaughter of Gen. James Clinton, and niece of DeWitt Clinton. Children:

705. 1. Henry Elijah, born Greenfield, March 11, 1844. "At the age of 18, being then a college student,

enlisted in the cavalry as a common soldier, nearly all his class enlisting with him. He has now risen through the various grades of Corporal, Sergeant, Orderly Sergeant, 2d Lieutenant, to the rank of 1st Lieutenant of Cavalry, and is now, having just past his 20th birth day, (March 16, 1864,) Provost Marshal of the Cavalry Station at Vienna, Va.

706. 2. Caroline M. C., born Greenfield, Mass., Sept. 17, 1846.

707. 3. Charles Dewey, born Greenfield, Mass., March 26, 1860.

708. 4. James Church, born Greenfield, July 24, 1862.

709. 5. Mary, born Greenfield, Oct. 9, 1863.

Received information from Hon. D. W. Alvord of Greenfield.

VI. 330. Caleb Alvord,

Born Wilmington, Mass., May 3, 1779; died 1840. Son of Caleb and Mary (Murdock) Alvord, who was the son of Elijah and Hannah (Huntington) Alvord, who was the son of John and Dorcas (Lyman) Alvord, who was the son of Thomas and Joanna (Taylor) Alvord, who was the son of Alexander and Mary (Vore) Alvord.

He married, 1, —— ——; married, 2,

Mrs. —— Ames.

Married, 3,

Mrs. —— Metcalf.

Children:

710. Lucy Melinda, born in 1836; died in 1843.

711. Mary Lucinda, born in 1838.

VI. 331. Pliny Alvord,

Born Greenfield, Mass., March 13, 1781; died Dec. 5, 1859 or 1858. Son of Caleb and Mary (Murdock) Alvord, who was the son of Elijah and Hannah (Huntington?) Alvord, who was the son of John and Dorcas (Lyman) Alvord, who was the son of Thomas and Joanna (Taylor) Alvord, who was the son of Alexander and Mary Vore Alvord. He married, Sept. 1, 1808,

Laurana Bardwell.

Children:

712. Elijah Smead, born July 11, 1809; resides in Indianapolis, Ia.; married, Aug. 23, 1830, Mary P. Lynde, and had children:
713. 1. Mary Pemberton Alvord, born Jan. 31, 1832; married, Oct. 27, 1852, Rev. David Stevenson, and had children:
714. a. Mary Alvord Stevenson, born June, 1854.
715. b. Emma Lynde Stevenson, born Sept. 1856.
716. c. James Elijah Stevenson, born Nov. or Dec. 1860; died July, 1861.

717. 2. Edwin Buckingham Alvord, born Feb. 22, 1835; married, July 9, 1855, Mary Hamed, and had children:
718. a. Mary Rebecca Alvord, born 1857.
719. b. Nellie Alvord, born 1860.

720. 3. Emma Lynde Alvord, born Aug. 6, 1838; married, July 11, 1855, R. F. Fletcher.
721. 4. Henry Beecher Alvord, born April 14, 1842.
722. 5. James Church Alvord, born Jan. 17, 1846.

723. Samuel Bardwell, born Aug. 27, 1811; died Nov. 4, 1811.
724. Lucy Bardwell, born June 16, 1813; married Sept. 9, 1834, Lewis Merriam, and had children:
725. 1. Edwin Alvord Merriam, born Feb. 7, 1837; died Aug. 26, 1838.
726. 2. Edwin Dwight Merriam, born Feb. 19, 1839.
727. 3. Lucy Alvord Merriam, born March 30, 1841; married, Oct. 8, 1861, Charles W. Russell, and had one child, viz.:
728. a. Laura Merriam Russell, born Sept. 14, 1863.

729. 4. Laura Bardwell Merriam, born March 30, 1841.

730. 5. Florence Merriam, born Nov. 26, 1844.
731. 6. Charles Merriam, born Nov. 21, 1846.
732. 7. Abby Fiske Merriam, born Jan. 7, 1855.

733. Laura Bardwell, born Oct. 29, 1815; married, Dec. 22, 1836, Thomas O. Sparhawk of Greenfield. (He is not living.) Children:
734. 1. Lucy Alvord Sparhawk, born Nov. 14, 1838.
735. 2. William Sparhawk, born Jan. 3, 1841; died Feb. 7, 1841.
736. 3. Edward Whitney Sparhawk, born Feb. 8, 1842.
737. 4. George Thomas Sparhawk, born April 26, 1844; died May 25, 1848.

Received information from Mrs. Sparhawk and D. W. Alvord, Esq.

VI. 347. Alpheus Alvord,

Born Greenfield, Mass., Jan. 17, 1787. Son of Caleb and Mary (Murdock) Alvord, who was the son of Elijah and Hannah (Huntington?) Alvord, who was the son of John and Dorcas (Lyman) Alvord, who was the son of Thomas and Joanna (Taylor) Alvord, who was the son of Alexander and Mary (Vore) Alvord. He married, Sept. 13, 1821,

Clara ——,

Born Aug. 28, 1799.

Children:

738. Fanny, born April 11, 1823; died Oct. 29, 1825.
739. Mary, born Sept. 6, 1826; married, Nov. 3, 1855, Rev. N. R. George.
740. Eliza, born Aug. 14, 1828; married, June, 1858, A. P. Hodges.
741. Elijah S., born April 23, 1830; married, June, 1856, Jemima Dupree.
742. Allen, born April 23, 1832; died Dec. 19, 1832.
743. Maria, born Aug. 19, 1834; married, Aug. 20, 1858, Joseph L. Hughes.
744. Allen, born May 10, 1840.
745. Amelia, born April 29, 1843.

VI. 348. Alfred Alvord,

Born Greenfield, Mass., Feb. 15, 1789; died Oct. 31, 1853. Son of Caleb and Mary (Murdock) Alvord, who was the son of Elijah and Hannah (Huntington?) Alvord, who was the son of John and Dorcas (Lyman) Alvord, who was the son of Thomas and Joanna (Taylor) Alvord, who was the son of Alexander and Mary (Vore) Alvord. He resided in Gill, and Northfield, Mass., and in Vernon, Vt.

He married, July 12, 1824,

Mary Allen.

Children:

746. Alfred Buckingham, born Gill, Mass., July 2, 1825; married, Sept. 1850, Cornelia A. Crittenden of Hartford, Ct., and had—

747. 1. Charles Lester Alvord, born Jan. 1852.

748. 2. Helen Isabella Alvord, born April, 1855.

749. James Brazer, born Gill, Mass., Oct. 7, 1826; married Sarah A. Wilson of Philadelphia, May 15, 1860, and had one child:

750. 1. James Leslie Alvord, born June 28, 1863.

751. Helen Melinda, born Gill, Mass., Oct. 13, 1829; died Jan. 1860; married, Sept. 1852, Joseph H. Washburn of Hancock, N. H., and had—

752. 1. Charles Alvord Washburn, born Oct. 1856.

753. Mary Catharine, born Northfield, Mass.; died Jan. 1833.

754. Sarah Isabella, born Northfield, Mass., Feb. 6, 1836.

755. Francis Albert, born Vernon, Vt., Aug. 26, 1839.

I. Benedict Alvord,

Born ——; died Windsor, Conn., April 23, 1683. He was of Windsor, Conn., in 1637; was in "Old England" in 1639; was in Massachusetts in August, 1640, (see page 92), and was of Windsor, Conn., in the fall of 1640, where he early had a grant of land, where he was married, where his children were born, and where he died. He was one of the 30 who went from Windsor, Conn., in 1637, to fight against the Pequots.

The Pequots had conceived the design of driving the whites from New England; and at a Court, convened May 1, 1637, "It is ordered that there shall be an offensive war against the Pequots."

"There shall be 90 men levied out of the three plantations, Hartford, Wethersfield and Windsor, in the following proportion Hartford 42 Windsor 30 Wethersfield 18."

"The decisive battle of May 26 had been fought—the Pequot power was broken, the victorious little army was on its homeward march full of joy and gratitude for success such as they had hardly dared to hope."

"A day of special thanksgiving was proclaimed throughout the colonies, and every where the song of exultant victory was blended with prayer and praise to him who ruleth on high. In all these rejoicings, we may well believe that the good people of Windsor had their full share."

"Capt. Mason the 'very foremost of them a'' was their townsman. '*So was brave Sergeant Alvord.*' So were Barber and Pattison whose valiant right arm caused seven Indians to bite the dust. So were lucky Thomas Stiles and John Dyer, who were singularly fortunate in escaping with their lives, being each of them struck by arrows which stuck in the knots of their neckhandkerchiefs, a twin like coincidence, which is justly commemorated by Capt. Mason in his account of the battle as among the 'wonderful providences' of the day. We have it upon good authority, that in the thickest of the fight an Indian drew 'an arrow to its head' full upon the Captain, whose life was only saved by an opportune thrust of a comrade's sword which cut the bow string, &c." [See History of Windsor.

He married Windsor, Nov. 26, 1640,

Jane Newton.

Her christian name is written Jane and Joan.

Children:

2. Jonathan, born Windsor, Conn., June 1, 1645; married, 1681, Hannah Brown, and had no children; resided in Westfield.

3. Benjamin, born Windsor, Conn., July 11, 1647; died New London, Aug. 12, 1709.

An ancient freestone table, in the ancient burial-ground at New London, "bears the following inscription":

"Interred
Under this Stone
is the Body of Col
Benjamin Alvord
Who departed this
Life Avgvst ye 12th
Ano. Dom 1709
in ye 63^D^ year
of His age."

We do not know of any descendants.

4. Josiah, born Windsor, Conn., July 6, 1649; removed to Simsbury, and there had wife and family, but particulars unknown. [Savage.

5. Elizabeth, born Windsor, Conn., Sept. 21, 1651; married Windsor, Conn., March 20, 1672, Job Drake of Westfield, who was the son of John and Hannah (Moore) Drake, who was the son of John, who probably came in the fleet with Winthrop to Boston or Dorchester, as we find his request to be made freeman, 19 Oct. 1630, and who moved to Windsor, Conn., where he was killed by a cart-wheel running over him, Aug. 17, 1659. She had children:

6. 1. Jonathan, born Jan. 4, 1673.

7. 2. Elizabeth, born Nov. 4, 1675.
8. 3. Sarah, born ——; (according to Savage.)
9. 4. Rebecca, born Jan. 16, 1689.
10. †Jeremiah, born Windsor, Conn., Dec. 24, 1655; married Jane Hoskins.

II. 10. Jeremiah Alvord,

Born Windsor, Conn., Dec. 24, 1655; died June 6, 1709. Son of Benedict and Jane (Newton) Alvord. He resided at Windsor, Conn.

Robert Hoskins of Simsbury, Jan. 3, 1710-11, names his sister, Jane Alvord, and his brother, Jeremiah Alvord, as dead.

He married

Jane Hoskins,

Born Windsor, Conn., April 3, 1671; died May 19, 1715. She was the daughter of Anthony and [Savage says Isabel (Brown)] Hoskins; History of Windsor says, daughter of Anthony and Mary Hoskins of Windsor, Conn. Her father died Jan. 4, 1707, leaving a large estate.

Children:

11. †Benedict, born Windsor, Conn., April 27, 1688; married, Jan. 12, 1714, Abigail Wilson.
12. Newton, born Windsor, Conn., March 24, 1689–90.
13. †Jeremiah, born Windsor, Conn., May 8, 1692; married Windsor, Conn., July 4, 1711, Sarah Eno.
14. Jonathan, born Windsor, Conn., March 4, 1696; died July 14, 1700.
15. Jane, born Windsor, Conn., Jan. 14, 1698-9.
16. Joanna, born Windsor, Conn., March 1, 1701-2; married, Dec. 9, 1725, Benjamin Loomis, Jr., and had children:
17. 1. Joanna Loomis, born July 31, 1726.
18. 2. Benjamin Loomis, born Jan. 12, 1728; died Feb. 8, 1728-9.
19. 3. Tabitha Loomis, born Oct. 16, 1730.
20. 4. Benjamin Loomis, born April 19, 1732.
21. 5. Rachel Loomis, born Aug. 5, 1735.
22. 6. Serajah Loomis, born Dec. 4, 1740.

23. Elizabeth, born Windsor, Conn., Nov. 22, 1703; died Jan. 10, 1703-4.

24. Elizabeth, born Windsor, Conn., April 27, 1706; married Windsor, Conn., Oct. 1, 1747, Jesse Hosford, son of Obadiah and Mindwell (Phelps) Hosford, who was the son of John and Phillury (Thrall) Hosford, and had,

25. 1. Jesse Hosford, born Windsor, Conn., Feb. 20, 1747–8.

26. Job, born Windsor, Conn., Aug. 26, 1708; (Stiles says that he was one of the first settlers in Harwinton, Conn.,) and had,

27. 1. Job, born July 3, 1736.

28. 2. Jonathan, born Sept. 4, 1738.

III. 11. Benedict Alvord,

Born Windsor, Conn., April 27, 1688; resided in Windsor, Conn. Son of Jeremiah and Jane (Hoskins) Alvord, who was the son of Benedict and Jane (Newton) Alvord.

He married Windsor, Conn., Jan. 12, 1714,

Abigail Wilson,

Born Windsor, Conn., March 3, 1683–4; died April 30, 1773, aged 91. Daughter of Samuel and Mary (Griffin) Wilson, who was the son of Robert and Elizabeth (Stebbens) Wilson.

Children:

29. †Benedict, born Windsor, Aug. 29, 1716; died Feb. 15, 1764; (?) married, 1, Aug. 1744, Jerusha Ashley; married, 2, Dec, 18, 1861, Rebecca Owen.

30. Abigail, born Windsor, Conn., Aug. 3, 1718; died Jan. 16, 1746.

31. Alexander, born Windsor, Conn., March 31, 1721.

32. Jerusha, born Windsor, Conn., April 3, 1723; died Feb. 15, 1753.

33. Azuba, born Windsor, Conn., Feb. 19, 1727; died June 2, 1786.

III. 13. Jeremiah Alvord,

Born Windsor, Conn., May 8, 1692. Son of Jeremiah and Jane (Hoskins) Alvord, who was the son of Benedict and Jane (Newton) Alvord. He married, July 4, 1711,

Sarah Eno,

Daughter of John and Mary (Dibble) Eno, who was the son of James and Anna (Bidwell) Eno.

Children:

34. Sarah, born Windsor, Conn., June 16, 1712; died June 9, 1815.
35. Jeremiah, born Windsor, Conn., June 1, 1714; died July ye 9, 1714.
36. Jane, born Windsor, Conn., June 1, 1715.
37. Sarah, born Windsor, Conn., Feb. 14, 1717–18.
38. †J[illegible]n, born Windsor, Conn., Sept. 16, 1720; married, Dec. 17, 1744, Charity Thrall.
39. Jeremiah, born Windsor, Conn., May 14, 1725; married Windsor, Conn., July 16, 1746, Annie Giles, and had,
40. 1. Jeremiah, born Windsor, Conn., Feb. 16, 1746–7; died Jan. 4, 1751–2.
41. Elizabeth, born Windsor, Conn., Aug. 2, 1727.

IV. 29. Benedict Alvord,

Born Windsor, Conn., Aug. 29, 1716; died Feb. 15, 1764.(?) Son of Benedict and Abigail (Wilson) Alvord, who was the son of Benedict and Jane (Newton) Alvord.

He married, 1, Aug. 9, 1744,

Jerusha Ashley,

Born 1723;(?) of Hartford, Conn.; died Jan. 18, 1761, aged 38 years. He married, 2, Dec. 18, 1761,

Rebecca Owen,

Born Nov. 6, 1736. She was the daughter of Elijah and Lydia (Clarke) Owen, who was the. son of Isaac and Sarah (Holcomb) Owen, who was the son of John and Rebecca (Wade) Owen.

Children of Benedict and Jerusha Alvord:

42. Deidemia, born Windsor, Conn., Jan. 13, 1744.
43. Abigail, born Windsor, Conn., Oct. 23, 1746; died Jan. 16, 1746–7.
44. Abigail, born Windsor, Conn., Dec. 3, 1747.
45. Jerusha, born Windsor, Conn., Aug. 21, 1750.
46. Alexander, born Windsor, Conn., June 25, 1752.
47. Lucrece, born Windsor, Conn., March 27, 1755.
48. Benedict, born Windsor, Conn., Feb. 21, 1757.
49. Anna, born Windsor, Conn., April 7, 1759.

Children of Benedict and Rebecca Alvord:

50. George, born Windsor, Conn., March 10, 1761.
51. Rebecca, born Windsor, Conn., Oct. 24, 1762.
52. Rocitter,(?) born Windsor, Conn., Nov. 18, 1763.

IV. 38. Jonathan Alvord,

Born Windsor, Conn., Sept. 16, 1720. Son of Jeremiah and Sarah (Eno) Alvord, who was the son of Jeremiah and Jane (Hoskins) Alvord, who was the son of Benedict and Jane (Newton) Alvord.

He married, Dec. 17, 1744,

Charity Thrall,

Children:

53. Jonathan, born Windsor, Conn., Dec. 21, 1745; resided at Windsor; married Elizabeth Reed, and had children:
54. 1. John, born Windsor, Conn.
55. 2. William, born Windsor, Conn.
56. 3. James, born Windsor, Conn.
57. 4. Nathaniel, born Windsor, Conn., 1784; died 1836; married, Nov. 13, 1808, Eunice Strong, and had children:
58. a. Nathaniel Alvord, born Windsor, Conn., Sept. 18, 1809; married, 1, Keziah Barber; 2, Eliza Ann Lord.

59. b. Elizabeth W. Alvord, born Windsor, Conn., Feb. 16, 1809.

60. c. Elijah Strong Alvord, born Windsor, Conn., Aug. 18, 1813; resides in Windsor, Conn.; married, 1, Julia Lord, who died Feb. 22, 1850; married, 2, Emily Sill, who was born June 30, 1824, and had children:

61. a. Henry Sill Alvord, born Dec. 15, 1851; died June 20, 1853.

62. b. Emma Alvord, born June, 1854.

63. c. Anna Alvord, born Dec. 30, 1856.

64. d. Carrie Alvord, born Aug. 17, 1859.

65. d. Samuel M. Alvord, born July 4, 1823.

66. e. Almira Enos Alvord, born March 4, 1830; died young.

67. 5. Chauncey, born Windsor, Conn.; single.

68. Joseph, born Windsor, Conn., July 6, 1748; married Lucy Griswold, daughter of Moses Griswold, and had children:

69. 1. Lucy Alvord, married Hermes Holcomb, and had,

70. a. William; b. Mary; c. Hermes; d. Almerin; e. Selina.

75. 2. William Alvord, born May 3, 1774; died Dec. 26, 1856; married, 1, Feb. 8, 1802, Clarissa Griswold, daughter of Isaac Griswold; she died Dec. 1, 1809. Married, 2, April 3, 1810, Selina Griswold; she died Feb. 4, 1821. Married, 3, July 4, 1837, Maria Barber, daughter of Gideon Barber. Children:

76. a. Felton Alvord, born July 2, 1802; died April 14, 1806.

77. b. William Alvord, born April 3, 1804; died March 14, 1806.

78. c. William Felton Alvord, born March 14, 1807; died Aug. 27, 1851; was never married.

79. d. Alanson Alvord, born Aug. 7, 1809; died April 3, 1810.

80. e. Euclid W. Alvord, born July 16, 1813; died April 24, 1859; resided in Poquonock, Conn., and married, Oct. 10, 1842, Mary E. Keeney, daughter of Leonard Keeney, and had children:

81. a. Celeste Alvord, born March 2, 1844.

82. b. Hester Alvord, born May 4, 1845.

83. c. William Alvord, born March 16, 1848.

84. d. Frank Alvord, born Dec. 27, 1856.

85. 3. Joseph Alvord; never married.

86. 4. Polly Alvord; married Ashbel Case.

87. 5. Rosewell Alvord; never married.

88. 6. Moses Alvord; married Rhoda Smith, and had,

89. a. Rosewell Alvord; b. Moses Alvord; c. Lucinda Alvord; d. Delia Alvord; e. Carlos Alvord.

91. 7. Abby Mathea Alvord, married Levi Pinney; no children.

92. 8. Sophia Alvord, married Anthony Demott; no children.

93. 9. Eleanor Alvord, married Amos Hathaway. Children:

94. a. Moses; b. Rodolpho; c. Duane.

97. Charity, born Windsor, Conn., June 20, 1750.

APPENDIX.

Appendix A—page 13.

ADMINISTRATION OF RICHARD BURKE'S ESTATE.

"*Mary and John Burck's Admcon Bond.*"

Know all men by these p^{r}sents that we Mary Burck Relict widow of Richard Burck of Sudbury in ye County of Midd^{x}. and John Burck of said Sudbury, yeoman and Abraham Holeman of said Sudbury and Richard Burck of Stow in ye County aforesaid and within their Majesties Province of ye Massachusetts Bay in New England, are holden and stand firmly bound, and obliged, unto James Russell Esq. in ye full sum of three hundred pounds current money of New England to be paid unto ye said James Russell, his successo^{rs} in ye office of Judge of Probate of Wills, and granting of Administration or Assigns to ye true payment whereof we do bind ourselves, our heires, Executors and Administra^{tors} jointly and severally firmly by these presents.

Sealed with our Seal. Dated in Charlestown the Seventeenth Day of January 1693–4.

The Condicon of this p^{r}sent obligation is such that if ye above bounden Mary Burck and John Burck Administrato^{rs} of all and Singular the goods, Chattells, Rights, and Creditts of Richard Burck late of Sudbury in ye County of midd^{x} Deced Intestate;

Do make a true and p^{r}fect Inventory of all & singular ye goods, Chattells, Rights & Creditts of ye Said Deced which have or shall Come to ye hands or possession or knowledge of ye said Administrators, or into ye hands & Possession of any other p^{r}son or p^{r}sons for them and ye same so made Do Exhibit into the Register's office of said County at or before ye Seventeenth day of April next Ensueing.

And the Same goods Chattells Rights and Creditts and all other ye goods Chattells Rights and Creditts of ye Said Deced at ye time of his Death which at any time after shall Come to ye hands or possession of said Administrators or any other p^{r}son or p^{r}sons for them.

Do well and truly administer according to Law. And farther Do make or Cause to be made a Just and true account of their said Administration at or before ye Seveenth day of January 1694–5, and all the rest and Residue of ye said goods, Chattells, Rights and Creditts which shall be found remaining upon ye Administrators account the same being first Examined and allowed of by ye Judge or Judges for ye time being of Probate of Wills and granting of Administrations within ye said County of midd^x^, shall deliver and pay unto such prson or prsons as ye said Judge or Judges, by his or their Decree or sentence p^r^suant to Law shall limit and appoint.

And if it shall hereafter appear that any last will and Testament was made by ye said Deced and ye Executor or Executors therein named Do Exhibit ye same into ye said Court of Probate makeing request to have it allowed and approved accordingly.

If ye said Mary Burck and John Burck within bounden being there unto required, Do render and Deliver ye said Letters of Administration approbation of Such Testament being first and made unto ye Register's Office of said County then this obligation to be void and of none effect or else to remain in full force and vertue.

MARY BURCK M her mark & seal
JOHN BURCK
ABRAHAM HOLMAN ( ) his mark & seal
RICHARD BURCK ( ) his mark.

Signed Sealed & Delivered in ye p^r^sence of us
Sam^ll^ Phipps Reg^r^
William Shattuck
John Simpson
Richard Burk of Stow to be added.

Inventory.

A True Inventory of Richard Burck Sen^rs^ estate.

He liveed in Sudbury in the county of middilssix. He is now Desicised. Taken the 29 day of January In the year of our lord 1693–4.

2 Oxen	07 10 00
4 Cows	10 00 00
2 young oxen coming three	04 00 00
2 hafers coming three	04 00 00
1 hafer coming Two year old	01 08 00
1 mare	02 05 00

8 swine - - - - - -	04 00 00
The cart and the oxen yoke - - -	01 10 00
2 Chains - - - - - -	01 03 00
A Grinstone - - - - -	00 06 00
2 axes - - - - - -	00 09 00
Bettel Rings and weges - - - -	00 10 00
Plow Irons And Plows - - - -	01 12 00
Horse trasis - - - - -	00 10 00
The corne enggen and ry and wheat - -	02 00 00
Corne sownen upon the land - - -	01 00 00
One Bed and beding - - - -	02 00 00
Another Bed and beding and curttains and bedstead	03 00 00
Linin - - - - - -	02 15 00
Saddel - - - - - -	00 12 00
warming Pan - - - - -	00 08 00
Frying Pan - - - - -	00 03 00
Putter - - - - - -	01 00 00
Two Guns - - - - -	01 15 00
Trammel - - - - - -	00 05 00
Two Pots and pot hooks - - - -	00 15 00
Brass cellet - - - - -	00 03 00
His wareing close - - - - -	04 04 00
Barrels - - - - - -	00 08 00
The tubs and other wooden lumber - -	01 00 00
Disis and spons - - - - -	00 10 00
Two wheels and other Smal things - -	00 08 00
Cheast, cobbord seive and other g[n] - -	00 18 00
In Books - - - - - -	01 00 00
Chairs and cousings - - - -	00 06 00
Cart rope and fork - - - -	00 05 00
the oger and bell - - - - -	00 02 00
	73 10 00
The house And Land lying in Sudbury being one of the New Grants which is a 136 acars of land was prised - - - - - -	100 00 00
	173 10 00

At A Hundred Pounds. This estate was prised all as money being the hol estate that goodman Burck Left.

Prised by

ABRAHAM HOLMAN
ISRAEL HEALL
THOMAS FOSTER.

Charlestown March 19th 1693–4—. By ye Honourable James Russell Esq.—Mary Burck Relict of Rich'd Burck and her son John Burk, admitted Administrat^ors p^rsonally appearing made oath that this Contains a true Inventory of ye Estate of Richard Burck late of Sudbury Dec'd, Intestate as far as comes to their Knowledge and when more appears they will cause it to be added.

Exa^Ex Sam^ll Phipps Reg^r

Juratur Coram Ja Russell.

Copied from the original, on file at the Prob. Office, Midd'x Co.

Richard Burke of Stow.

Know all men by these p^rsents that I Richard Burk of the Town of Stow in ye County of Middx. in New England, have received of the administrators of my deceased father's estate the full and just claim of Eight pounds Twelve shillings and four pence, which I accept for my whole proportion of my father's Estate, and do hereby for my selfe, my heirs, Executors, adms. and assigns; fully, clearly, and absolutely, release, &c., &c.

In witness whereof I ye said Richard Burck have put to my hand & seal this 9 of March 1694–5.

RICHARD BURK and a Seal.

The Acct. of Mary Burck and John Burk Administrators of all and Singular the good, Chattells, rights & Creditts of Richard Burk late of Sudbury Deces'd Intestate as well of as and for such and so much of ye same goods, & Chattells as came to their hands as for their payments and disbursements out of ye same, as followeth viz;

	£ s d
The said Accompt^ts charges themselves with all & singular ye goods, Chattells, Rights, Estate of the said Deced, specified in an Inventory thereof made & Exhibited into ye Registers office of said County March 19: 93–4 amo^ts as by the same to ye sum of - - - -	163 07 00

A Petition for allowance as follo^{os}.

For so much pd Docto^{r} Minot for attendance &c -	01 00 00
To so much paid Docto^{r} Prescott - - -	00 12 00
To Mr Sherman Clerk - - - -	01 05 02
To John Butterick - - - -	00 03 00
To Roger Chandler & Tho ——— - -	00 04 00
To Taking Inventory to 3 men - - -	00 06 00
For a bondsman Journey to ye office - -	00 03 00
To charge of Adm̅con & Inventory at ye office -	00 10 00
To Sam^{ll} How for ye meeting house - -	00 12 02
To our Son & Brother Richard Burk in full of his Portion to his Content as per his discharge and or hand and seal appears - - - - -	08 12 04
To so much for ye Adm^{rs} charge & Trouble -	02 10 00
To Drawing & Registering ye Acct of Adm̅con -	00 04 06
To allowing ye said ——— - - -	00 05 00
To Commission for settle^{t} - - - -	00 05 06
	16 08 08

Charlestowne March 11. 94–5.

JOHN BURCK.

By ye Honble James Russell Esq.

Jno Burk one of ye Administrato^{rs} of ye Estate of Richard Burk of Sudbury Deced. Intestate; personally appeared, &c., &c.

From the original on file at the Prob. Office for Mid. Co.

Settlement of Richard Burk's Estate.

Pursuant to an order Recev^{d} ffrom ye Honoured James Russell Esqr. Judge of Probate of Wills and settling of Intestate Estates.

We whose names ar hear vnto subscribed being appointed by said Judg to make an Equal a estrebushan of the estate of Richard Burk late of Sudbury Deceased, who died intestate which wee have atended accor to our best judgment and Directions Given vs in the Law.

Imprimas

Ye widows thirds of moveabels

by two steares and two heifers - - -	8 0 0
by linning and a Mare - - - -	5 0 0
by two pots: brass scillet a warming pan and friing pan - - - - - - -	1 9 0
by a chest and a cubbord - - - -	0 12 0
totll - - -	15 1 0

Mary Burk Juners Legacey or portion.

by two oxen - - - - -	7	10	0
by two cows - - - - -	5	0	0
by bedding bed curtings & bedstead - -	3	0	0
by tabel and othr wooden lumber - - -	1	0	0
by two wheeles, sive, and other tooles - -	0	14	0
by dishes, spoons, cheires, cushens - -	0	16	0
by a tramill and barrels - - - -	0	13	0
by a gun - - - - - -	0	17	6
	19	10	6

John Burk his Division of land.

By two third of the housing and two thirds of the field and vpland behind the dwelling house; two thirds of ye pasture and a part of back medow with the vn Improved land as it is now butted and bounded.

Of ye moveabel estate

by a gun; Cart wheels, yoake, fork and rope - - 2 12 06

Joseph Burk's division of land.

Lands lying on the north side of ye farme, Joyning to ye new grant of left. John Rudduk on ye nor easterly sid: and runs easterly: home to the hy way, that devids ye new Grant lots: and Southerly, buts on his brother Thomas his division, and westerly on his brother John's division.

Of ye moveable estate,

by 2 chaines; grinstone, beetel rings wedges horsetraces 2 10 06

Jonas Burk's Division of Land.

butting on ye east with the land of his brother John burk, on ye south with ye lands of Mr Abraham Holman, westerly with ye lands of Stow, northerly with the land of Leuet Rudduck.

Of ye moveable estate

by one cow - - - - - - 2 10 00

The widdos thirds of ye house & lands.

by half an acre of orchod, and the 3^d^ pt of small pasture, Both joyning together, lying South and South westerly of ye house.

By ye third part of the vpland in the field on ye back sid of ye house being bounded with stakes: by a third pt of ye dwelling house.

by the third pt of the feild lying before ye house and joyneth to the land of Mr Abraham Holman; said holman land lying South westerly thereof.

by a third pt of ye little feild; that lyeth at the westerly end of the farme the nearest end next ye dwelling house.

by a third pt of the medow caled spruce medow being ye south west sid.

by a third pt of the medow, called river medow; lying on ye nor est side.

by a third pt of ye medow caled back medow lying on the north side thereof.

by a third pt of the medow caled wasp medow.

Ye widows pt is next Left Rudducks lyne with a third part of all ye wast lands in all ye divisions.

Thomas Burk's Division of land.

Bounded on ye South with ye land of Mr Abraham holman: easterly with ye middle hy way of ye new grant lots and northerly with the land of Joseph Burk and westerly with the land of John Burk.

Moveables.

by pillows bed and bedding, - - - - 2 12 00

April 1, 1695 pr
allowed pr
James Russell

THOMAS BROWN
JOHN GOODENOW
JOHN HAYNES
JOHN BUTTERICK.

by a saddle not showed.

The above from Court files.

APPENDIX B—page 32.

CÆSAR AND FLORA BRACKEY.

Flora Brackey, servant of Solomon Burke, was a Guinea negro. She was brought to this country, supposed to Providence, R. I., by Capt. Snell, who was master of the vessel. He considered her to be the "smartest female negro" that he had, and he took her to his own house, but she desired to get away, and Mrs. Snell persuaded her husband to sell her.

He sold her to "Massa Lyon" of Woodstock, Conn. This happened previous to the emancipation of slaves in New England. Her first husband's name was Biberto.

Cæsar Brackey, her second husband, was raised by a minister of the name of Bugbee, of Woodstock, Conn.

Priest Bugbee gave Cæsar Brackèy a lot of land in Hartland, Vt., and Cæsar, with his wife Flora, who was a number of years older than himself, moved upon the said land, and there made their home.

They had a number of children, who all died young, and they became disheartened and lonesome, so that they neglected to improve their homestead, and went out to work at different places. Mr. Solomon Burke and his wife manifested sympathy when they came to work for them, and treated them with kindness.

The town authorities of Hartland gave their consent to have Cæsar and Flora Brackey go to Mr. Burke's and make their home with him, and Mr. Burke to have their homestead in Hartland, he giving bonds for their future maintenance.

A small house or tenement was provided by Mr. Burke, near his own house, for Cæsar and Flora as their own.

Cæsar was a short, thick-set man, well proportioned, very active, and at the time of his death would do as much work as any young man. He was a pleasant person, and was universally esteemed.

Mr. Stephen Conant, who kept the tavern in Windsor, Vt., employed Cæsar "to do chores," to build fires, tend ovens, &c. He was troubled with the gravel, and went up into an attic in the tavern and laid down and died.

The father of Stephen Conant went on horseback to inform Mr. Burke of Cæsar's death. Mr. Burke took the remains to Hartland and buried them upon the land which was formerly his own, and there subsequently Flora was buried.

Flora Brackey was a very black negro, but late in life became somewhat lighter colored. She was a very peaceable woman, and was an excellent cook, and capable of doing any kind of woman's work. Mr. Solomon Burke in conveying his property to his son Jonathan Burke, makes provision for himself and wife, and provides for the maintenance "of a negro woman by the name of Flora Brackey." Dr. Nahum Trask of Windsor, Vt., said that, according to the best information he could get, she lived to be one hundred and four years old.

APPENDIX C—page 33.

BENJAMIN.

1. I. *John Benjamin,*

Born about 1598; died in Watertown, June 14, 1645. Immigrant maternal ancestor of Mr. Benjamin Burke, (see page 33, also V. No. 75, page 64,) came to Boston, Mass., in the ship Lion, Sept. 16. 1632, and was made freeman the 6th of November following. May 20, 1633, he was chosen constable of New Town, (Cambridge,) by the General Court. Nov. 7, 1634, he was exempted from training on account of age and infirmity, but was required to have, at all times, arms for himself and servants.

He was of New Town, (Cambridge,) in Oct. 1636, and settled in Watertown about the year 1637. His homestall of sixty acres in Watertown was situated east of Dorchester Field, and bounded south by Charles River. He owned three other large lots. Besides these, it is supposed that he purchased several homestalls in Watertown of those who migrated to Wethersfield. Gov. Winthrop designated him as *Mr. Benjamin;* the title *Mister* being rare in those days. His will, dated 12 (4) 1646, is upon record at the Probate Office for Suffolk Co. The following is an abstract of his will:

I *John Benjamin* being in pfect memory, as touching my outward estate—do bequeath to sonne *John* a double portion, beloved wife two Cowes, fourty bushels of Corne out of all my lands, to be allowed her towards the bringing vp of my smale Children yearly such as growes vppon the ground, one part of fower of all my houshold stuffe, all the rest of my lands goods and chattels shall be equally divided between seven other of my children. Provided that out of all my former estate my wife during her life shall enjoy the dwelling house I live in, and three Acres of the broken vp ground next the house, & two Acres of the Meddowe neere hand belonging to the house. That this will be truly pformed I do appoint my brother *John Eddie* of Watertowne & Thomas Marrit of Cambridge that they doe theire best Indevor to see this pformed. JOHN BENJAMIN.

Witnes *Georg Muniage* [Muning].
the 15 (4) 45.

This was proved to be the last will & testament of *John Benjamin* & that he did further declare (as an addition to this his will) that his wife should have liberty to take wood for her vse vppon any of his Lands dureing her life vppon the Oath of

John Eddye Before

(5) 3. 1645. THOMAS DUDLEY Govr.
Jo: WINTHROP Dep. Gov.

His Inventory, proved July 3, 1645, amounted to £297, 3s. 2d.

Abstract of Inventory:—House and meadow next the mill, lot bought of John Bernard, £50; house and sixty acres (homestall), £75; ten acres in Rocky Meadow, £13; eight acres in Great Dividens, £12; sixteen acres in Watertown, bought April 20, 1645, of Capt. Robert Sedgwick of Charlestown, £10, &c. [See N. E. H. & G. R., Vol. 3, p. 177.] Fathers, in those days, at the marriage of their children, gave them large portions of their own property, which would make their estate small at the time of their death, although they were formerly possessors of considerable property. He married

Abigail ——,

Born 1600; died in Charlestown, Mass., May 20, 1687, aged 87. She outlived her husband, and went to Charlestown about the year 1654, with her son-in-law, Joshua Stubbs, where she died. Probably she did not live in Charlestown all the time, for, in March 28, 1670, Abigail Benjamin, spinister, of Watertown, for twelve pounds, sold to John Wellington of Watertown, three parcels of land in Cambridge.

Children:

2. †John, born England, (?) 1620; died in Watertown, Dec. 22, 1706, aged 86. He resided in Watertown, and married Lydia Allen.
3. Abigail, born England, (?) 1624; married about 1640–1, Joshua Stubbs of Watertown, who was admitted freeman May 2, 1649. They moved to Charlestown, Mass., and had children: Samuel, born Aug. 3, 1642; Mary, who married John Train; Elizabeth, who married Jonathan Stimson. Nov. 8, 1654, Joshua Stubbs, then of Charlestown, and wife Abigail, with consent of mother, Abigail Benjamin, sold to Joseph Underwood, for £30, their homestall, (a house and twelve acres,) and several other parcels of land in Watertown. Her husband died about the year 1654–5, and she united with the church in Charlestown, March, 1656. She afterwards married John Woodward, son of Richard, by whom she had children. She was again left a widow. "Mrs Abigail Woodward was witness in Court, June, 1671, then aged 47, showing that she was born in England about 1624."

4. Samuel, born England,(?) 1628; died Hoccanum, Hartford, Conn., about the year 1669; he resided in Watertown, and took the oath of fidelity in 1652. Oct. 28, 1667, he, with his wife Mary, sold to Daniel Medup, three lots of land; 1st, 120 acres adjoining lands of his mother; 2d, six acres in little Nonesuch Meadow; 3d, farm lands elsewhere surrounding. In the same month, Oct. 19, 1667, he sold to his mother Abigail, for £35, ten acres, with the mansion house, &c. He moved to Hoccanum, in Hartford, Conn. He married Mary ——, who out-lived him, and by whom he had children: Samuel, John, Abigail, and Mary, born in Watertown, May 12, 1666.

9. Mary, born ——; died Watertown, April 10, 1646. Her will, proved June 4, 1646, was set aside by the General Court, as not valid, she being under age, and her mother Abigail was appointed administratrix. Abstract of will: I *mary Benjamin* of Watertown do give to Pastor Knolls fyve Acres of Marsh at the Rocky Meddow in Watertown bounds. I giue to my *Aunt Wines* one Cowe, I giue to my sister Abigail Stubbs two Cowes my best clothes wth my best seary Peticoate. I giue to my brothers in generall one Cows worth To my Cosin Anne Wyes [Wines] my best wastcoate. MARY BENJAMIN

Witnes to this will her owne act & deede.

Jane Mahew
Elizabeth Child } both sworn in Court 4 (4) 1646.

10. Caleb, born ——; died in Wethersfield, Conn., May 8, 1684, intestate. He settled in Wethersfield, Conn., and was admitted freeman of Connecticut in 1669. He married Mary Hale, born 1649, daughter of Samuel and Mary (——) Hale of Wethersfield, and had children: 1, Mary, born Sept. 15, 1671; 2, Abigail, born April 27, 1673; 3, Sarah, born Feb. 17, 1675; 4, John, born Nov. 5, 1677; 5, Samuel, born Feb. 14, 1680; 6, Martha, born Jan. 19, 1681; 7, Caleb, born 1683. Administration of his estate was granted to his widow Mary, who afterwards(?) married Walter Harris of Glastenbury.

18. Joseph, born ——; he married, 1, June 10, 1661, Jemima Lambert, daughter of Thomas and Joice Lambert of Barnstable. "Oct. 30, 1686 Joseph Benjamin of Barnstable sold land in Cambridge bounded on land of Abel Benjamin, my brother, which was devised by Will of my honored father Mr. John Benjamin sometime of Watertown deceased." He resided in

Barnstable, and lived some years at Yarmouth. He had children: 1, Abigail; 2, Joseph; 3, Jemima; 4, Sarah; 5, Keziah; 6, Hannah, born Feb. 1668; 7, Mary born April, 1670; 8, Mercy, born March 12, 1674; 9, Elizabeth, born Jan. 14, 1680; 10, John, born 1682.(?) He married, 2, Sarah Clark.(?) He removed to New London, Conn., where he died, 1704, leaving widow Sarah and children; Joseph, aged 30; John, 22; Abigail, Jemima, Sarah, Keziah, Mary, and Mercy. Barnard Lumbert, aged 60, testifies, that William Clark of Yarmouth gave, by nuncupative will, his property to *Joseph Benjamin*, 28th 12 mo. 1668. Clark died Dec. 7, 1668. Inventory, £8, 3s. 0d. [See N. E. H. & G. R., Vol. 3, 178.

29. Joshua, born Watertown, 1641; died Charlestown, Mass., May, 1684, aged 42; resided in Charlestown, and married Thankful ——, who out-lived him, but had no issue.

30. Abel, born Watertown; resided in Charlestown, Mass., and married *Amithy Myrick*, Nov. 6, 1671. She was admitted to full communion to the church of Christ, in Charlestown, May 14, 1676; and he was admitted to full communion, Sept. 8, 1700. His will, dated July 3, 1710, mentions wife Amithy, son 1, John; gr. son John; dau. 2, Mary; dau. 3, Abigail, born Aug. 26, 1680, and brother Joshua.

II. 2. *John Benjamin*,

Born England, (?) 1620; died Watertown, Dec. 22, 1706, aged 86. Son of John and Abigail (——) Benjamin, the immigrant. He resided in Watertown. John Benjamin, upon his petition to the General Court, April 5, 1681, aged about 61, was exempted from training. He sold to his sons Daniel and Abel, sixty acres in Dorchester Field, bounded south by Charles River, east by land of William Bond and Dorchester Field, west by land of John Loveran, north by land of Robert and J. Goddard. He married

Lydia Allen,

Daughter of William Allen.(?) Mr. Savage says, "William Allen of Boston made his will 15 Dec. 1674, and died soon. In it he gives all his property, in hands of Jonathan Tyng or elsewhere, to Lydia, wife of John Benjamin of Watertown, from which Bond seems to be justly authorized to infer that Lydia was his daughter, but it may be doubted, for on 26 of next month John Benjamin renounces the benefit of the will. She may have been his sister, for the will does not call her daughter, nor can I find any children on Boston records of births; but sister or daughter, probably the value of his goods was small."

Children:

34. John, born Watertown, Sept. 10, 1651; died Watertown, Nov. 18, 1708; resided in Boston and Watertown. He married Mehitable ——, by whom he had children: 1, John, born Boston, Sept. 4, 1679; 2, Sarah, born Boston, May 8, 1686; 3, Lydia, bapt. Sept. 10, 1699; 4, John, born Watertown, April 15, 1699.

39. Lydia, born Watertown, April 3, 1653; married Thomas Batt of Boston, son of "Christopher Batt, who came from the city of Salisbury, Co. Wilts, in the Bevis, embarked at Southampton in 1638," and settled first in Newbury, Mass., afterwards moved to Boston, and was a tanner by trade. Thomas Batt likewise carried on the business of tanning in Boston, after his father. He left one child, Elizabeth, who died in Watertown in 1692.

41. Abigail, born Watertown, July 14, 1655.

42. Mary, born Watertown, Aug. 2, 1658.

43. Daniel, born Watertown, Sept. 12, 1660; died Sept. 13, 1719; married, March 25, 1687, Elizabeth Brown; and was licensed to keep an inn. He had children: 1, Daniel, b. Jan. 15, 1687–8; 2, Daniel, born Dec. 27, 1688; married, Nov. 23, 1738, Mary Bond, and died Sept. 15, 1768; 3, John, bapt. Nov. 23, 1690; died young; 4,(?) Jonathan, married, 1, Annabella Eve, dau. of Adam Eve of Boston; married, 2, May 7, 1734, Hannah, widow of William Bond of Boston; 5, Samuel, born Jan. 30, 1695–6; married, Nov. 28, 1723, Mary Hammond of Newton; 6, Elizabeth, born March 22, 1697–8; married, Aug. 20, 1718, William Bond; 7, Lydia, born Sept. 8, 1699; 8, Patience, born Oct. 17, 1701; married, March 24, 1719–20, David Sangar; 9, Mary, born Sept. 21, 1705; married, June 3, 1725, John Ball; 10, John, born Aug. 4, 1709;(?) died Dec. 1729.

54. Ann, born Watertown, Aug. 4, 1662.

55. Sarah, born Watertown, 1663; married, March 30, 1687, William Hagar, Jr., and had children: 1, William,(?) married, Dec. 13, 1711, Mary Flagg, and settled in Waltham; 2, Sarah, married, May 13, 1712, John Flagg; 3, John, born April 28, 1725; married Sarah ——; owned the covenant, Aug. 26, 1722;

4, Ebenezer, born Aug. 13, 1698; married, Feb. 23, 1725–6, Lydia Barnard; 5, Joseph, born Jan. 1, 1701–2; married, Jan. 1, 1729–30, Grace Bigelow; 6, Mehitable, born May 7, 1704; married, Feb. 28, 1726–7, Joseph Traverse of Sherburne; 7, Mary; (?) 8, Mercy, died in Waltham, Nov. 23, 1772, aged 65.

64. †Abel, born Watertown, May 20, 1688; died in Watertown, March 4, 1720.

III. 64. *Abel Benjamin,*

Born Watertown, Mass., May 20, 1668; died Watertown, Mass., March 4, 1720. He was the son of John and Lydia (Allen) Benjamin, who was the son of John and Abigail (——) Benjamin, the immigrant. He resided in Watertown, where he was admitted to the full communion of the church of Christ, Feb. 6, 1697–8. He married

Abigail ——.

Children:

65. Abel, born Watertown, 1696; died in infancy, in Watertown, 1697.
66. Jonathan, born Watertown, Feb. 18, 1697; died 1731; married, Feb. 1, 1719–20, Susanna Norcross, and had children: 1, Joshua, born Feb. 13, 1721; married, March 25, 1745, Sarah Ball of Concord; 2, Susanna, born Nov. 10, 1723; 3, Mary, born May 24, 1726: married, July 4, 1753, John Whitney of Waltham; 4, Abel, born Sept. 15, 1731; married, April 24, 1753, Elizabeth Nutting. Abel Benjamin belonged to Capt. Jonathan Brown's Company, that went to Fort William Henry in 1758, and on the return list he is marked as deceased. He was father of Lieut. Samuel, a revolutionary soldier, who settled in Livermore, Me.

72. Abigail, born Watertown, Sept. 7, 1699.
73. Susanna, born Watertown.
74. †Caleb, born Watertown, Jan. 28, 1702; died Windsor, Vt., March 8, 1775.
75. Ann, born Watertown, Jan 21, 1703–4; married, March 5, 1723–4, Nathaniel Bond, who was ensign in Captain Jeduthan Baldwin's Company in 1759; and it is supposed that he moved to Sturbridge, and was 2d lieutenant in Captain Fletcher's Company, Nov. 1760. They had children: 1, Anna, bapt. March 28, 1755; 2, Nathaniel, born Sept. 15, 1726; 3, Jona-

than, born Sept. 25, 1728; 4, Abigail, born Dec. 11, 1730; 5, Elizabeth, bapt. Feb. 4, 1732–3; 6, Seth, bapt. Dec. 22, 1734.

82. Abel, born Watertown, March 31, 1706; died Watertown,(?) 1729.

83. Rebecca, born Watertown, June 11, 1708; married, Jan. 29, 1733–4, Edmund Livermore, and had children: 1, Elizabeth, born Nov. 12, 1734; 2, Samuel, born June, 1736; 3, Josiah, bapt. Dec. 31, 1738; 4, Josiah, bapt. April 6, 1740; died in the army. Rebecca administered on the estate, in Sturbridge, Aug. 21, 1750.

88. Elizabeth, born Watertown, Jan. 1710–11.

89. Elizabeth, born Watertown, July 3, 1712;(?) married, Aug. 12, 1735, Samuel Mansfield, and had children: 1, Elizabeth, born Dec. 11, 1736; died Jan. 1737–8; 2, Samuel, born Dec. 1738; died, aged 13 mos.; 3, Daniel, born Oct. 8, 1740; married, July 2, 1761, Eunice Fiske; 4, Elizabeth, born June 20, 1743; married, April 16, 1761, David Fiske; 5, David, born Sept. 25, 1745; 6, Lois, born April 18, 1748; 7, Samuel, born Dec. 22, 1750; 8, Jonas, and 9, Lois, (twins,) born Oct. 14, 1753.

99. Mary, born Watertown, Aug. 8, 1714.

IV. 74. *Caleb Benjamin,*

Born Watertown, Jan. 28, 1702; died Windsor, Vt., March 8, 1775, aged 73. Son of Abel and Abigail (——) Benjamin, grandson of John and Lydia (Allen) Benjamin, and great-grandson of John Benjamin, the immigrant. He resided in Watertown and Hardwick, Mass., and in Windsor, Vt., where he died and was buried. His grave-stone is somewhat marred. April 5, 1725, Caleb Benjamin of Watertown conveyed land in Southborough, and land in Marlborough, to Joseph Ball, Jr. Benjamin Grover of Hardwick, husbandman, conveys to Caleb Benjamin of Hardwick, husbandman, one tract of land lying and situated in Hardwick, on the easterly side of Ware River, northerly upon the highway.

March 1, 1743, Caleb Benjamin was chosen a surveyor of the highways in Hardwick, and in March 4, 1744–5, was chosen constable, and surveyor of the highways, and in 1746 served as constable.

He married, Aug. 16, 1726,

Abigail Livermore,

Born ——; died at Hardwick, June 24, 1756. Dr. Bond says, that she died 1786, aged 87. We find upon the Hardwick Records, that "Abigail wife of Caleb Benjamin died June 24, 1756." We also find upon the same records, that "Wid Abigail Benjamin died March 30 1755." We suppose the Widow Abigail Benjamin to be the mother of Caleb and the wife of Abel Benjamin.

Children:

100. Anna, born Lexington, Nov. 23, 1725. Out of wedlock.
101. Abigail, born Watertown, June 3, 1726–7; married Hardwick, Dec. 25, 1751, Joseph Powers.
102. Caleb, born Watertown, May 26, 1729; died Wendell, Mass.; married ——.
103. Keziah, born Watertown, April 18, 1731; died young.
104. John, born ——; died in Barnard, Vt. "He married a sister of a Mr. Gibb's wife of Windsor," and had children: Caleb, John, Daniel, Ezra, and Abigail.

110. Abel, born ——; married Hardwick, Mass., March 22, 1759, Susannah Carpenter, and died in Wendell, Mass.
111. Mary, born Hardwick, Mass., Sept. 1, 1743, bapt. Oct. 16; died West Windsor; she married John Smead.
112. Anna, born Hardwick, June 5, 1746; died March (?) 15, 1814, aged 68; married Hardwick, Sept. 19, 1769, Eliphalet Washburn. He was celebrated as a school teacher. He died Dec. 14, 1816, aged 75. Their grave-stones are in the ancient burial-ground at Hardwick.
113. Keziah, born Hardwick, May 6, bapt. June 25, 1749: died Windsor, Vt., Sept. 24, 1835, aged 86 years, 4 months. She married Solomon Burke. [See Burke IV., No. 40, p. 33.

Appendix D—page 64.

AN ADDRESS DELIVERED AT THE FUNERAL OF BENJAMIN BURKE, ESQ., AT NASHUA, N. H., SEPTEMBER 30, 1855.

BY REV. GEORGE B. JEWETT,

PASTOR OF THE FIRST CONGREGATIONAL CHURCH, NASHUA, N H.

Selections of Scripture.

What man is he that liveth, and shall not see death? shall he deliver his soul from the hand of the grave? Selah.—PSALM 89: 48.

One generation passeth away, and another generation cometh: but the earth abideth forever.—ECCL. 1: 4.

There is no man that hath power over the spirit to retain the spirit; neither hath he power in the day of death; and there is no discharge in that war; neither shall wickedness deliver those that are given to it.—ECCL. 8: 8.

When a few years are come, then I shall go the way whence I shall not return.—JOB 16: 22.

Then shall the dust return to the earth as it was; and the spirit shall return unto God who gave it.—ECCL. 12: 7.

Jesus said unto her, I am the resurrection and the life: he that believeth in me, though he were dead, yet shall he live; And whosoever liveth and believeth in me shall never die. Believeth thou this?—JOHN 11: 25, 26.

Precious in the sight of the Lord is the death of his saints.—PSALM 116: 15.

And I heard a voice from heaven saying unto me, Write, Blessed are the dead which die in the Lord from henceforth; Yea, saith the Spirit, that they may rest from their labors; and their works do follow them.—REV. 14: 13.

Remarks.

Such are a few, among many passages of inspired truth designed and adapted to impress upon our memories the thought that death is inevitable; that human life is transitory and vain; so that to the servants of God, death, especially if it overtakes us in a good old age when we are ready to be gathered to our fathers in peace, is not only not to be dreaded, but even to be desired. And if these truths were not constantly repeated in the Word of God, the frequent monitions of his providence could not fail to keep them in remembrance. Occasions like the present are of almost daily occurrence. One day it is the little child over whose grave we are called to weep; yet not sorrowing as those who have "no hope." The next day the man of middle life is cut down in all the strength of his manhood and in the midst of his usefulness. And again we are called to stand by the grave of one who died full of years and honors, like a shock of corn fully ripe for the Master's use. In this last case we feel, instinctively, that the transition from earth to heaven is easy, natural, and earnestly to be desired. We feel that it would be wholly unreasonable to wish to detain our aged Christian friend here upon earth; to hold him back from the presence of his Saviour, and from the purity, the fellowship, and the bliss of the heavenly state. As we watch by his bedside, and witness his sufferings, we feel almost tempted, like the poor peasant on the Welsh mountains, every morning to open our casement towards the East and look out to see if the Lord Jesus Christ is not coming to release our friend and his from the bondage under which he here groans. In the death of the aged Christian there is much, very much, to comfort and sustain surviving relatives. You will allow me to say, that I trust the death of him whose remains are now before us was that of a believer in Jesus. My acquaintance with him has been, it is true, a short one, but one which I shall always recall with pleasure and satisfaction.

On entering upon the labors of the ministry, in this place, my eye singled him out, in my congregation, as an attentive and apparently devout hearer of the Word. I noticed the extreme effort it cost him and his aged companion, enfeebled, as they both were, by the infirmities of years, to present themselves in the Sanctuary. They were among the first whom I visited; and one of my last visits, before leaving home on my recent absence, was paid at the bedside of our departed friend. In every interview, which it has been my privilege to have with him, the subject of religion, either in its relations to the individual heart, or to the Church of Christ, or both, has been the principal, and in fact almost the only topic of conversation; and that, too, because this subject was the one of his choice; the one which seemed to be in his estimation the most important; the one on which he loved to dwell. At his request, these interviews were, in every instance, if I mistake not, sanctified by prayer. Very frequently and earnestly did he express to me his desire to see the work of God revived, and the Church of Christ built up. I well remember the joy it gave me, just after I had preached a discourse on the text, "O Lord, revive thy work," to hear him say, that he went directly from the house of God to his own place of secret prayer, and there poured out his soul in supplication for a revival of pure and undefiled religion in this community. Correspondent to this is the testimony of those who have been with him during his last hours. At the lucid intervals he was permitted to enjoy, his thoughts seemed to be much on spiritual themes. His prayers for forgiveness of sin and for acceptance with God through the merits of His Son have left a lasting impression on the memory of those who stood by his bedside even until the angel of death gave him at last a gentle release from the pains of this mortal body. Can we doubt, then, that his prayers were heard, and that, while we are assembled on the evening of this Sabbath, to pay him our last tribute of respect, can we doubt, I say, that his freed spirit is enjoying not merely its first, but its endless Sabbath in heaven? and that, too, "in a city which hath no need of the sun, neither of the moon, to shine in it; for the glory of the Lord doth lighten it, and the Lamb is the light thereof."

Allow me, therefore, to administer to you who mourn the loss of a companion, or a father, the full consolation which these thoughts are calculated to impart. Let me remind you that far beyond the allotted period of human life have you been permitted to enjoy his society. Let me remind you how much occasion you have for gratitude that, during the long period of his physical and mental weakness, you were permitted and enabled to minister to his wants and alleviate his sufferings. Let me assure you, his children, if indeed you need the assurance of a stranger, that all your filial affection and devotion was by him most fully appreciated and most gratefully acknowledged. I know whereof I affirm, when I say that your welfare for time and for eternity lay very near his heart. And let me say to you, my venerable friend, that your separation from him with whom you have spent so many years of your earthly pilgrimage will be short at longest; and that when your fellowship with your beloved companion is renewed, I trust it will be under circumstances more favorable to unalloyed enjoyment than are those of time and sense. I trust it will be where there is no more sickness, nor sorrow, nor sighing, nor sinning, nor separation, nor death; but in a world where those who have known and loved each other on earth will be permitted to dwell together in the purest and sweetest followship, unchangeably and forever! And let us all, my friends, learn from these scenes, which are passing before us, a lesson of our own mortality. To my mind, one of the most impressive chapters of Scripture is that which contains the genealogy of the patriarchs from Adam to Noah, of whom it is said in every instance except in the case of Enoch, notwithstanding the number of years which they lived, notwithstanding the sons which they begat, the wealth they accumulated, the works they performed, and the blessings and honors they received; yet of every one of them it is said, with impressive brevity, "and he died!" "The fathers, where are they? and the prophets, do they live forever?" Nay! few at most and evil at best are the days of the years of our earthly pilgrimage. We know—we know it from our own consciousness of frailty; we know it from our daily observation of the course of God's providence; we know it from the evidence which is this moment set before us,—that, when a few years are come, we must, "we shall go the way whence we shall not return." We know, too, on the authority of God's Word, that "after death cometh the judgment." Seeing, then, that our days are determined, and that there is a bound which we cannot pass, how important is it that we so number our days as to apply our hearts unto wisdom; so live, that we can say, "for me to live is Christ, to die is gain;" so live, that "when our earthly house of this tabernacle is dissolved, we shall have a building of God, a house not made with hands, eternal in the heavens;" so live, that we shall hear at last a voice from heaven saying unto us, "Blessed are the dead which die in the Lord from henceforth; yea, saith the Spirit, that they may rest from their labors; and their works do follow them."

Appendix E—page 96.

WILL OF ALEXANDER ALVORD.

Northampton decemb^e 6. 1689 at ye Co^re of Common pleas ye aforesaid Will was p^rsented the witnesses thereto mr Joseph Hawley & Jno. Lyman Examined concerning there being prsent at ye tyme of Allexander Alvord signeing & sealeing it wch they acknowledged and set their hands thereto and further made Oath that ye sd Allexand^r was then of sound diposeing mynde. JOHN PYNCHON.

Hampshire Co., Vol. 1, 265. JAMES CORNISH.

Will.

May 23, 1687. Whereas I Alexand^r Alvord of Northampton in ye Countie of Hampshire in ye Massachusets Bay in New England being weak and deceased in strength and well stricken in years, dayly Lookeing w^{n} I shall go hence vnto ye place appointed for all liveing doe therefore make, ordaine constitute & appoint this my Last Will and Testament, I being of perfect memory and sound Understanding I comitt my soul to God y^{t} gave it and Jesus that redeemed it.

Hopeing through his merrits to receive pardon of all my sins and to be accepted in ye sight of God.

I leave my Body to be buried in comely manner at ye discretion of my Executor herafter mentioned & as for that portion of outward estate y^{t} God hath given me I dispose, alienate and bequeath it as followeth viz:

Whereas my son John Alvord; my daughter Abigaile wife to Thomas Roote; Mary Weller deceased; and Elizabeth Birth deceased; having received ye full of their portiones already, I only give as follows viz.

To John Alvord twenty shillings; to Sam^{ll} Root son to Thomas Root twenty shillings; to two of my sons Weller's children, Experience, and Abigail, to each of ym 20^{s}., to Henry Burt's child 20^{s}.

Item to Thomas Alvord twentie shillings and to his two sons Thomas and John twentie shillings to each of them.

To my son Benjamin Alverd I give that part of my old house joyneing to that wch my son Weller lived in, togeather with that piece of Land it standeth upon which was given me by the town.

Item to my son Jeremiah Alvord I give thirtie pounds. To my daughter Sarah Alvord I give thirtie pounds.

Item, to my son Jonth Alvord I give twentie pounds;

The rest of my Estate my just and due debts being pay^{d} I give to my son Ebenezer Alvord viz: my house barne, orchard, pasture, meadow land, stock, debts, household stuff and all my estate whatsoever, both moveables and immoveables.

Alsoe my will is that ye Legacies be paid out of ye stock, debts & in moveable Estate, and to be payd to each of them, the one half at my decease, the other half within two years after; & my will is y^{t} my son Ebenezer shall not alianate any part of ye lands given him but shall make such disposall of ye same to the heirs of his body as shall see cause.

And I do hereby constitute and appoint my son Ebenezer Alverd to be ye sole Executor of this my last will and testament.

In witness hereunto I have subscribed and sealed this 23^{d} May 1687, and I desire my trustie ffriende Mr Hawley to see this my will to be accomplished and to take speciall care of my unmarried children; to advise them in matching & to have ye oversight of y^m while they remayne in a single condition.

ALLEXANDER ALVORD
his A. A. marke.

Signed sealed in ye p^rsence of us
Joseph Hawley
John Lyman.

[Northampton Reg. of Probate, Hampshire Co., Vol. 1, p. 265.

APPENDIX F—page 111.

WILL OF JOSEPH ALVORD.

[Copied from Hampshire County Probate Office Court Files.]
See Alvord No. 49.

In the [illegible] of God Amen, I Joseph Alvord of Northampton, in the County of Hampshire, in his Majesty's Province of the Massachusetts Bay, in New England, being in health, and of sound mind, and memory; Blessed be God; do this eighth day of Anno Domini, 1774, make and Publish this my last will and testament, in manner following; that is to say, Principally, I commend my soul to God the Father of Spirits, hoping for pardon, and Gracious acceptance with him, only, on account of the Glorious and perfect Mediator, and atonement, made for miserable sinners by the Lord Jesus Christ; and I desire my body, may be decently interred, at the direction of my Executor, hereafter named, in full faith of the great Christian Doctrine of the Resurrection of the Body; and what followeth is my last will and testament;

As to worldly estate wherewith the Lord has been pleased to bless me; to wit in the first place;

I give, and bequeath, to my beloved wife Clemence, the vse, and improvement, of one half of the Homestead I now live upon, together with the vse, of the one half of my house, and half of the barn, also the improvement of ten acres of my meadow land where she shall please to take it; also the one half of my Inner Common's land; to have, and to hold so long, and for such term of time, as she shall remain the widow of me the Testar, and no longer, also I give & bequeath to my sd wife all my household stuff to her disposal forever.

I give, and devise, to my son Elisha, four acres of my pasture land, being inclosed within the meadow fence under the hill, on the south side of the pasture; also one acre lying on the hill, adjoining the sd four acres; also two acres and three quarters of land lying in the meadow in Venturer's field;

Also woodland lying in the Long Division, so called that I had of my uncle 'John Alvord, from the east end of sd lot the North Branch Manham River, to have, and to hold, to him, and his heirs forever.

To my son Joseph I give and devise the homestead he now liveth upon, on the east side of the County Road, that I purchased of Henry Curtis, it being three acres and twenty rods.

Also two acres of land lying in the meadow at the Walnut tree, called Clapp's lot; also one acre and half of land lying in the meadow at the upper end of Young Rain Bow at the Point; also my second draught in the Inner Common land, lying near to Fortification Hill, to have and to hold to him and his heirs for ever.

I give and devise to my son Stephen twenty shillings more than I have already advanced him.

I give and bequeath to my son Medad the homestead I now live upon together with the house and barn and all other buildings standing thereon allowing to my wife the improvement of the one half as above said.

I give and bequeath to my son Medad five acres of land lying in the pasture within the meadow fence on the north side of sd pasture; also five acres and one quarter lying in the Upper Meadow in the Second Division;

Also five acres and one half lying in the old Rainbow, also my lot of land at the Walnut trees containing three acres; also two acres and one half of land, lying at the upper end of Young Rainbow, also all my land in the Long Division that was originally laid out to my Hon[d] Father Ebenezer Alvord, deceased; from the east end of sd lot running westward, to the north Branch of Manham River, except that part of it which I have conveyed to David Clark by deed of sale:

Also my first draught in the Inner Common land lying on the Boggy Meadow; to have, and to hold, to him and his heirs forever.

I give to my son Simeon ten shillings more than I have already advanced to him in full satisfaction for his part and portion of my estate.

I give to my daughter Lucy Parsons five shillings more than I gave her at her marriage.

The remainder of my estate both real and personal if any there should be after my just debts are paid, I give to my son Medad to be to him and his heirs forever. Lastly I hereby constitute and appoint my son Elisha my sole Executor of this my last will and testament.

In witness whereof I have hereunto set my hand and seal the day and year above written.

Signed, Sealed, Published and Declared by the before named Joseph Alvord the Testator as his last will and testament.

JOSEPH ALVORD.

In the presence of us who have hereunto subscribed our names as witnesses in presence of the Testator and in the presence of each other.

Samuel Mather
Timothy Mather sworn
Daniel Strong sworn.

Codicil.

A Codicil to be added to and to be taken as a part of the last will and testament of Mr. Joseph Alvord of Northampton in the county of Hampshire, Yeoman.

Whereas I have made and published in writing bearing date the eight day of November Anno Domini 1774; which will, and the devices, and bequests therein contained were at that time according to my best judgment and discretion; Yet on the account of the decease of my wife, which has happened since that time and diverse other alterations in my circumstances which have since taken place too many here to recite and as it has pleased God not only to continue my life but also my understanding and judgment so that I am still (Blessed be God) of a sound and disposing mind and memory I do this seventh day of November A. D. 1782 make and publish this Codicil that is to say all the lands and tenements which in and by my above mentioned will, it is declared that I give and devised to my son Elisha Alvord, which I still own, I do hereby give and devise to my three grandsons, and the sons of the said Elisha, to wit; Eleazer Elisha and William, to have and to hold to them in fee simple by equal shares as tenants in common and not as joint tenants on and under the conditions, restrictions limitations and provisoes herein after expressed and declared and not otherwise, that is to say if every and all of my said grandsons should die without issue of his body lawfully begotten and living at the time of the death of the father before he shall attain the age of twenty one years and living, my grandson Daniel Alvord the son of my son Elisha then my will is that he the said Daniel shall take and have in fee simple all the said lands and tenements subject to all conditions and provisions which are herein after provided and declared relating to the taking and holding of the same lands by my said grandsons Eleazer Elisha and William so far as the said conditions or provisions respect any duties or payments to be made and performed by them to my said son Elisha or his present wife Mary.

And in case of the death of any one or two of my said grandsons Eleazer Elisha or William without issue of his body lawfully begotten and living at the time of the death of the father before he shall attain the age of twenty one years, in that case the survivors or the surveyors of the said Eleazer Elisha and William together with him the aforesaid Daniel shall take and hold in fee simple by equal shares as tenants in common and not as joint tenants all the said lands and tenements always subject to the conditions provisoes injunctions directions here expressed and declared respecting the having and holding of the said lands by my said grandsons and any of them the heirs or assigns of any of them To wit;

That each of my said grandsons, &c., &c., shall annually from the respective times when the said lands shall fall to them, respectively in the life time of my said son Elisha or after his decease, the said Mary his now wife living and being his widow, pay to him my said son Elisha and after his death to his widow aforesaid during such widowhood such and part of the sum of four pounds of the now lawful silver money of this Commonwealth as shall be in proportion to four pounds, &c., &c.

And to my grand daughter Sarah Alvord, the daughter of my son Joseph, I give and bequeath my spare feather bed and bolster and the two rugs belonging to the said bed also three of my pewter plates as good as one with another.

And all the residue of my household stuff, I give and bequeath to my daughter Lucy the wife of Mr. Elisha Parsons forever.

And I do hereby constitute, make & ordain my son Medad Alvord to be joint Executors with my aforesaid son Elisha of my last will and testament, &c., &c.

In witness whereof I hereunto set my hand and seal the seventh day of November A. D. 1782.

JOSEPH ALVORD.

Signed, sealed, &c., &c.
Joseph Hawley
Ebenezer Wright
Enos Wright.

A Second Codicil.

Not much different from the former codicil. Confirms his will dated Nov. 8, 1774; codicil dated Nov. 7, 1782; and this codicil, dated Aug. 15, 1785. Prob. Feb. 4th, 1786.

JOSEPH ALVORD.

APPENDIX G—page 118.

WILL OF JOHN ALVORD.

In the Name of God Amen The sixteenth day of March An Dom 1758.

I John Alvord of South Hadley in the County of Hampshire in the province of Massachusetts Bay in New England, being weak in body but of perfect mind and memory; thanks be given to God therefore calling to mind the mortality of my body and knowing that it is appointed for all men once to die; do make and ordain this my last will and testament, that is to say principally and first of all;

I give and recommend my soul to the hands of God that gave it; and my body I recommend to the Earth to be buried in decent Christian burial at the discretion of my Executor's nothing doubting but at the General Resurrection, I shall receive the same again by the mighty power of God.

And as touching such worldly Estate wherewith it has pleased God to bless me in this world I give, demise, and dispose of the same in the following manner and form, my just debts & funeral charges being first paid.

I give to Azariah my second son six pounds lawful money and the remainder of my estate both Real and Personal I give and bequeath to my children, namely, Moses, Azariah, Abigail, Jerusha, Dorcas, Rachel, Phineas, Luther, and Rebecca, to be divided to each of them in equal proportions;

My daughter Abigail to have the use and improvement of my daughter Rebecca's part until said Rebecca arrive at the age of eighteen years or to the time of her marriage (which shall first happen) provided my said daughter Abigail shall take care of, provide for, and bring up said Rebecca until she arrive to the above said time, and I do will and appoint my brother Thomas White and brother Saul Alvord executors of this my last will and testament & I do hereby utterly disallow all other testaments or wills by me in any ways before named ratifying and confirming this and no other to be my last will and testament.

In witness whereof I have hereunto set my hand & seal the day and date abovesaid.

Signed, sealed, published, pronounced & declared by the said John Alvord as his last will and testament in presence of us subscribers who also; signed in his presence.

JOHN ALVORD. [Seal.]

Elijah Alvord
Gad Alvord
Daniel Nash.

Codicil.

Codicil to the above will. South Hadley, July 6th, 1758.

Probate of the above will and codicil, July 11, 1758. For Inventory see Vol. 9, 42–3 pages.

APPENDIX H—page 125.

ELISHA ALVORD.

Who formerly owned the land in Northampton on which the Court House now stands, and also the land under the Old Town Hall?

Answer.—Elisha Alvord, son of Joseph and brother of Stephen Alvord. [See Alvord No. 95.

The town has built a new Town Hall on another site.

What can the land or buildings thereupon be used for?

Sept. 23, 1767. A warrant was issued for a town meeting, to be held Sept. 28, 1767, at 9 A. M., then and there to determine whether the town will grant any sum of money towards purchasing Elisha Alvord's house lot for the town's use, and particularly for the purpose of setting the New Court House on, which is soon to be set up.

After considerable debate and conversation about the clause in the warrant. The question was put, whether the town would grant any sum of money towards purchasing Elisha Alvord's house lot, with a view of setting the New Court House, soon to be erected, on a part of the same, and it passed in the negative. [Abstract. Joseph Hawley, Moderator.

Deed of Elisha Alvord of Northampton to sundry persons.

To all People to whom these presents shall come, Greeting;

Know ye, that I Elisha Alvord, of Northampton, in the County of Hampshire, & Province of the Massachusetts Bay in New England, Shopkeeper, for, and in consideration of the sum of One hundred and thirty pounds lawfull money, to me in hand, before the Ensealing hereof, well and truly paid by Ebenezer Hunt, Timothy Dwight Junr. Seth Pomeroy, Caleb Strong, Solomon Stoddard, Samuel Clarke, Epraim Wright, William Lyman, Seth Lyman, John King, Samuel Parsons, Jonathan Allen, Selah Wright, Joseph Allen, ———, Joseph Cooke, Joseph Lyman, Benjamin Sheldon, Jun., Quartus Pomeroy, Elisha Lyman, Gid[illegible]larke, George Hodge, Hezekiah Russell, Thomas Bridgman, Elijah Southwell, Asahel Clapp, Abner Barnard, Daniel Hitchcock, William Mather, Levi Shephard, Eliphaz Strong, Seth Clapp, Aaron Wright, Eliphaz Clapp, Elnathan Wright, Joseph Parsons, Simeon Parsons, Haines Kingsley, Aaron Kingsley, Timothy Parsons, Enos Kingsley, Asa Wright, Josiah Parsons Jun, Titus King, Oliver Lyman, Elihu Lyman, Elkanah Burt, Ebenezer Clapp, Elihu Clark, Pliny Pomeroy, Abijah Wait, John Parsons Jun. Simeon Clapp, Joseph Clapp, Joseph Hutchings, Lemuel Lyman, David Lyman, Elias Lyman Jun. and Asahel Danks all of Northampton aforesaid, and Samuel Fairfax of Hatfield in the county and province, aforesaid; generous Subscribers of the Consideration above mentioned; for the purchase of the premises hereinafter described for the public use of erecting a Court House thereon for the sole use and benefit of the Inhabitants of the county of Hampshire, the receipt whereof I do hereby acknowledge and am therewith fully satisfied and contented have given, granted bargained, sold, alienated, conveyed and confirmed, and by these presents do freely, fully, and absolutely, give, grant bargain, sell, alien, convey & confirm unto the Inhabitants of the county of Hampshire aforesaid and their successors forever a certain small tract or parcel of land in Northampton aforesaid, situated near the meeting house; there in quantity about seventy three rods; being the houselot where I now dwell; surrounded and described by the following lines and bounds, viz; beginning at a young buttonwood tree in a corner of said houselot standing east thirteen degrees & thirty minutes south of the south east corner of the Belfrey & at the distance of one chain & twenty three links of Gunter's chain therefrom, & from said tree runs east, forty three degrees north, one chain and one link; thence north, ten degrees and thirty minutes east, two chains & forty seven links; thence west thirty five degrees north, one chain and twenty links; thence South twenty four degrees West, one chain and thirty three links; thence south twenty six degrees and thirty minutes west, one chain and sixty two links; thence south twenty six degrees east, twenty five links; thence east forty degrees south, one chain and twenty links to the button wood tree abovesaid; always excepting, and reserving to myself, the several buildings standing on the same land, with liberty of egress & regress for the purpose of taking down said buildings, and removing the materials thereof, which is to be done with all convenient speed.

To have and to hold the said granted premises with the appurtenances (saving only the buildings standing on the same as above excepted & reserved and liberty to demolish them and take off the materials) to the proper use of the Inhabitants of the said County of Hampshire, in succession for the Term of & so long as Courts are or shall be held by law in said town of Northampton, for the purpose of a green or common & for the erecting a Courthouse or Courthouses thereon as shall be ordered by the proper authority for setting up and erecting the same; and whensoever that term shall cease and determine, and the Courts are removed & shall be held at some other town or place pursuant to law, which are now held there then the same premises shall be and remain as an open uninclosed common for the use and benefit of the inhabitants of the said town of Northampton in succession for ever; for erecting any meeting house for public worship, or town house for town affairs, or meeting and for no other purpose whatsoever;

And I the said Elisha Alvord for myself & my heirs, executors, and administrators, do covenant and grant to, and with the said inhabitants of said county of Hampshire, and their successors that before, and at the ensealing hereof I am the true sole & lawfull owner of the above bargained premises and am lawfully seized and possessed of the same in my own proper right as of a good and absolute estate of inheritance in fee simple & have in myself good right to sell and convey the same as aforesaid, and that the same shall & may be held by the said inhabitants of said county of Hampshire in succession for the use and purpose aforesaid and enjoyed by them free and clear of, and from all manner of let molestation or incumbrance whatsoever that might in any measure make void or obstruct this present deed; and I and my heirs, &c., will at all times for ever hereafter warrant and defend the same to them and their successors for the use and purpose aforesaid.

In witness whereof I the said Elisha Alvord have hereunto set my hand and seal this sixth day of October in the seventh year of the reign of our Sovereign Lord George the Third over Great Britain France and Ireland, King, &c. Ano Dom̄ 1767.

Sam[l] Mather. ELISHA ALVORD.
John Row.

I Mary Alvord wife of the above named Elisha Alvord in consideration of what is acknowledged to be received above do relinquish and give up to the said inhabitants of said county all my right of dowers in the above described premises and do hereby absolutely debar myself from my demand thereof forever hereafter.

In witness whereof I have set my hand and seal the day and year above said. MARY ALVORD.

Signed sealed by the said Elisha and Mary in presence of
Samuel Mather
John Rowe.

[Copied from a deed in the office of Clerk of Courts—Northampton, Mass.

At a town meeting held Northampton, Sept. 3, 1852, The question of the removal of the Old Town Hall being brought before the town and freely discussed by several gentlemen, Dr. Allen presented the following vote:

"Voted, That the Town will remove the Old Town Hall, and give the land under it to the Inhabitants of the County of Hampshire, to be used forever for the purposes mentioned in the deed of the Alvord lot, dated A. D. 1767." The above vote was rejected by five yeas and eighty nays.

The following preamble and votes were then submitted to the town and passed by a large majority:

Whereas, a petition is pending before the County Commissioners, requesting some action in reference to the revocation of a license to erect a Town Hall on the Alvord lot, so called, and a removal of the building; and whereas, there is a difference of opinion as to the rights of the Town in the premises, and as to the location of the Alvord lot, and whether said building is upon it—

"Voted, That the Town, not conceding any rights or title already gained, and not admitting the building to be in any part upon said Alvord lot, hereby declare, that the lapse of time hereafter shall not operate to give the Town further title than is already acquired, or to deprive any party adversely interested of title to the same, provided the County or County Commissioners take no measures to deprive the Town of possession or to eject them."

It would improve the appearance of the village of Northampton if the Old Town Hall was moved off of the Alvord lot, and the land, under and around it, was used for a Green.

Appendix I.

BIRTHS.

[From Northampton, Mass., Town Records.]

Ebenezer, son of Alexander and ——	Alvord b.	Dec.	23, 1665.
Jeremiah, son of Alexander and Mary	" "		1663.
Jonathan, son of Alexander and Mary	" "	April	6, 1669.
John, son of Thomas and Johannah	" "	Aug.	10, 1682.
Thomas, son of " " "	" "	Aug.	28, 1683.
John, " " " "	" "	Oct.	19, 1684.
Josiah, " " " "	" "	Feb.	7, 1687.
Abigail, daughter of Benjamin	" "		1691.
Ebenezer, son of Ebenezer and Ruth	" "	Aug.	24, 1693.
Benjamin, " Benjamin and Deborah	" "	Sept.	1695.
Jonathan, " Jonathan and Thankful	" "	April	9, 1694.
John, " " " "	" "		1696.
Joseph, " Eliezer(?) and Ruth	" "	March	1697.
Deborah, daughter of Benjamin and Deborah	" "	May	1698.
Mary, " Ebenezer and Ruth	" "	June	24, 1699.
Experience, " Benjamin and Deborah	" "	Oct.	5, 1700.
Patience, " Jonathan and Thankful	" "	June	22, 1701.
Noah, son of Ebenezer and Ruth	" "	June	27, 1701.
Josiah, " Benjamin and Deborah	" "	April	13, 1704.

Zebadiah, son of Jonathan and Thankful Alvord, b. Oct. 30, 1705.
Sarah, daughter of Benjamin and Deborah " " May 28, 1707.
Mary, " Jonathan and Thankful " " July 21, 1707.
Thankful, " " " " " " Aug. 10, 1709.
Thomas, son of Thomas and Mary " " May 18, 1710.
Ruth, daughter of Ebenezer and Elizabeth " " Aug. 24, 1710.
Jonathan, son of *John* and Mary " " Nov. 16, 1711.

(I think the last should be Jonathan, son of *Thomas* and Mary.)

John, son of John and Dorcas Alvord, b. Oct. 29, 1711.
James, " Ebenezer and Elizabeth " " July 22, 1712.
Aaron, " Thomas and Mary " " July 16, 1713.
Mindwell, of John and Dorcas " " Aug. 4, 1713.
Elizabeth, daughter of Ebenezer and Elizabeth " " Sept. 7, 1713.
Seth, son of Thomas and Mary " " Nov. 13, 1714.
Rebecca, daughter of Ebenezer " " Oct. 25, 1716.
Rebecca, " " and Elizabeth " " Feb. 10, 1717.
Saul, son of John and Dorcas " " April 13, 1717.
Elijah, son of John and Dorcas " " Jan. 17, 1718-19.
Dorcas, daughter of John and Dorcas " " March 28, 1720.
Asahel, son of Thomas and Mary " " Dec. 16, 1720.
Ebenezer, son of Ebenezer and Elizabeth " " Dec, 17, 1720.
Elisha, " Thomas and Mary " " June 19, 1717.
Zebadiah, " John and Prudence " " April 20, 1722.
Mary, daughter of Thomas and Mary " " Sept. 3, 1724.
Zebadiah, son of John and Prudence " " Feb. 14, 1724.
Sarah, daughter of " " " " " March 21, 1726.
Eunice, daughter of Benjamin and Eunice " " June 14, 1727.
John, son of John and Prudence, " " Jan. 16, 1728.
Rachel, daughter of John and Prudence " " March 26, 1730.
Mary, " " " " " " Feb. 19, 1734.
Martha, " Saul and Martha " " June 29, 1747.
Lydia, " " " " " " Sept. 7, 1748.
Thankful, daughter of Jonathan and Elizabeth " " Jan. 16, 1749.
Saul, son of Saul and Martha " " May 20, 1751.
Saul, " " " " " " July 9, 1753.
Ann, daughter of Saul and Martha " " Oct. 7, 1755.
Eunice, " " " " " " Jan. 2, 1758.
Jonathan, son of Jonathan and Elizabeth " " Nov. 29, 1751.
Beriah, daughter of " " " " " Feb. 3, 1754.

Jehiel, son of Jonathan and Elizabeth	Alvord,	b.	Jan.	7,	1756.
Eliab, " Ebenezer and Catharine	"	"	Sept.	4,	1755.
Elizabeth, daughter of Ebenezer and Catharine	"	"	Feb.	15,	1757.
Rachel, " Phineas	"	"	Sept.	28,	1783.
Naomi, " "	"	"	Aug.	10,	1789.
Samuel, son of "	"	"	Jan.	5,	1792.
Timothy, " "	"	"	Oct.	5,	1804.
Lewis, " "	"	"	April	11,	1807.

MARRIAGES.

[From Northampton Town Records.]

1666.	Thomas Root and Abigail Alvord.
March 24, 1669–70.	John Weller and Mary Alvord.
March 22, 1680.	Thomas Alvord and Johannah Taylor.
1685.(?)	Hinry Burt and Elizabeth Alvord.
1691.	Ebenezer Alvord and Ruth Baker.
1691.	Jeremiah Alvord and Mehitable Root.
Dec. 29, 1708.	John Alvord and Dorcas Liman.
Jan. 24, 1712.	Preserved Bartlett and Elizabeth Alvord.
Jan. 13, 1714.	Samuel Judd and Abigail Alvord.
April 4, 1716.	Henry Burt and Deborah Alvord.
July 30, 1730.	Joseph Alvord and Clemence Wright.
Aug. 4, 1720 or 21.	John Alvord and Prudence Baker.
Jan. 17, 1733.	Benjamin Alvord and Ruth Alexander.
Feb. 2, 1743.	Zebadiah Miller and Rebecca Alvord.
June 28, 1749.	Noah Edwards and Jerusha Alvord.
July 16, 1760.	Isaac Morgan of Springfield and Ruth Alvord of Northampton, by Joseph Hawley, Justice of the Peace.
June 11, 1778.	Jehiel Alvord and Dorothy French, by Rev. Solo[m] Williams.
Oct. 11, 1781.	Daniel Warner, Jr., and Phebe Alvord.
July 11, 1706.	*Judah Wright and Sarah Burke.*
May 10, 1731.	*Jonathan Burke and Thankful Wait.*
Feb. 21, 1782.	Eleazer Alvord and Eunice Clarke.
July 5, 1782.	Phineas Alvord and Rachel Judd.
March 20, 1783.	Daniel Alvord and Susannah Judd.
Dec. 28, 1790.	Israel Bridgman and Sarah Alvord—Rev. S. Williams.

May 10, 1791. Medad Alvord and Betsy Partridge—Rev. S. Williams.

Feb. 27, 1794. Phineas Alvord and Salome Judd—Rev. S. Williams.

June 19, 1797 or 6. Luther Hunt and Eunice Alvord—Rev. S. Williams.

June 18, 1805. Reuben Smith of Northfield and Mrs. Elizabeth Alvord.

June 12, 1806. Mr. Eliab Alvord of Westhampton and Miss Dorothy Parsons.

Sept. 8, 1808. John I. Rogers of Springfield and Miss Naomi Alvord.

Nov. 27, 1816. Cyrus Alvord of South Hadley and Asenath Smith.

April 21, 1803. Percy Alvord and Ann Elizabeth Pelton.

Jan. 17, 1822. Henry Judd of S. Hadley and Maria Alvord of Northampton.

Oct. 7, 1824. Elisha Alvord, Jun., and Naomi Rogers, both of Easthampton.

Oct. 10, 1843. Mr. Amazia Lyman of Hadley and Miss Amanda M. Alvord of Northampton.

RETURN OF MARRIAGES.

South Hadley.

1789. Abiather French of N. and Naomi Alvord of S. Hadley.

Hatfield.

Feb. 6, 1788. Abiather French, Jun., and Beriah Alvord, both of Northampton.

Feb. 27, 1787. Robert Powell of Lanesborough and Clemence Alvord of Northampton, Feb. 27, 1787.

Westfield.

Sept. 22, 1756. John Miller, 3^{d} of Northampton and Hannah Burke of Westfield, by Rev. Ballentine.

Dec. 28, 1722. Wm. Clark of Northampton and Abigail Burke of Westfield, by Capt. John Ashley, J. Peace.

[From Northampton Church Records.]

Dec. 19, 1754.	Ebenezer Alvord and Katharine Strong.
Oct. 27, 1757.	Elisha Alvord and Mary Hamilton.
Dec. 29, 1759.	Joseph Alvord and Sarah Knight.
Feb. 2, 1773.	Joseph Alvord and Submit Chapin.
Jan. 25, 1762.	*Seth Burke and Rebecca Stearnes.*
March 22, 1770.	Elisha Parsons and Lucy Alvord.
Nov. 25, 1773.	Elisha Jones and Sarah Alvord.
Jan. 26, 1775.	Ebenezer Stearns & Thankful Alvord.
June 11, 1778.	Jehiel Alvord and Dorothy French.
July, 1776.	Elisha Alvord and Sarah Danks.
Feb. 21, 1782.	Eleazer Alvord and Eunice Clarke.
1782.	Phineas Alvord and Rachel Judd.
March 20, 1783.	Daniel Alvord and Susannah Judd.
Dec. 28, 1780.	Israel Bridgman and Sarah Alvord.
[Town 1790.]	
May 10, 1791.	Medad Alvord and Betsey Partridge.
Nov. 6, 1794.	Gaius Burt and Hannah Alvord.
June 19, 1796.	Luther Hunt and Eunice Alvord.
Nov. 24, 1800.	Luther Alvord and Eunice Strong.
June 18, 1805.	Capt. Reuben Smith of Northfield and Riem Elizabeth Alvord.
June 12, 1806.	Eliel(?) Alvord of Westhampton and Wid. Katharine Parsons.(?)
June 12, 1807.	Eliel Alvord of Westhampton, and Wid. Dorothy Parsons.(?)
Nov. 27, 1816.	Cyrus Alvord of S. Hadley and Asenath Smith.

DEATHS.

[Northampton Town Records.]

Alexander Alvord had a child still born		1671.
John, son of Thomas Alvord,	died Aug.	25, 1682.
Alexander Alvord	" Oct.	3, 1687.
Thomas Alvord	" July	22, 1688.
Josiah Alvord	" Dec.	13, 1691.
Jeremiah Alvord	" March	4, 1691
Thomas Alvord	" July	22, 1688
Ruth Alvord	" March	4, 1706
Jonathan Alvord	" Nov.	8, 1703.

Jonathan Alvord, son to Jonathan, - - died April 11, 1706.
Mary Alvord - - - - - " Aug. 12, 1708.
James, son of Ebenezer Alvord, - - " July 28, 1712.
Sarah, dau. of Ebenezer and Elisabeth, - " Nov. 29, 1716.(?)
John Alvord, Sen., - - - - " Mar. 17, 1726–7.
Rebecca, dau. of Ebenezer and Elizabeth, - " Nov. 29, 1716.
Jonathan Alvord - - - - " Aug. 13, 1727.
Eunice Alvord, wife of Benjamin, - - " Oct. 8, 1732.
Thankful Alvord, widow, - - - " March 30, 1738.
Ebenezer Alvord - - - - " Nov. 28, 1738.
Thankful Alvord, dau. of Jonathan, - - " Aug. 7, 1747.
Rachel, dau. of Jonathan & Prudence, - " Aug. 22, 1748.
Lydia, dau. of Saul and Martha, - - " June 22, 1750.
Saul, son of Saul and Martha, - - " July 5, 1753.
"Died, the aged Wid° Alvord, said to be about one hundred and two years old, said to have been born in the same year this town was first planted," - - - - Aug. 26, 1756.
Mr. Benjamin Alvord died in his chair suddenly and alone - - - - - Oct. 22, 1772.
Medad Alvord, son of Joseph Alvord, - died May, 1798.

[Northampton Church Records.]

Abigail Alvord, aged 103, - - - died Aug. 26, 1756.
Zebadiah Alvord's child - - - " Nov. 7, 1758.
Aged Joseph Alvord, in March next 89, - " Jan. 9, 1786.
Patience Alvord - - - - " Jan. 16, 1766.
Joseph Alvord's wife - - - - " 21,
Two of Zebadiah Alvord's children - - " April 28, 1767.
Benjamin Alvord's wife - - - " June 6, 1770.
John Alvord's child - - - - " Feb. 2, 1771.
Benjamin Alvord - - - - " Oct. 21, 1772.
Ebenezer Alvord's wife - - - " Sept. 12, 1773.
Jonathan Alvord's wife - - - " Feb. 14, 1775.
"Major Jonathan Alvord was accidently shot in ye War by Mr Seth Wyman. Two balls went into his body, one through his arm. He was shot at about one o'clock and he lived to be brought home and died about 7½"—[Williams.] 1780.

DEATHS.

[From a printed book in possession of Dea. Williams of Northampton.]

Thomas Alvord's son - - - -	died	Aug.	25, 1682.
Alexander Alvord - - - -	"	Oct.	3, 1687.
Josiah Alvord - - - -	"	Dec.	13, 1691.
Jeremiah Alvord - - - -	"	March	4, 1692.
Jonathan Alvord - - - -	"	Nov.	8, 1703.
Ruth Alvord, - - - -	"	March	4, 1706.
Jonathan Alvord, Jr., - - - -	"	April	11, 1706.
Esther Alvord, drowned - - -		Oct.	3, 1707.
Mary Alvord - - - - -	died	Aug.	12, 1708.
James Alvord, son of Ebenezer, - -	"	July	28, 1712.
Rebecca Alvord - - - -	"	Nov.	29, 1716.
Gad Alvord - - - - -	"	Sept.	5, 1723.
Sarah Alvord - - - -	"	April	11, 1724.
John Alvord - - - - -	"	March	17, 1727.
Jonathan Alvord - - - -	"	Aug.	13, 1727.
Eunice Alvord - - - -	"	Oct.	8, 1732.
Benjamin Alvord's child - - -	"	Nov.	3, 1732.
Wid. Thankful Alvord - - -	"	March,	1738.
Ebenezer Alvord - - - -	"	Nov.	29, 1738.
———, daughter of Jonathan Alvord, -	"	Aug.	7, 1747.
Joseph Alvord's child - - -	"	Sept.	1748.
Prudence Alvord - - - -	"	Aug.	1752.
Abigail Alvord - - - -	"	Aug.	26, 1756.
Zebadiah Alvord's child - - -	"	Oct.	17, 1756.
Thomas Alvord, - - - -	"	Dec.	27, 1756.
Jonathan Alvord's child - - -	"	Nov.	29, 1757.
Sarah Alvord - - - -	"	March	2, 1758.
Zebadiah Alvord's child - - -	"	Nov.	7, 1758.
Joseph Alvord's wife - - - -	"	Jan.	21, 1766.
Widow Alvord, aged, - - - -	"	March	1, 1767.
Zebadiah Alvord's two children - -	"	April	28, 1767.
Wife of Benjamin Alvord - - -	"	June	6, 1770.
John Alvord's child - - - -	"	Feb.	2, 1771.
Benjamin Alvord - - - -	"	Oct.	21, 1772, (or 1771.)
Mary Alvord - - - - -	"	March	14, 1773.
Ebenezer Alvord's child - - -	"	Sept.	12, 1773.

Ebenezer Alvord's wife - - -	died	Sept.	12, 1773.
Patience Alvord - - - -	"	Jan.	16, 1766.
Wife of John Alvord - - - -	"	Feb.	14, 1775.
(Jonathan Alvord's wife - - -	"	Feb.	14, 1775?)
Wife of Joseph Alvord - - -	"	March	25, 1776.
——— Alvord died in the army - -		Sept.	1776.
Child of Medad Alvord - - -	"		1778.
John Alvord, aged more than 70, - -	"		1780.
Infant of Medad Alvord - - -	"		
Aged Joseph Alvord (in March next 89) -	"	Jan.	1, 1786.
Child of Phineas Alvord - - -	"	March	25, 1786.
The wife of Medad Alvord, aged 48 last Nov.,	"		1790.
Wife of Elisha Alvord, aged 66—Obstruction, did not speak, - - - -	"	Jan.	2, 1794.
Mary Alvord—"her father was John Alvord—never married, died of Fits in her 70 y.,"		March	2, 1803.
Phineas Alvord's daughter - - -	died	Aug.	16, 1803.
Timothy Alvord, Jr., "in his 20 or 21 year," -	"	Oct.	7, 1804.
Luther Alvord, of a fever; left a widow and two children; aged 28.			
The wife of John Alvord of the farms, aged 56,	"	Oct.	6, 1810.

[From Windsor, Conn., Town Records.]

BIRTHS.

Elizabeth, dau. of Jeremiah Alvard, - -	April	27, 1706.
Job, son of Jeremiah Alvard, - - -	Aug.	26, 1708.
Sarah, dau. of Jeremiah Alvard, - -	June	16, 1712.
Jeremiah, son of Jeremiah Alvard, - -	June	1, 1715.
Benedict, son of Benedict Alford, - -	Aug.	29, 1716.
Jonathan, son of Jeremiah Alfort, - -	Sept.	16, 1720.
Alexander, son of Benedict Alford, - -	March	31, 1721.
Jerusha, dau. of Benedict Alford, - -	April	3, 1723.
Jeremiah, son of Jeremiah Alford, - -	May	11, 1725.
Elizabeth, dau. of Jeremiah & Sarah Alford, -	Aug.	2, 1727.
Azuba, dau. of Benedict & Abigail Alford, -	Sept.	19, 1727–8.
Job, son of Job Alford & Margaret, - -	July	3d, 1736.
John, son of Job Alford & Margaret, - -	Sept.	4, 1738.
Deidemia, dau. of Benedict Alvord & Jerusha, -	Jan.	13, 1744–5.
Jonathan, son of Jonathan Alvord & Charity, -	Dec.	21, 1745.

Jeremiah, son of Jeremiah Alford, Jun., & Ann, -	Feb.	16, 1746.
Joseph, son of Jonathan Alford & Charity, -	July	6, 1748.
Dorothy, dau. of Azuba Alford, - - -	July	28, 1750.
Charity, dau. of Jonathan Alford & Charity, -	June	20, 1750.
Abigail, dau. of Benedict Alford, Jun., & Jerusha,	Dec.	3, 1747.
Jerusha, " " " " " " " -	Aug.	21, 1750.
Alexander, son of " " " " " -	June	25, 1752.
Lucrece, dau. of " " " " " -	March	27, 1755.
Abigail, " " " " " " " -	Oct.	23, 1746.
Benedict, son " " " " " " -	Feb.	27, 1757.
Anna, dau. " " " " " " -	April	7, 1759.
George, son " " " " and Rebecca,	March	31, 1761.
Rebecca, dau. of " " " " " -	Oct.	24, 1762.
Rocitter, " " " " " " -	Nov.	18, 1765.

MARRIAGES.

Jeremiah Alford and Sarah Enno, daughter of John Enno, were married - - -	July	4, 1711.
Benedict Alford & Abigail Wilson, - -	Jan.	12, 1714–5.
Jonathan Alford & Charity Thrall, both of Windsor,	Dec.	17, 1744.
Benedict Alford, Jun., of Windsor, and Jerusha Ashley of Hartford, - - -	Aug.	9, 1744.
Jeremiah Alford, Jun., and Anna Gile, both of Windsor, - - - - -	July	15, 1746.
Benedict Alford, Jun., and Rebecca Owen, both of Windsor, - - - - -	Dec.	28, 1761.
Nathaniel R. Alford and Keziah Barber were lawfully married - - - -	April	14, 1829.
Cyrus Attleton and Eliza Ann Alford, both of Springfield, Mass., - - - -	Feb.	6, 1825.
George Andrews of Waterbury and Cordelia Alford of Windsor, - - - -	May	26, 1839.
William Alford & (Maria?) Barker, - -	July	9, 1835.
James Burke of New Yorke and H. J. Halsey of this town, - - - - -	Oct.	12, 1836.
Jesse Hofford & Elizabeth Alford, both of Windsor,	Oct.	1, 1747.
Benj'n Loomis, Jun., & Joanna Alford, both of Windsor, - - - - -	Dec.	9, 1725.
Jacob Phelps & Abigail Alford, both of Windsor,	Dec.	30, 1745.

DEATHS.

Jeremiah Alvard Dyed - - - -	June the 6, 1709.
Jeremiah Alford, son of Jeremiah, dyed - -	July ye 9, 1714.
Widow Jane Alford - - - -	May 19, 1715.
Sarah, daughter of Jeremiah Alford, - -	June ye 9, 1715.
Elizabeth Alford Dyed - - - -	May 18, 1727.
Jeremiah, son of Jeremiah Alford, Jun., and Ann his wife, Dyed - - - -	Jan. 4, 1751–2.
Abigail, dau. of Benedict Alford, Jun., and Jerusha,	Jan. 16, 1746–7.
Jerusha, dau. of Benedict Alford, Jun., and (Jerusha?) - - - - -	Jan. 18, 1761.
Benedict Alford - - - - -	Feb. 15, 1764.
Abigail Alford (91 years?) - - -	April 30, 1773.
Azuba Alford - - - - -	June 2, 1786.

[From Windsor, Conn., Church Records.]

BAPTISMS.

Joscias Alvard baptised - - - -	July 8, 1649.
Elizabeth Alvord baptised - -	Sept. 21, 1651.
Jeremiah Alvard, son Benj. Alvard, baptised -	Jan. 31, 1655.

Births upon the Church Records.

Benjamin Alvard married Jane Newton - -	Nov. 26, 1640.
his sonn Jonathan was born - - -	June 1, 1645.
his sonn Benjamin was born - - -	July 11, 1647.
his sonn Josias born - - - -	July 6, 1649.
his dau Elizabeth was borne - - -	Sept. 21, 1651.
his son Jeremy was borne - - -	Dec. 24, 1655.
Alexander Alvord married Mary Vore - -	Oct. 29, 1646.
his daughter Abigail was borne - - -	Oct. 6, 1647.
his sonne John was borne - - -	Aug. 12, 1649.
his daughter Mary was borne - - -	July 6, 1651.
his sonne Thomas was borne - - -	Oct. 27, 1653.
his daughter Elizabeth was borne - -	Nov. 12 1655.
his sonne Benjamin was borne - - -	Feb. 11, 1657.
his daughter Sara was borne - - -	June 24, 1660.

INDEX OF NAMES.

The figures before the name denote its consecutive number in the genealogy. The figures after the name show the page, and the small figures denote that the name is found more than once upon the page. The Appendix I is not indexed.

L.

M.

N.

O.

P.

Q.

R.

S.

www.ingramcontent.com/pod-product-compliance
Lightning Source LLC
Chambersburg PA
CBHW070904270326
41927CB00011B/2451

* 9 7 8 0 7 8 8 4 1 5 5 7 9 *